Walking wit

I.S.B.N. 978171

Copyright © 2006 Juli

The right of Julia R Merrifield to be identified as the Author of the Work has been asserted by her in accordance with the Copyright, Designs and Patents Act 1988. Apart from any use permitted under UK copyright law, this publication may only be reproduced, stored, or transmitted, in any form, or by any means, with prior permission in writing of the publishers or, in the case of reprographic production, in accordance with the terms of licences issued by the Copyright Licensing Agency.

Dedication

To Chris and Merv.

Like most things in life, when it comes to friends it is quality that counts, not quantity.

Also by Julia R May

My Feet and Other Animals

Walking Pembrokeshire with a Fruitcake

Pedals, Panniers and Punctures

Walking with Hadrian

I've Cycled Through There

Cycling Across England

Cycles and Sandcastles

Bicycles, Boats and Bagpipes

A Week in Provence

Bicycles, Beer and Black Forest Gateau

Dawdling Through The Dales

Cycling Through a Foreign Field

Ever heard of a bloke called Offa? King of Mercia, he instigated the building of a defensive dyke. 12 centuries later a long distance path was laid out, roughly following the line of Offa's Dyke, and thirty years later still two friends set out to walk it.

How difficult could it be, walking from one end of Wales to the other? Loaded down with maps, guide books and global positioning systems they were soon to find out and only 5 minutes after leaving Chepstow were monumentally lost! Soon they were enjoying the scenery, watching the wildlife and overdosing on dried apricots. Staying in haunted English castles and heavenly Welsh guest houses they made their way north.

Chapter One

Ever heard of a bloke called Offa? His name recalled a distant memory of Primary School history lessons, a swashbuckling xenophobic King during the Dark Ages, who had a particular dislike of the Welsh. I know, that doesn't differentiate him from most other English kings who took exception to this song-loving nation with a nice line in tea bread and griddle cakes. But as I had sat in that sweaty little classroom over thirty years ago listening to a history lesson recounted with the aid of picture books instead of multimedia projectors and interactive computer programmes, I had no idea that one day I would be walking along the borders he had laid out more than a thousand years before. Funny how things turn out, isn't it?

My initial reaction to the suggestion of my friend, colleague and walking companion Chris, that we try Offa's Dyke Path had been somewhat reserved.

"You've got to be joking! There's no way I'm going on a walking holiday with another woman on a path that has the word 'Dyke' in the name. You can forget it. Think of something else. Are you mad? Can you imagine the comments we're laying ourselves open to?"

"It's very popular amongst the Dutch," replied Chris, ignoring my objections.

"Well, it's bound to be. You can't move in Holland for dykes."

"Lots of Dutch walk Offa's Dyke every year according to the Association's handbook."

"Yes, well – they probably think it's a stroll along some sea defences," I mumbled, beginning to get the feeling I was losing the discussion. "Er, what association?"

"The Offa's Dyke Association. It's a charitable organisation set up to promote the footpath and it seems to be very well organised. When you join you get a handbook, an accommodation guide and lots of other useful information. Look."

"You've joined?"

"Yes, we have," she replied assertively. "You can't keep repeating the coastal national trails. You need to try something different."

"But it's all inland. I'll miss the sea at our side, the sound of the waves, the cry of the gulls, the ice cream vans at every beach."

"You can't just rule out the dyke, you need to try it, experience new things. You never know, you might enjoy it!"

"Well you can tell people where we're walking this year. I'm having nothing to do with it."

And so a few days later I found myself surrounded by maps, brochures and guidebooks about Offa's Dyke as Chris and I began to plan our next walking holiday.

"Read that grid reference out to me, will you please? I don't seem to be able to find this B&B on the map."

"Which one?" I replied, thumbing through an accommodation guide.

"The one for the farm near Pandy," Chris replied, peering at the map over the top of her varifocals. "It begins 0154 something."

I turned my attention to our list of prospective accommodation and ran my eye down the page. "There is no grid reference beginning 0154 anything," I sighed.

"Yes there is, I just saw it."

"Chris," I said, adopting my most sensitive and caring tone, "the only things on this list beginning 0154 are telephone numbers."

"Oh, must have read it wrong!"

And thus began our adventure along Offa's Dyke National Trail; not the most auspicious of introductions, lost before we even set foot on the path. As with all our walking holidays we planned our itinerary with care and booked all our accommodation well in advance. We had done the best we could to ensure the daily mileages would be achievable whilst still allowing us time to stop and explore our surroundings, and to ensure that each night's accommodation would be clean, comfortable and reliable. All that was left to do was to wait for August and book our train tickets to the start of the path at Chepstow.

August came, and so eventually did the 1305 Nelson to Preston diesel locomotive. We stepped onto the crowded local train and were whisked away amongst a growing assortment of small children, big adults, large dogs and over-engineered baby buggies; the two carriage Sprinter train could barely contain us all. Just when it looked like no one else could possibly squeeze onboard, a scruffily dressed man and his huge, slobbering Alsatian forced his way into the carriage. Space miraculously appeared for this menacing looking pair but not out of fear from the other passengers; it soon became apparent that either the man, or the dog, or possibly both, had a severe odour control problem. As the train rumbled its way to Preston and points west, every possible window was opened but the smell in the hot, crowded carriage soon became unbearable. Relief came with every station as the doors opened allowing the smell, and a few lucky travellers, out and refreshing blasts of diesel fumes, and more unfortunate travellers, in. With every stop we hoped the noxious pair would alight but it seemed they too were travelling at least as far as Preston. As if the smell was not bad enough, the dog lunged at every passing person. When a young mum dragged her push chair on board and left it next to the dog, it seemed the tiny baby would end up as a dog's dinner. It was the quick actions of Mr Smelly himself that prevented infanticide.

With immense relief and bursting lungs we staggered out of the train onto the busy platform at Preston station and made our way to the platform for our connecting train to Crewe. Soon we were onboard the latest investment in our wonderful rail network and settled back in clean, plush velour seats wondering if we had blundered into first class by mistake. Conversations drifted around us and with growing interest and amusement we listened in to other peoples' lives.

"Yes, so we sold those shares and bought the flat in Kensington," droned a suited gent in a loud pink shirt.

"Really?" replied his pin striped companion. "Didn't consider investing off-shore then?"

"So I told him, cos I always have to remind him, you know," nattered an old lady at the seat in front of us. "'Brian', I said, 'Brian, you've forgotten to put the condoms on the table.' Well, he knows I can't abide cabbage without a bit of salt and pepper."

Chris and I dissolved into fits of giggles and even the two business men briefly suspended their own conversation to stare across the aisle at the elderly lady and her bemused companion.

"They must be salesmen," whispered the woman to her friend, referring to the gentlemen across the aisle. "You can tell you know – high powered suits, leather briefcases. I bet they spend their time driving round in their fancy BMXs."

Hilda Baker lives.

It was with some disappointment at the thought of missing more of this lady's verbal gems, that we left the train at Crewe to catch a third train to Newport. The information board directed us to a lonely little two carriage train all by itself at a lonely little platform round the corner from the main concourse; climbing onboard we found we were the only passengers.

"Is this really our train?" asked Chris, examining the frayed and faded upholstery and the sagging seats. "Or is it on its way to the railway museum?"

With a plethora of empty seats to choose from we settled into two exhausted seats and dumped our rucksacks on the seats facing us. Adverts pasted to the walls seemed to hark back to the halcyon days of rail when Britain had a train service to be proud of. This carriage must surely remember those better times. As we sat, examining the sepia ads, I noticed a dirty smudge on my arm: where had that come from? I rubbed it, making it worse. Then I noticed another dark smut on my shirt, then one on Chris' shirt and another on my trousers. What were they and where were they from? The answer was the train itself. This ancient relic was emitting smoke and smut all over the platform and any unfortunate body that happened to pass by. We rubbed at the smudges to no avail. An hour later as we got off the train at Newport we resembled rejects from the Black and White Minstrel Show.

It was tea time at Newport and passengers came and went on the small platform, hurrying home from a day at work. We sat and watched them go and waited impatiently for our connecting train to Chepstow. One crew cut ginger haired young man, who didn't look as if he had ever worked, sauntered down the platform, scratching his bare chest and clutching a scruffy T-shirt and a can of lager. Reaching the end of the platform he turned and wandered back. When our train arrived he climbed aboard. Exchanging glances, Chris and I boarded a different carriage. But we had not avoided him; soon he was wandering through the carriages in a seemingly aimless manner. However, when the conductor appeared his aimless wanderings gained sudden purpose: he had not got a ticket.

"Is this the train for Cardiff?" he muttered.

"No, mate. You're on the wrong train," replied the conductor, with a knowing look.

"Aw, god! Sorry pal, I've made a mistake."
Insincerity dripped from every syllable but the man seemed too drunk to notice.

"Well, if you get off at the next station, there'll be a train going the other way in about fifteen minutes," explained the conductor, with more patience than I could have mustered.

"Oh, right, cheers," replied the ginger crew cut, toasting the conductor with his can of lager.

At the next station the ginger drunk got off, still clutching his lager but now wearing his T-shirt. As the train pulled away he was sitting on the platform, obviously waiting for the next train to take him a bit further up the line, away from Cardiff! He seemed to be train hopping his way to Chepstow.

Having taken the more conventional and legal option of paying for our journey we reached Chepstow before the ginger drunk, and with no help from a very confusing town plan we blundered around the town until we stumbled across our Bed and Breakfast quite by chance. Finding accommodation in Chepstow had proved rather difficult, the choice was limited to places that either appeared rather run down or prohibitively expensive. We had eventually picked the best of a mediocre bunch purely on the grounds that they were willing to take a one night booking. From the outside it looked okay, and indeed the room was comfortable, boasting a brand new en suite. That, however, was the best that could be said about it. Standing at the reception desk our greeting was a little brusque.

"Would you mind paying now," asked the owner. "We're full and will be too busy in the morning to take payment."

A little taken aback at the request, Chris dutifully produced her credit card and paid in full before we had even seen the room. Shown to our room along a maze of passageways, we were given instructions about the security and about breakfast times then the landlady left, we never saw her again. Dumping our rucksacks on the floor and making hasty use of the loo we grabbed the guide book and Chris' global positioning system, on which she maps all our walks, and rushed out to 'do' the first part of Offa's Dyke Path.

The way we had broken down our mileage meant we intended to walk out to the start of the path and then back to Chepstow that first evening. It was a total distance of four miles and a pleasant stroll on that balmy August evening. We crossed the bridge over the fast flowing River Wye, leaving Chepstow with its Norman Castle guarding the town, it was the first of many castles we would encounter as we followed the border path north. Through a collection of houses, estates, roads and urban footpaths we made our way to the start of the path, marked by a stone monument at the southern end of Offa's Dyke.

At this point on the path the dyke was arguably at its most impressive, a tree-covered embankment running down the hill from its start at the top of Sedbury Cliffs. We posed for photos by the monument and then set off down a path to emerge a couple of slippery minutes later on the banks of the River Severn. The silent grey waters of Britain's longest river slipped by towards the distant span of the huge Severn crossing. Traffic flowed over the bridge faster than the waters flowing underneath, and the sound of rumbling wheels and growling engines carried clearly to us across the flat expanse of river banks and marsh. The sinking sun flashed golden beams along the bridge's suspension wires. Further downstream was the second Severn crossing, opened in the summer of 1996 the bridge had cost over £300 million pounds to construct and was quite possibly the most expensive of the one hundred bridges spanning the River Severn.

Turning our backs on the river we climbed back to the start of Offa's Dyke Path and followed, briefly, the dyke as it began its long, winding journey north along the old borders of England and Wales.

Opinions differ not only as to when Offa's Dyke was constructed but how and even why. The Welsh borders have long been fought over. From Roman times and earlier, defensive hill forts marked out the boundaries, separating different tribes. Offa was a powerful King of Mercia, a land that stretched between the rivers Mersey, Trent and Thames and to the Fens in the east and the Welsh borders in the west; his reign lasted from 757 to 796 A.D. By a series of political marriages for his offspring he expanded his kingdom and as such was possibly one of the first true kings of England. It is the writings of a chap called Asser, biographer of King Alfred, that originally credit King Offa with the building of the dyke, and it is thought work began on the dyke in about 785. Dispute still exists as to whether the dyke was built as a defensive line or a territorial boundary. Much discussion also continues as to how the dyke was constructed: was it built by one team of workers or, as seems more likely were local teams of forced labour made to each build their own section? What is known is that the dyke consists of a ditch and a raised mound, with the ditch on the western side. It is thought that originally the dyke would have been some twenty-six feet high and an astounding ninety feet in width. With the passage of time and effects of erosion and interference by man much of the remaining dyke falls far short of these remarkable dimensions, it is only in a few places where the walker experiences the impressive size of the dyke as it must have been over one thousand years ago.

By the time of the Norman Conquest the dyke had already become part of history, and it was William the Conqueror and his Norman Lords who established the chain of defensive castles along the border of England and Wales. Frequent fighting and invasions followed until things eventually quietened down with the defeat, in 1410, of Owain Glyndwr. This legend of Welsh history was finally defeated not only by the victorious armies of Henry IV but by deprivations brought on by the horrendous winter of 1408/09 when many communities starved and froze to death.

Offa's Dyke Path, by necessity, does not follow faithfully the line of the dyke. Due to problems of access, practicality, erosion and, in some areas, complete destruction of the dyke over the centuries, the national trail has been laid out so that it links stretches of the existing dyke, passing as it does so places of interest and natural beauty and taking the walker through stunning border scenery. For approximately half of the 177 miles of the Offa's Dyke National Trail we would be walking in the company of this ancient defensive boundary. But on that first evening we soon left both the dyke and the footpath as we diverted back across the Wye to Chepstow in search of something to eat.

We crossed the Wye on the distinctive cast iron bridge, designed in 1816 by John Rennie. A famous and successful bridge builder, he died only five years later whilst work on his last project, London Bridge, was still on-going. The bridge, adorned by baskets of beautiful begonias, was a truly impressive structure, and positioned as it was at the bottom of the hill leading into Chepstow, gave fine views of the castle and the town rising up the hillside. Many previous wooded bridges here had succumbed to floods over the centuries.

Situated on the broad sweep of the River Wye, Chepstow was not only a significant border town but an important port. Trade with other parts of Britain and Europe brought prosperity to the borough and it was from Chepstow that the leaders of the Chartist Insurrection were transported to Tasmania, then called Van Diemen's Land, in 1840. The Chartists were calling for political reform, hoping for a fairer system of government for all, not just the ruling classes. It was in 1839, following an organised demonstration by thousands of Welsh miners that the Chartist movement was finally suppressed. During the demonstration which took place in Newport, the army fired on demonstrators, killing twenty and wounding many more.

Chepstow has a castle, a racecourse, the ubiquitous supermarket that no town nowadays can do without, and a rather appealing high street running up from the river to pass beneath ancient town gates. As we climbed the sloping main street, eagerly on the look out for a quiet restaurant or appetising takeaway, I dawdled along examining the carvings in the pavements and on the ornate walls of the town square. Lines of poetry had been carved into the pavement and beautifully worked carvings of fruit, fish, fowl, meat, loaves and other goods decorated the honey coloured stone work around the multinational bank. The carvings celebrated the past of this historic market town. In front of the shops, again carved into the pavements, were trades listing the past businesses that had occupied all the different premises from centuries ago up to the present day. In front of one shop, where tulips and anemones decorated the window, was carved 'Butcher, Haberdasher, Costermonger, Florist'. Further up the hill stretching across the front of a window adorned with CAT boots and Sketcher trainers I read 'Tanner, Wheelwright, Cobbler, Shoe shop'. Other premises had similar carvings: in front of the next shop with colourful displays of the latest mobile phone tariffs: 'Tailor, Dressmaker, Hairdresser, Telecommunications'. I dreaded reading what might be carved in front of the window displaying lingerie and whips: 'Grocer, Florist, Solicitor, Sex Shop'? Hmm, how times change! I could imagine the long dead businessmen would be shocked at what their respectable premises had become, and maybe just a little curious?

At the top of the high street music, laughter and beer fumes floated out of an old coaching inn as a group of giggling young women flounced in. Just beyond the town gates we found a sudden selection of takeaways and drawn by the smell of garlic and basil hastened into a pizza and kebab shop. Ten minutes later we were sitting on a bench watching the passing traffic and hungrily devouring a couple of nine inch pizzas. A string of melted cheese and a dollop of tomato sauce fell onto my trousers, just adding to the black smudges already there.

"Great, these trousers have to last two and a half weeks and they're filthy on the first night!" I exclaimed, rubbing at the stains with a tissue and only succeeding in spreading them.

"I don't know how you manage to be so sloppy," remarked Chris, before dropping a slice of mushroom down her front.

"You were saying?"

Cars sped by on the one-way system, their drivers giving us curious glances as they passed. When the nearby traffic lights changed to red we were treated to Eminem's latest offering of crap, (sorry think that should be rap, although actually the former is more accurate) as the driver waited with revving engine, pounding stereo and miniscule manhood, for the green light.

"That car's been round twice since I started on this slice of pizza," said Chris, as a Nissan Micra with alloy wheels, wide tyres and a noisy exhaust thundered past. "And look at that one, surely that can't be safe?"

A little two-seater open-topped sports car cruised past, with an infant strapped into a baby seat.

"Frivolous expense," I muttered, through strings of melting cheese.

"I take it you mean the baby."

"Yes."

Back in the bedroom of the B&B we sorted out our rucksacks and settled down for a cup of tea. Nothing like a nice cup of tea. And what we had was nothing like a nice cup of tea. Either the water was soft or the teabags were foul. The brown scummy sludge floating in the dainty china cups suggested both options were likely. Neither of us could manage to drink it.

A sudden chirruping cheep distracted us both from the terrible tasting tea. I began looking for a trapped bird, thinking one must have flown into the room or be lodged in the chimney but Chris was frantically groping in her pocket. What? She had a budgie in her pants?

"It's the new tone for when I receive a text message," she explained, seeing my bemused look.

While Chris perused the guidebook I perused the painting on the wall over the beds. It was not to my taste, a stylised wishy washy and rather revealing image of a young woman, entitled 'Broken Silence'. Broken bra strap would have been more appropriate.

"Bigsweir, according to the guidebook," read Chris, "is the highest tidal point on the river. We walk through there tomorrow. I wonder if that is where the Severn Bore reaches."

"Shouldn't think so. Bigsweir's on the River Wye."

Our sleep was disturbed that night not by pounding traffic or nightmares of horrible tea but by a sudden thud and then a pathetic but increasingly annoying meowing. A cat had let itself in through the open window. With Chris still fumbling for her glasses it was left to me to put the cat out. Stumbling about in the unfamiliar room without the aid of my own specs I found the cat, picked it up and put it on the windowsill. But before I could find a gap in the net curtains it had jumped off and was running round the room. I caught it twice more before I could eventually shove it out through the curtains and onto the flat roof below our window.

"It must have heard your mobile earlier and thought there was an easy meal in here," I remarked as I climbed back into bed, brushing cat hairs from my pyjamas.

Chapter Two

The dining room was full of people as we sat waiting for our juice that morning. As we helped ourselves to cereal we read the framed breakfast menu on the wall. The waitresses seemed to be overworked and rushed about, dumping pots of tea and racks of cold toast on tables with unceremonious haste. When our cooked breakfasts were finally delivered to us, plonked on the table with enough force to break a more delicate set of crockery, we hurried to eat them before they could be removed as had been the case at the neighbouring table. It was 'Fawlty Towers' meets 'I'm a Celebrity Get Me Out of Here' with the diners being grateful for any decent food they could get. Where were the promised yoghurt, fruit salad, juice, homemade marmalade, mushrooms and beans? Eventually, faced with only the unpalatable tea to drink, Chris asked a passing waitress for some fruit juice. It seemed Chris' request was an aide memoir to the staff, for suddenly juice was served to every guest. Maybe she should have mentioned yoghurt, fruit salad, marmalade, beans and mushrooms too.

At just before nine o'clock, clad in shorts, shirts and walking boots we set off to walk to Prestatyn, er via Tesco, where we stocked up on flapjack, bread rolls, bananas, apricots and hair bobbles. The food should keep us going for a few days and the hair bobbles were vital as the one that had served me well for several weeks had chosen that morning to snap, twanging across the bedroom and nearly blinding Chris in the process, as it was finally defeated in its brave battle to control my unruly mop of hair. With food in rucksacks and hair in a ponytail we set off out of the car park and past the petrol station.

"That bloke looks like Peter Snow," I said, nodding to a tall, grey haired chap crossing the road towards us.

"It sounds like him too," replied Chris. "Even if he's not mentioned Labour, Conservative, Lib Dems and swings. Perhaps he's here for the racing."

Chepstow not only has a castle and a supermarket, it has a popular race course that attracts many visitors to the town. Most of our fellow guests at the B&B had been going to the races. I had counted seventeen guests at breakfast that morning, making the landlady a nice sum for just one night.

Across the river and back into England for the third time we stepped onto Offa's Dyke Path where we had left it the evening before and began to walk to Prestatyn. Straight away we found ourselves climbing a steep hill, which eventually crested a rise near to a ruined tower, thought to have been a lookout tower. We were in a field high above the river, surrounded on a couple of sides by mature trees. It was at that point that we were distracted by a rickety old wooden bridge that crossed the path in front of us. After Chris posed for a photo we set off under the bridge and down a path into the wooded slopes and limestone cliffs of a nature reserve. An information board foretold of rare snails, peregrines and small leafed lime. We saw a male peregrine, lots of squirrels and great tits as we descended the rapidly deteriorating path until we were almost back at river level. It was then that I looked at the guidebook and discovered we should never have entered the nature reserve at all. Chris was out of sight somewhere ahead of me, I called and faintly her reply drifted back through the undergrowth. Hurrying to catch her up, I battled through increasingly dense elder and buddleia bushes until I caught up with her.

"You've taken me the wrong way," I sighed, picking bits of purple and lilac coloured flowers out of my hair.

"Are you sure?" she asked, taking the book from my hands. "Oh, we shouldn't have come down here. You got carried away with that little wooden bridge, didn't you?"

"Me? I was following you!"

On hands and knees I crawled back under the low growing branches that overhung the rock strewn path. Once able to stand upright, I straightened with a creak from my knees to find they had become pebble-dashed with soil, seeds, twigs and small stones. Chris, much shorter than I, walked under the branches without difficulty.

"That's one of the few occasions when being short is an advantage," she said smugly, watching as I tried to clean off my knees.

Back at the entrance to the nature reserve, half an hour after we had first entered it, we found the Offa's Dyke Path sign prominently pointing us in the right direction. How had we missed it? I checked my pedometer, hoping to estimate how far we had walked out of our way, but it had been re-zeroed, possibly whilst I had been crawling about. Shortly afterwards I abandoned the pedometer completely, shoving it into a pocket of my rucksack when it became apparent that it was not working properly. From then on we relied on Chris' G.P.S. which gave us a far more accurate mileage in any case.

Following the signs, instead of our noses, we emerged onto a road, walking along in the gutter for a few yards until signposts led us onto a narrow track above the steep cliffs on the River Wye. From the top of the cliffs there were wide views along the curving sweep of the river, its banks covered in thick, verdant woodland. Below us a female peregrine swooped gracefully and effortlessly past, perhaps the mate of the male we had seen earlier.

At the road once more we nearly missed our next turn off. A spaniel grinned at us from the narrow entrance to the well hidden path, his pink tongue hanging from the corner of his mouth. Seeing he had got our attention he turned and disappeared down the path, almost as if his mission was accomplished. Thanks to him we avoided taking a wrong turn there, only to miss the next turn a mere fifty yards further on! Too busy chatting, we carried straight on at a field boundary, but we quickly realised our mistake. The field path had cut out a busy section of road but the road could not be avoided for long and soon we were walking along a pavement, passing large houses set back from the road. At one a container of water, a Tupperware box of plastic cups and even a dog bowl had been set out, with a sign on the wall stating they were for O.D. walkers. A thoughtful gesture on the part of the owners, perhaps they were walkers themselves. It was a complete contrast to a house we had passed in Cornwall when walking a very isolated part of the South West Coast Path a few years ago. There, a notice pinned to the gate informed walkers there was 'no water and no toilets, so please do not ask'.

Following a woodland path high above the grand meandering curves of the river our route stuck closely to the line of the dyke, at this point of the walk a very obvious dyke and ditch. Sometimes the path ran along the top of this ancient monument and sometimes in the ditch on its Welsh side. In one place the path had been realigned to prevent erosion of the dyke, we were to encounter similar preventative realignments several times along the path's length. Badgers had built their setts into the high embankment of the dyke, digging deeply into the red soil. Whilst in some parts, too rocky for their tunnels, the dyke remained undisturbed save for the gnarled roots of trees.

We walked near the edge of this dense woodland, where steep tree-covered slopes led down to the river, passing through Worgan's Wood, Passage Grove and Caswell Wood. Sunlight dappled through the patchwork of leaves above our heads and birds flew in the branches. Squirrels feasted on the glut of hazelnuts, leaping from branch to branch at our approach and racing across the path to scale trunks with consummate ease. There was not a day of walking the path that we did not see either hazels or squirrels.

Tintern Abbey appeared tantalisingly through the trees, a grey stone ruin on the opposite bank, the Welsh side of the Wye. At Devil's Pulpit, a precipitous stack of rocks on the edge of the wooded cliffs, we stopped for lunch. Sitting against a tree we hungrily consumed the bananas, bread rolls and some of the flapjack, whilst admiring the leaf-framed view of the Lilliputian abbey far below. We had met no other walkers all morning so it was something of a shock to suddenly realise that a couple had appeared on the path behind us. But they were not your average friendly 'hale walkers, well met' sort of rambler, both chose to ignore us. The man came to stand in front of me as he took a shot of the abbey, and for a minute or so my picturesque view was replaced by the less than scenic sight of his denim-clad bum.

"I wonder why it's called Devil's Pulpit?" I mused.

"Ah, the guidebook says that legend has it the devil stood here and preached to the monks at the abbey below in an attempt to corrupt them," explained Chris.

"Ridiculous! How could they have heard him from up here?" I muttered.

"Pardon?"

"Exactly."

"No, what did you say?"

"Exactly."

"No, before that."

"Are you taking the Michael?"

"No, I'm being serious. I didn't hear you. I think I've got a problem with this ear," Chris explained, rubbing her right ear lobe.

"I said, oh never mind. It wasn't important, I was just being flippant."

"Pardon?"

"Oh, for goodness sake. What's up with your ear ?"

"There's no need to shout," replied Chris indignantly. "It's a bit blocked up. I might have to get some ear drops."

"Sawdust, I shouldn't wonder," I muttered.

"Pardon?"

"Never mind, have an apricot," I offered, reading the back of the brightly coloured packet. "They're good for you – full of iron, vitamins and er, sulphur dioxide."

Above the riverside village of Brockweir, we left the woodland to emerge in a sloping field of long grass and thistles. The signposting was a little vague and faced with a choice of paths we chose the wrong one, following a sheep track until we realised our mistake and retraced our steps.

"I told you we were going the wrong way, but you obviously didn't hear me," I fibbed. "That's the second time you've got us lost today. Are you sure it's not your eyes you've got a problem with?"

Chris gave me her 'mother's getting cross' look and I grinned and shut up. Winding one another up was a mutual hobby that on one occasion had left one friend convinced we were about to have an argument.

Down the field, on the correct path, with the dyke a barely discernable hump in the grass, we climbed a stile and emerged onto a track. Very soon we reached a collection of wooden stables and outbuildings and found ourselves at the home of H.A.P.P.A., a charity dedicated to the rescue and protection of horses and ponies. I wondered if we could hire a pack pony for a couple of weeks, it would save us carrying our rucksacks, although we might have difficultly getting the pony over the hundreds of stiles that O.D. Path is notorious for.

Leaving H.A.P.P.A. and all possibility of luggage transport behind, we reached Brockweir. Little more than a hamlet by the river, the place consisted of a few old houses, some undergoing renovation, and a cast iron bridge. It was at Brockweir that the national trail divided, giving the walker a choice of two routes between there and St Briavels a few miles further up the river. We had opted to follow the lower route, which ran along the banks of the river, rather than the high level route over St Briavels Common. Our decision to keep to the river was rewarded by sightings of swans, ducks, a kingfisher, jumping fish and, finally, biting ants.

For the first mile or so we strolled along the wide sweeping loop of the broad Wye. Gently sloping, tree-covered hillsides on the opposite bank provided thermals for several buzzards that we watched as we walked along. Immediately next to the river on our side of the Wye flat land had been utilised for crops and cattle, a field's width inland the trees and sloping hillsides took over once more, stretching up to the more open land of the common. Leaving the grazing animals behind we entered an arable field where we had to battle through a towering crop of maize, edging our way between the thick stems on one side and succulent stems of Himalayan Balsam on the side of the path next to the river.

We passed an unfriendly sign forbidding picnics, fishing, boating and breathing, before stopping on the grassy river bank to have a piece of flapjack. Off came the rucksacks, boots and socks, out came the sit mats and flapjack and then, quite without warning, out came the expletives as Chris was attacked by ants.

"It's biting my toe!" she shrieked, leaping to her feet, hopping about and batting at her toes with a sock.

Chris has an unhappy knack of always choosing an ants' nest as a likely picnic spot. It was no comfort to note that on this walk, as on all our previous ones, she was reliably on form once again. Shoving our bare feet into our boots and grabbing socks, sit mats, rucksacks and flapjack we hurried along the path, searching for ant-free pastures as we went. When Chris was eventually convinced we had gone a safe distance we stopped and finally ate our flapjack.

"Look! It's drawn blood," she exclaimed, thrusting her foot towards me.

"Take that foot away from my flapjack, will you."

"It's stinging," she moaned.

"Well, it's bound to sting isn't it? All that formic acid it injected into your toe. Why don't you put some tea tree oil on?"

"Pardon?"

"Oh, for goodness sake! PUT SOME TEA TREE OIL ON!" I bellowed.

"That won't do any good."

"It might. It's supposed to be good for everything is tea tree oil. You could try dropping some in your ear," I added.

The glance Chris gave me suggested she had heard my sarcastic reply only too well. Nevertheless, she did apply a drop of tea tree oil to her red and bleeding toe.

Leaving the field we joined the road at Bigsweir Bridge, the limit of the tidal reach on the Wye, and rendezvoused with the alternative path coming down from St Briavels Common. Our Offa's Dyke walking for that day was over but we still had almost two miles to walk up the hill on the rather busy lane to reach the village of St Briavels and its youth hostel, where we had beds booked for the night. We plodded on along the hard tarmac, squirrels leaping in the trees at the side of the road, greedily harvesting the bounteous hazelnuts that grew in profusion all through that part of Gloucestershire. All day we had been treading on the empty shells of hazelnuts and the still unopened green cases of clusters of nuts. This was to be an almost daily occurrence on our walk and the sound and sensation of crunching hazelnuts underfoot formed, for me, lasting memories of Offa's Dyke Path.

At last the steep road levelled out and we entered the village of St Briavels. On our left was the old parish church of St Mary the Virgin and on the right, the imposing moated castle. The moat had long since dried up and today local volunteers tended the nature reserve that had been created in the wide, curving depression of the old moat. The Norman castle was built in 1205 as a hunting lodge for King John and was further fortified, on the orders of Edward I, by the addition of the towers in 1293 when the castle formed part of the 'Ring of Stone around Wales.' In 1947 it became a youth hostel and is the oldest building used as such in England and Wales, it must rate as one of the most interesting hostels in the YHA network.

We walked up the cobbled passage between the towering gateways, passing under the remains of the portcullis to enter a courtyard. Near a wall of the courtyard old stocks tempted hostellers to pose for photos, previous occupants of the stocks must have gone to them with far more reluctance. Studded oak doors, firmly closed against intruders and early hostellers, were set into the mossy stone walls which towered above our heads three storeys high.

We had arrived a little before five o'clock, and the hostel reception was not yet open. We sat at some picnic benches in the cobbled courtyard and waited with a growing crowd of fellow hostellers. Three macho, mud-covered mountain bikers were craving attention, talking loudly about their exploits of the day and comparing cycles. Two French families and a large organised group of American teenagers completed the multinational assembly. Dead on five the iron studded oak door was unlocked and the hostellers formed a disorderly queue to register. By the time we took our turn at the front of the queue all the most popular options from the evening meal menu had been sold out.

"Soup, then sausage and mash and fruit crumble, please," I requested.

"Er, sorry," said the Australian receptionist. "Sausage and mash has all gone."

"Okay. Chris, you order while I have a rethink."

"Pardon? Oh, order? Okay, I'll have the soup, sausage and mash and fruit salad please," Chris said.

"Sorry, the sausage and mash has still all gone," grinned the receptionist.

"Erm, chicken pie then please."

"Make that two, please," I added.

"The chicken pie has gone as well. Sorry."

"Okay, what's not gone?"

"Chilli's good, so's the fish, and the veg curry."

"Pardon?" asked Chris.

"Two chillies please!" I decided, fearing we were doomed to spend the evening going over everything twice for the benefit of the hard of hearing.

With the food finally sorted out, the receptionist took our money and gave us directions to our dorm room. We had stayed at this youth hostel once before, en route for Cardiff it had made a good stopping point on the journey. At the time all the Ashford family and I had slept in the Prison Room. That room had once housed condemned prisoners and the walls and windowsills exhibited lots of old graffiti of the 'Cedric woz here in the year of our Lord 1634, I was stitched up' variety. Whether he did it or not, Cedric was banged up but at least he had a nice view from the windows. The same windows were also used to hang prisoners from, the stone plinths stretching out at right angles to the castle wall above the windows had been purposely designed for nooses.

On our second stay at the hostel we found ourselves in the top room of one of the towers at the front of the castle: the Chaplain's room. Leaving reception we crossed the courtyard to enter a narrow passage, climbing first a worn stone spiral staircase to the first floor, and then a dark, narrow-treaded creaking wooden staircase, that bent sharply halfway up, to the top floor of the tower. Our aching knees protested with every step as we staggered up the narrow stairs, our rucksacks bashing and scraping the rough stone walls and threatening to unbalance us. How the chaplain managed those stairs if he was old and bad on his feet and with failing eyesight I do not know. Pushing open the fire door at the top we found ourselves in a round room with two window alcoves, several bunk beds and two single beds, one in each alcove. As we were the first hostellers in there we grabbed the two single beds and set about unpacking our rucksacks before heading for much needed showers.

With our freshly laundered clothes attempting to dry in the damp, enclosed drying room we went in search of the self catering kitchen and a cup of tea. It always amazes me just how much better you feel after a shower, change of clothes and a cup of tea. We sat in the lounge, in front of the empty hearth, oak panelled walls surrounding us and stretching up to the ceiling, and sipped our tea. It was a good choice to go into the lounge when we did – I found a one pound coin on the floor and as no one was about out of whose pocket it might have dropped, I gave this lonesome coin a home.

At seven o'clock all the hungry hostellers crowded into the grand dining room, more bare stone and oak panelling, to have their evening meal. Despite the food not being our first or even second choice, it was rather good. The standard of hostel food varies from one hostel to another, as there is no set menu for youth hostels to follow, but we have never had a bad meal in a hostel yet. Well, there was one, but I cooked that myself! There is a limit to how al dente pasta should be; and on that particular occasion I exceeded that limit.

Food eaten and tea drunk we went for a stroll round the village to find a post box. Chris had postcards to write and we sat at a bench beneath an ancient oak. Just as she was sticking on the last stamp it began to rain and we hurried off to post the cards before returning to the hostel. The rain increased in intensity as the night went on and we were both convinced it heralded an unwanted change in the weather.

Back at the castle, the drying room was proving to be a misnomer, with our washing seeming to be wetter now than when we had done it. Was it absorbing moisture from the old stones? Owls hooted and bats swooped around the courtyard as we hurried through the rain to the main part of the castle and the self catering kitchen to make a cup of hot chocolate.

I was the last into the dorm that night. Since we had arrived several other women had joined us in the dorm, until only one bed was left unoccupied. I crept up the stairs, trying to be as quiet as possible, totally futile as each tread creaked, cracked and groaned like an old galleon pitching on a stormy sea. The door screeched hideously as I entered the room. Not wishing to create even more disturbance I felt my way timidly across the room in the dark, choosing not to turn on the light for fear of waking anyone, although only a deaf person and Chris could have failed to hear my approach and entry. Once at my bed I fumbled about, undressing in the dark, before climbing into bed and snuggling down under the thin duvet. After an hour of listening to the owls hooting and when the church clock struck midnight, I realised my bladder was unlikely to have sufficient capacity to last until morning. Soon after that thought entered my head I must have fallen asleep.

Do you believe in ghosts? Well, do you? No? Yes? Don't know?

Had I been asked earlier I would have said the jury's still out on that one. I'm logical, scientific, daft as a brush, but intensely sceptical about things that can't be proven or that I can't see for myself. Maybe seeing really is believing. Or should that be feeling is believing?

I woke in the night: bladder full, body cold. The room felt cold. It must have been the open windows and the strong wind. Too cold to want to get out of bed and venture down two flights of stairs in the night to the nearest toilet on the ground floor, I pulled the duvet up around my shoulders. Drifting off to sleep again I felt a sudden weight on the bottom of the bed. I was dreaming, right? It was the cat, jumping onto the foot of the bed, right? But I wasn't asleep. And I wasn't at home. And there wasn't a cat in the castle. How strange, our night-time brain plays tricks on our semi conscious. I was convinced a ghost was sitting on my bed. I could feel its weight on the duvet, pinning my legs into the mattress. I lay still, half on my side, not daring to move. Thoughts of being cold overcome by thoughts of the ghostly presence only feet away. I felt myself starting to drift into sleep again and mentally shook myself. Maybe the ghost wanted me to fall asleep? Eventually, after what seemed like many, many minutes, I bravely kicked out with my legs. There was no weighty resistance, the ghost had gone.

I became acutely aware of my full bladder. What time was it? How long till daylight? The room was in total darkness. Rain lashed at the window and wind shook the branches of the trees. I knew with a certainty I have rarely known anything that a ghost waited for me in the dark at the bottom of the stairs. And I knew I would have to wait for daylight before I could go to the toilet. I slept with crossed legs until morning brought enough light for me to slip out of the dorm and down the stairs in safety to the toilet.

St Briavels Castle, like all old buildings, claims its fair share of ghosts and hauntings. Until my night time experiences in the Chaplain's Room, I had taken all such claims with a stroke-threateningly large pinch of salt and a healthy dose of 'yeah, yeah go along with the tradition of it all' scepticsism. In fact, ghost walks around the castle were a regular feature, one had been run by the staff that evening, but neither Chris nor I had taken part. Relating my nocturnal experiences to Chris the next day met with jocularity, teasing and plain, scientific, unarguable logic. She thought I had imagined the whole thing. And in the cold light of day, I began to wonder myself. It was a couple of months later that Helen, a friend of Chris' daughter, Clare, got a temporary job as an assistant at St Briavels youth hostel.

"Ask her about the ghosts," I implored Chris. "See if she can tell us which rooms they haunt and what they do."

The reply came in the form of an email a week later when Helen began work at the hostel.

"Oh, Julia!" exclaimed Chris, reading her emails. "Helen says that one of the ghosts has been seen at the foot of the spiral stairs. And several people have reported feeling a weight on the end of their bed and something pulling at the bed covers when they are lying in bed."

Perhaps my night time brain hadn't been so over imaginative after all

Chapter Three

The morning was as damp as our laundry. Chris' silk socks, hand knitted with care by her sister, remained wet for most of the day, although our blouses were dry enough to wear.

Breakfast was the usual noisy, hostel affair of clattering crockery, chattering diners and scraping chairs. I experienced a moment of panic when it became clear that the automatic tea vending machine had gone on the blink. It was dispensing half measures of a wishy washy liquid that might have been tea or then again might have been washing up water. Tepid and tasteless, the tea did little to satisfy my early morning craving for a decent cuppa, and it looked as if I would have to go without, until one of the kitchen assistants arrived with an odd collection of tools with which she set about the innards of the vending machine. A crowd of thirsty hostellers crowded round to watch proceedings, the men giving useless advice as is often the case when they spot a woman with a screwdriver. A couple of whacks with the handle of the screwdriver did little to effect an improvement and the woman eventually gave up, muttering something about contracts and plumbers. She returned sans tools and avec a large, steaming teapot. Problem solved!

Having collected our packed lunches from reception we were soon on our way, down the steep lane and into dense woodland once more. There was dampness in the air and moisture on the ground as we followed the woodland track between the massive trees but the rain held off. More diversions to conserve the dyke led us along a wide muddy track away from the original line of the trail. Sudden movement to the right caught our attention and we swung our heads in time to watch a wood mouse scurrying across a pile of slowly rotting logs before disappearing out of sight in the leafy undergrowth. Shortly afterwards a diversion took us up a steep slope, the path zigzagging up the muddy hillside on rough cut steps, to rejoin the dyke once more.

Desperate for some urinary relief I hunted round for a wide-trunked tree to provide adequate screening but voices carrying to us up the slope put a stop to my plans. Killing time, we broke open the apricots and awaited the arrival, and departure, of the advancing walkers. Individually they arrived at the top of the slope, stopping, much to my distress, for a chat. They were doing a circular day walk that would eventually return them to Bigsweir Bridge along the other side of the river. After exchanging the usual sort of walker talk – weather, path condition, route – they said their farewells, clambered over the stile and disappeared across the next field.

Once they were out of sight, I dived behind the nearest tree, broad-trunked or no, for my long overdue relief. Too much haste on that occasion nearly resulting in a nettle enema. Look before you squat!

We climbed the stile to cross a few fields, now walking above both the woodland and the dyke that formed its upper boundary. The sun came out, dispelling the last of the morning mist and promising a warm day to come. We followed field paths for a while, passing Coxbury Farm before plunging into woodland again at the Woodland Trust managed Oxpasture Wood. More conservation work meant another small diversion but it was a well marked route and easy to follow. According to information boards, dormice live in the wood, feasting on the glut of hazelnuts and berries. I found much evidence of this delightful little mammal in the form of distinctively eaten hazelnuts, but actual wildlife sightings were non-existent, even the ubiquitous grey squirrels seemed to be keeping out of sight for once.

Beyond Highbury Wood the path dropped towards the river, leaving the shady woodland to pass a collection of ramshackle farm buildings and a brand new telephone mast, from which the sharp aroma of bitumen still emanated. The chemical odour cut across the organic smell of wild flowers and leafy woodland. After the heavy rains in the night the dry day had become quite warm and very sunny, a fact we had been oblivious to whilst walking in the shady woods.

We met the river once more at Lower Redbrook which, together with Upper Redbrook, was once a small industrialised community. From the hilltop above, the view of Lower Redbrook, sitting on a curving stretch of the river where a steel railway bridge crossed the glistening water, gave little hint of the bustling industry that must have once filled the valley. Iron ore had been smelted here and a busy wharf had existed on the riverbank where now a memorial park provided an ideal lunch spot. The buildings themselves, cottages once home to families whose livelihoods depended on the iron industry, were not the only clues to the industrial heritage: a wall we had passed had been constructed of a mixture of stones and blocks of clinker, no doubt from the foundries.

Chris cannot pass a sign, a memorial or a notice without stopping to read it. And the computer printout A4 sheet of paper pinned to a telegraph pole was no exception. Someone had lost their parrot. 'African, grey, answers to the name of Flint. Hand tame but nervous,' read the description. What did that mean? Flint would perch on your arm but then poo on it?

We had barely sat down on a cast iron bench and began our packed lunch, listening to the sounds of ducks and swans on the river, when a lone woman walker approached.

"Hello there!" she called cheerfully. "Do you mind if I join you for lunch?"

"Hello," we replied in unison, somewhat bemused at her request.

She threw herself down onto the adjoining bench, slung off her capacious rucksack and began unfastening various parcels of food from the numerous straps and bungees adorning the outside of her pack. Out of a plastic carrier bag came a pair of socks and a sandwich. The socks, obviously wet, were draped in the sun and the sandwich was quickly consumed. Between mouthfuls the woman chattered away, asking questions about our intentions (purely honourable madam, we're both married, thank you!) and commenting on her experiences of the path so far. Walking on her own for over a week, she was obviously in need of a good chat, but although she asked lots of questions she seemed barely to listen to our responses before launching into her next sentence.

"Can't beat a good cheese and pickle sandwich," she remarked, biting into the said sandwich with gusto. "What are you on?" she continued through a mouthful of Cheddar, Branston and bread.

"Pardon?" asked Chris.

"Tuna mayonnaise," I butted in, coming to the rescue.

"And bananas! They're excellent too. I see you've got apricots," the woman added, as I took the packet of supermarket fodder out of my rucksack.

"Yes, we like them," I remarked. "Full of iron, vitamins and sulphur dioxide."

The woman cast me a strange glance and took another bite of her sandwich before continuing unfazed,

"There aren't many benches further north on the path. This is one of the first I've come across."

"Really?" I asked.

"Or signposts. It's very badly signed coming from the north, I've found."

"We thought the signposting has been rather good," commented Chris, taking another bite of her sandwich."

"Oh, it's been dreadful! Is that a bought packed lunch?" she asked, eyeing our identical paper bags.

"Yes, we stayed at the youth hostel in St Briavels last night and ordered it from there," I explained.

"Prefer to make my own. You know what you're getting. No dirty fingers!"

Chris and I both eyed the remains of our lunches before taking another bite. Considering what we had touched that morning – stiles, gateposts, fungi, half eaten hazelnuts, my knickers – it was likely our unwashed fingers were dirtier than the hostel sandwich-maker's had been.

"Yes, very few benches," continued the woman, as bananas took over from cheese and pickle sandwich. "And the stiles are so dirty! Far too dirty to sit on."

"Hm, it's probably all those walkers' muddy boots standing on them," I commented, at a loss for something sensible to say. Chris for once, with her blocked ear, was proving rather unhelpful in the talking to strange walkers situation.

"Some people are walking the path without maps, you know! Can you believe it? I hope you've got adequate maps."

"Oh, yes," assured Chris, coming to life suddenly. "I love maps, find them fascinating, we always have maps."

I cast a sideways glance at her, half expecting her to produce the evidence. We had maps, or rather sections of maps; several of them in fact, as the long narrow route of Offa's Dyke Path covered a proliferation of Ordnance Survey maps that would have given us unnecessary additional weight had we brought every map in its entirety. These map sections were carefully numbered in sequence and were, we thought, a foolproof method of route finding for us. But like all well thought out plans ours was to come adrift later in the holiday when we realised one of the sections was missing! Fortunately the guidebook we were using also contained maps.

Our food consumed we began packing up our litter and preparing to set off.

"Have a nice walk!" said the woman, adding cheerfully: "You've a long, long climb out of this village."

Gee, thanks for that!

The woman began preparing to leave and as we looked back a minute after setting off ourselves we saw her wandering along the road in the wrong direction.

"Where is she going?" I asked. "I thought she was walking north to south."

"She is," replied Chris dryly. "But it's very badly signed coming from the north, you know!"

Leaving the park, the river and the lost lone female walker, we set off up the long, long climb to find it wasn't that bad. Long perhaps, but not persistently steep. After four and a half miles and climbing approximately 875 feet, the summit was reached when we emerged at the lookout point by the Kymin above Monmouth. But before that the climb followed first the road for a short distance, then a track and then through fields, alongside the woods once more. I noticed that many of the fields had padlocked gates, making me wonder if cattle or horse theft was a problem in this idyllic rural area.

A strange bird call reminded us both of the missing parrot.

"Was that Flint?" asked Chris, searching round in the hope of spotting a tame but nervous African Grey.

"Nah, didn't sound much like 'pieces of eight' to me," I responded sarcastically.

Nearing Kymin we passed through an old, rusted, ornamental kissing gate, before walking along a narrow fenced path. Last autumn's leaf litter crunched underfoot and looking down Chris noticed, just in time, a pair of pink-tinted sunglasses before they too were crunched underfoot. I picked them up and tried them on, coming over all Anastacia but was prevented from bursting into song (perhaps no bad thing for anything in the vicinity with half decent hearing and Chris) because the ground tipped, the horizon shifted and everything blurred dizzyingly.

"Uh! They're prescription sunglasses," I gasped, hurriedly taking them off. "Far too strong for me!"

Chris took them from me as I gladly put my own comfy pair of specs back on.

"They're okay for me," she commented, turning to look at me.

"Take them off, you look ridiculous!"

"These must have cost a bit of money. Someone will be miffed," she remarked, replacing the loud sunglasses with her own much tamer pair.

"Do you think Anastacia could be walking Offa's Dyke?" I wondered. "Don't suppose she'd miss one pair of specs, she's got dozens."

"I think you've overdosed on the apricots," Chris sighed, shaking her head. "Too much sulphur dioxide – it's affected your brain."

"Thank you."

"What for?"

"The implied acknowledgment that I even have one."

We put the sunglasses on top of a fence post, in case Anastacia or whoever had lost them, came back to look for them, and went on our way. Soon we reached a small car park and then the edge of the high ridge above Monmouth: we had reached the National Trust owned land of the Kymin. Crowning this impressive wooded ridge there sits a cream painted Round House and a Naval Temple.

Both buildings were built in the late eighteenth century by members of a dining club called the Kymin Club, an early forerunner of the Pudding Club I suppose. The two storey Round House, with its castellated tower, contained a kitchen and banqueting room. The diners would no doubt admire the view from the escarpment before consuming quantities of fine food and wine, after which they were probably more likely to fall into the view than appreciate it. The Round House had recently been restored by the

National Trust and was open to the public, just not on the day we were there! We had to content our selves with peering through the windows, shielding our eyes with our hands to cut out the reflections. The nearby Naval Temple, complete with a large statue of Britannia sitting resplendent on the top, was erected in 1800 by members of the Kymin Club in celebration of Britain's naval victories of that time.

Nelson breakfasted there, together with his mistress Emma Hamilton and her husband. A case of 'two's company and three's a crowd' I should think. It is said they all admired the view. Nelson and Emma's relationship seemed to have occurred, if not with the blessing of Sir William Hamilton, at least with his acceptance. Almost twice as old as his wife, Sir William regarded Nelson as "my dearest friend ... the most virtuous, loyal and truly brave character I have ever met". Nelson's relationship with his own wife had deteriorated considerably and when she finally told him to choose between herself and Lady Hamilton his decision was not a difficult one: Emma Hamilton had borne his daughter, Horatia, at the beginning of that year. Nelson bought a house in Surrey in which he lived with both Hamiltons. Sir William died in 1803 and of his death Nelson wrote: "The world never lost a more upright and accomplished gentleman". But alone at last the lovers' happiness was brief, Nelson died during the Battle of Trafalgar in 1805. His body was preserved in a barrel of brandy and brought back to Britain where he was buried in the crypt of St Paul's Cathedral. Emma soon spent all their wealth and died in poverty in France.

Horatia was returned to England and grew up in the charge of Nelson's sisters; she married a curate from Norfolk and eventually died aged eighty-one after a much less colourful life than either of her parents.

We stood with a small crowd of sightseers, leaning against the metal railings and looking out across the countryside below. The views from the Kymin were extensive. In the immediate foreground wooded slopes dropped away to fields, then the river and the market town of Monmouth. Beyond the town a patchwork of colourful fields, woods and rolling hills stretched away to the Black Mountains on the horizon. We would be walking across that unfolding landscape over the next few days and it was fascinating to try to pick out points on the ground that we could relate back to the map of our route. Hills such as Skirrid Fawr, Sugar Loaf and Hatterall were easy to locate, but as for our exact route through the valleys and over the less pronounced hills we could only make rough guesses.

As we began our descent through the woodland towards the Wye with Monmouth sitting on the far bank, my mobile phone suddenly burst into life.

"Ooh, I'm vibrating," I called to Chris, as the top pocket of my rucksack emitted the theme music from the Pink Panther. I hastened down the slope to Chris, who after a brief struggle managed to extract the vibrating handset from my rucksack.

"Hello!" I called, fumbling with the keypad and clamping the phone to my ear.

"It's me," came a calm and weary sounding Roger.

"I know it's you. I've got your number set to play the Pink Panther." My choice of tune for calls from Roger's mobile had seemed rather appropriate as the music always reminded me of the bumbling Inspector Clouseau. "How's things?"

"The cats are fine. The car is fine. I'm fine, thank you for asking. Thought I'd ring you, as you've not been in touch."

"We've been in remote places with no signals," I excused feebly.

"For three days?"

"I've only been away two and a half!"

"What number is on our wheelie bin?" he asked, in a complete change of subject.

"Pardon? Our wheelie bin? You're phoning me to talk about our wheelie bin! I'm in the middle of Wales, or it might be England – difficult to keep track with all this cross border walking – and you're asking me about our wheelie bin!"

Wheelie bins were a new introduction to our backward little borough and had been causing unmitigated confusion with some residents who had failed to grasp the concept of recycle one week, bin the next. Bins had been left out on the wrong days, in the wrong place and with the wrong contents. Eager to do my bit to save the planet I had happily and keenly taken wheelie bins and doorstep recycling to heart, following all instructions to the letter; unfortunately not all our neighbours had proved to be quite so enthusiastic.

"Yes, I want to talk wheelie bins. After sixteen years of marriage you should be grateful we can still find subjects to discuss. So, if you can tear your mind away from borders and dykes for two minutes, will you please tell me what number our wheelie bin has on it?" repeated Roger with mounting irritation.

"Well, six, of course. What other number would it have on it, for goodness sake! What a stupid question."

"Not twenty-two?"

"Roger, have we moved house while I've been away? Hmm? I don't think so! In which case why would our wheelie bin have twenty-two on it when we live at number six?"

"Because the wheelie bin now sitting on our drive has number twenty-two on it."

"Well, some gormless sod's taken our wheelie bin by mistake then!" I exclaimed with disbelief. "Have you been down to number twenty-two to see if our bin's there?"

"Yep, you can't get into number twenty-two's drive, the gate's locked."

"Well, we'd not had the bin long. It's not like I've grown attached to it. So why don't you just change the number?"

"Oh, I suppose so. I didn't think of that," he muttered. "Okay, then. Have a nice time. Bye."

"Oh, yeah. Thanks. It's been nice talking to you," I replied sarcastically. "Bye yourself."

I turned to hand the mobile to Chris for her to put back in my rucksack, only to find she was leaning against a tree doubled up with laughter.

"Yes, yes, very funny. My wheelie bin's gone AWOL. Whilst you're enjoying yourself might I remind you of a phone conversation you had with your husband once when we were walking the South West Coast Path? Do you remember – the one when he phoned to say he'd won chocolate body paint and handcuffs in a radio phone-in competition? Makes my wheelie bin seem rather tame."

But if I thought a chat about wheelie bins was bad enough, worse was to come when I phoned my mum later that evening.

The steep woodland path descended to a quiet lane which we followed before turning off into a field. The path across the field passed several trees and coverts and long bracken grew up in some parts. Monmouth was slowly getting closer and with the loss in height, the town was gradually hiding itself from view but it was not the only thing that was hiding.

"There's a horse in this field," Chris informed me nervously. She is not comfortable with anything equine and usually goes to great lengths and detours to avoid walking near horses, ponies, donkeys, mules and probably zebras too if we ever encountered any.

"Where?" I asked, glancing around. "I can't see a horse."

"It's hiding behind that bush!" she whispered, as if afraid it would hear her and come galloping out.

"What do you mean? Horses don't hide behind bushes. It's not lying in wait to leap out and terrorise you!"

"It is," she insisted. "It's hiding. I saw it."

"There's really nothing to worry about," I said, adopting my most caring voice. "Horses, given a choice, rarely run people down. They are much more likely to try and avoid them."

"Try telling that to Emily Davison," muttered Chris anxiously, still continuing to look around.

As we continued down the field, the horse seemed to have disappeared, had it ever been there at all. Yet Chris persisted in her wary search for the hidden equine. Her comical, slow progress and anxious glances from side to side became too much for me, and in a state of rapidly growing hilarity I crept up behind her and executed a fair imitation of a whinnying horse. Her reaction was immediate: she leapt into the air with a shriek and, on landing, set off at a run, only stopping when she realised I was in hysterics behind her.

"You.... You..."

"Oh, god! You should have seen yourself," I laughed.

With Chris ignoring me, we crossed the border for the fourth time, walking over the Wye along the busy road bridge and entered the lovely market town of Monmouth. As well as the ruins of the castle, Monmouth is awash with other historical architecture. Medieval churches, a thirteenth century gatehouse on the bridge over the River Monnow, Georgian halls and a fifteenth century priory sit alongside the ornate buildings of the Haberdashers' Monmouth School. The school, originally opened in 1615 as a free boys' grammar school at the bequest of William Jones, a member of the Haberdasher's Company, is still providing education today but now they take girls too. The ornate building with its coat of arms above the gate was the first building we came to in Monmouth.

Nelson and Lady Hamilton are not the only persons of note to be linked with Monmouth. Geoffrey of Monmouth, that famous chronicler of English history, attended school in the town. Henry V, Agincourt and all that, was born in Monmouth Castle in 1387, and as we walked down the main street we could not help but notice the statue to Charles Rolls who lived nearby. The co-founder of the most famous car manufacturer in the world, he was a keen racing cyclist who progressed to ballooning and then aviation, before founding the Rolls Royce Company with American F H Royce. Rolls died in 1910, when his French built plane broke up in mid air, despite a fall of only twenty feet he died of a fractured skull; rather an ignominious end to the first man to fly non stop both ways across the English Channel.

Near the imposing red bricked grammar school we passed a large group of black suited men and women, standing chatting. Curiosity overcame annoyance and Chris spoke to me to ask what I thought the occasion was.

"Funeral?" I ventured. "They're all wearing black ties. It must be a funeral."

"But they're drinking champagne," Chris observed.

"Funeral of a teacher they didn't like? You know: 'thank Gawd the old blighter's gone, far too keen on the old cane if you ask me, what?'" I said in a silly upper class accent. Chris gave me a strange side long look and once again muttered something about apricots.

We found the toilets and having found them and used them, quickly found a small cake shop which also sold ice cream. Sitting outside the shop on a collection of wooden benches ranged in front of the plate glass window and surrounded by beautiful hanging baskets and tubs of flowers, we chilled out with the delicious farmhouse ice cream and watched the locals passing by. A young woman and her elderly mother approached, laden down with a vast assortment of bulging shopping bags, and dumped them on a spare seat next to me. Ordering the young woman to 'go and get her dad' the elderly lady then stood wearily in front of us and waited. We watched the daughter head off to a nearby car and begin an animated conversation through the window with an elderly chap. With the daughter still trying to persuade her dad to join his wife for a cup of coffee, the elderly lady wandered into the cake shop. Muffled voices reached us from inside the shop, before the lady came out and began complaining to her returning daughter that the shop had run out of milk.

"It's gone off," she said, tilting her head in the direction of the shop.

"Sit down mum," ordered the exasperated daughter.

The mother sat down tiredly at a table outside the adjoining tearoom and a waiter came out.

"I want a takeaway coffee," demanded the old virago. "I'm worn out."

"Sorry madam, we don't do takeaways. The cake shop next door does."

"They've run out of milk," she snapped. "It's gone off."

The man went into the tearoom and quickly emerged carrying a bottle of milk, which he carried into the cake shop. From inside the shop we could hear him asking if they had run out of milk. But apparently the cake shop did not require any milk. As we got up to go, heaving our rucksacks on, we could clearly hear the two assistants in the cake shop.

"She's sitting on their bloody chairs, telling him our bloody milk's gone off," ranted the first girl. "It's her bloody fault! Putting her bloody shopping bags on our seats and then complaining she needed to sit down."

Having enjoyed the ice cream and the floorshow we left to find our B&B, stumbling across it quite by chance near the church. Chris was sure it was the right place, convinced she could remember the name of the house but I was not so sure.

"Are you positive this is it?" I questioned her. "We can't just knock at the door and then discover they're not expecting us and we've got the wrong place."

"Yes, I'm sure," Chris insisted. "I remember the name."

"Perhaps we had better get our list out and double check."

As we stood there on the pavement bickering and fumbling through our accommodation list, we heard a creaking noise and the front door opened and a friendly lady smiled out at us.

"Told you!" smiled Chris smugly as we were ushered inside.

The house was a wonderful old town house, with creaking oak floors, casement windows and bowing ceilings. Originally, several hundred years ago, it had been a coaching inn but over the centuries its shape and its purpose had changed, passageways had been converted into rooms and the building had grown in size.

Having shown us the bathroom and arranged a convenient time for breakfast, the owner added one final comment: "The festival is on this week, it's likely to get a bit noisy later this evening."

"I'm sure we'll be okay," I replied. "We've got earplugs. Past experience has proved they are very useful in youth hostels. We can always use them."

"Oh, good!" she replied with far more relief than seemed warranted, and with that she left us with an apologetic smile.

"I don't think we'll be too disturbed by the music, do you?" remarked Chris. "The stage that we saw being set up was quite a way from here."

"Well, you shouldn't be. An elephant could sneeze next to you and you wouldn't hear it at the moment!"

Later that evening we walked through the town, watching a stage crew putting the final touches to the stage: lights, smoke machines and speakers. Over the next few days of the Monmouth Festival there were various artist and bands performing live. Groups like Dr and the Medics and The Stranglers, which I remembered from my teenage years, and plenty of other groups whose names I didn't recognise.

We headed down the main street until we found a quiet fish and chip restaurant away from the crowds of early evening revellers. I opted for fish and chips but, with reminiscences of childhood, Chris ordered faggots.

"Er, what exactly are faggots?" I asked, as the waitress brought her plate with several brown lumps covered in steaming gravy.

"Pardon?"

"WHAT ARE FAGGOTS?" I reiterated in louder tones. My repeated question raised an eyebrow and some sniggers from a nearby table where four men were tucking into sausage and chips.

"Oh!" gasped Chris. "Er, well, sort of... I prefer not to think about it actually. But it's sort of meat with herbs and very it's nice."

The high street in Monmouth was lined with small shops and businesses and had very few national chains. One big name store that had infiltrated this lovely market town was Marks and Spencer. Tempted by the thought of fresh juice or fruit for supper we went inside. But the healthy supper option was quickly forgotten when we saw the tempting array of mousses and desserts in the chiller cabinet. Into the shopping basket went two rich chocolate desserts, and as we made our oblivious way past the fruit counter to the checkouts Chris was distracted by a chilled drinks cabinet. Healthy juice? No, alcoholic mixers and gin in cans.

"Ooh, look! They've got cans of ready-mixed G and T," squealed Chris with excitement.

"That's nice," I replied absent-mindedly.

"I could have a gin and tonic tonight. Just what I need after a day's walk. Good for my knees."

"Will it help your hearing as well?"

But Chris either was not listening or did not hear. In any case she was far too busy selecting a can of Gordon's finest.

As we wandered back up the main street, Chris got out her mobile and began composing a text message to a friend. Soon a reply came back. Reading it, Chris began to laugh. "Julie says I should ditch everything in my rucksack and fill it with M&S G&T instead. She thinks it will be much more useful."

By the time we reached the stage in the market square, the first act was performing to a growing crowd of people who thronged across the now closed main street. The atmosphere was relaxed and good humoured as locals and holidaymakers with their children in tow listened to the music, brought drinks out from the nearby pubs, and ate burgers, hot dogs and candyfloss purchased at several hastily erected street vendors' stalls. Amongst the crowd we saw a couple who had ignored our cheerful 'hellos' at Sedbury Cliffs, they ignored us again but this time it was mutual. Overlooking the stage, residents at a pub watched from the bedrooms as the acts got into full swing and full volume.

"Glad we're not staying there," remarked Chris. "We'd need more than earplugs to get to sleep."

We walked back to the B&B along a different road that followed the line of the river Monnow at the back of the town. The evening sun was setting beyond the fields across the river, its mellow light illuminating the russet tones of the red sandstone buildings of the old priory. Below us a streak of electric blue and a high-pitched call drew our attention as a kingfisher skimmed low across the surface of the river. And on the overgrown path below the elevated pavement on which we stood, a lone black and white cat crept stealthily through the grass, picking her way between discarded beer cans and scattered litter. A lovely spot on the edge of the river: spoiled by the inconsiderateness of people too lazy to find a litterbin. How I hate litterbugs.

I decided to phone my mum before it got too late and dialled her number as we watched the sun sink below the line of trees on the horizon.

"Hello, it's me," I said cheerfully when she answered the phone. "How's things?"

"Oh! You've remembered my number then? Are you having a nice time? Oh, shut up will you!" she shouted. "Sorry, the cat's driving me mad."

"Er, right. Yes, we're having a very nice time."

"Company's terrible." I heard Chris mutter.

"What's wrong with the cat?" I asked.

"I don't know, she keeps being sick."

"Fur ball? Worms?"

"No, none of that."

"You've not been cooking again have you?"

"Don't be so cheeky!" retorted my mum. "I wouldn't care if she did it in the kitchen. But she seems to think it has to be distributed about the house, the only place she hasn't thrown up is in the toilet."

I barely retained my composure as I was suddenly faced with a mental image of my mum's cat kneeling in front of the toilet, gripping the seat with its forepaws and wishing it hadn't had so much to drink the night before, like something out of a Louis Wain painting.

"Maybe it's the heat. It has been warm today," I pacified. "She'll probably be fine tomorrow. How are you?"

"Me? I'm worn out, spent half the day on my hands and knees."

"Oh, well, look on the bright side – at least you don't have to worry about your wheelie bin."

Back in our room, with the laundry drying suspended at the open windows, we ate our sickly desserts, drank our respective tea and gin and went to sleep to the lullabies of rock acts performing half a mile away. It must have been around eleven o'clock when the concert finished, the sudden silence waking us. But the live music was soon replaced by a hideous racket from the ugly flats across the road. One of the flats, totally out of character from the surrounding buildings, seemed to be home to a tone deaf, inconsiderate lout with terrible taste in music. The noise blared from the open windows of his flat long into the early hours and where earplugs had not been necessary for the festival, we found ourselves frantically cramming the spongy plugs into our lug holes to block out the din. The sound was successfully silenced but the bass seemed to pound across the road and into the foundations of the old house, through the floors and into our beds. It was like trying to sleep on a subwoofer.

Chapter Four

The music (I use that term loosely) had stopped sometime in the night, possibly because the lout had eventually turned it off but more likely I thought because one of his neighbours had broken in and bludgeoned both him and his hifi system to death with anything they could lay their hands on. Or maybe the credit on his electricity meter had run out? Who knows? Who cares? The silence, broken only by the occasional rumble of traffic, was bliss.

We were both full after the wonderful breakfast and it was almost with digestive meltdown that we took receipt of our packed lunches of wholemeal sandwiches, apples and a packet of biscuits. Then we were on our way but not very far, soon stopping at a greengrocer's shop. Yes, we were full – and so were our rucksacks – but we could not resist the fruity display spilling out onto the pavement at the local greengrocers. Living in a town where greengrocers are limited to a couple of ethnic shops selling mainly dried rice with the odd bunch of chilli peppers and bindi, and where the only alternatives are supermarkets with their regimented rows of identically shaped and fairly tasteless foreign fruit available all year regardless of season, it was a pleasure for both of us to come across a genuine greengrocer, selling seasonal English and foreign fruit.

Leaving me guarding the rucksacks, Chris went inside to buy as much as we could carry and eat before it spoilt. She came out, arms full of brown paper bags, and began distributing them between our rucksacks.

"Plums, cherries, nectarines," she rhymed off. "And the shop keeper says he'll set up a stall at the roadside as we pass through Pandy, so we can stock up again."

"I wish!"

We followed the main street, passing the stage, now surrounded by discarded litter and plastic beer glasses; the market stalls were already erected and doing a bustling trade with local shoppers, selling everything from vegetables to mobile phones. Our next stop on that busy Saturday morning was Millets. I was desperately in need of a new hydration system. Hydration system! Doesn't it sound wonderfully hi-tech? It is a plastic bottle with a long hose and a mouthpiece, a simple idea but one that saves having to take off your rucksack every time you want a slurp of water, or gin in Chris' case. My old Platypus hydration system that I had carefully cleaned with sterilising solution after it was last used, was dispensing a foul tasting liquid I was reluctant to bathe my feet in, never mind drink. Having got a new bottle, I then had to buy something to put in it. Gin was not an option: one glass of alcohol was enough to make my world spin, my brain ache and my legs go funny. I would have to settle for water. Somerfield provided the solution at 18p for a bottle of 'table water'.

"Table water!" I exclaimed, reading the label. "Define table water! It's another of those marketing ploys to make the unsuspecting, and quite possibly brain dead, consumer spend money on yet another unnecessary product. Look, there's no mention of it being spring water. I bet its tap water. People pay 18p for a litre of tap water and a bit of plastic packaging with all the associated environmental issues of disposal and recycling. It's not even spring water. What are we doing as a nation? I mean can you believe we import foreign spring water? Don't we have enough springs in this country? What about the food miles? The pollution? Why, for goodness sake is it necessary to buy bottled water at all?"

"Because," interrupted Chris, as I paused to draw breath, "you've nothing to drink for the rest of the day otherwise!"

All the thoughts of water had had a detrimental effect on my bladder and as we left Monmouth we made use of the public toilets, it would be days before we came across more on the path. We crossed the Monnow, walking under the arches of the thirteenth century gatehouse that guarded the bridge. The gatehouse is the only one of its kind in Britain but it reminded me very much of one I had seen in Strasbourg. The difference was the river flowing under the bridge and gatehouse in Strasbourg was free of shopping trolleys and motorway cones, and the flower tubs and hanging baskets were spectacular as opposed to nice.

A mile or so of road walking took us out of Monmouth through a new housing estate and along a quiet country lane. Field and woodland paths carried us on a gradual ascent to the rolling hills above the town. As we walked through King's Wood it began to rain, a light drizzle that barely penetrated the canopy of hazel, oak and sycamore. The woodland floor was awash with hazelnuts and the branches alive with squirrels. Bright yellow fungi sprouted, like discarded lemon peel, from a decaying log. And in the overgrown shrubbery at the side of the path Chris found an old boundary stone that rated a mention in the guidebook. A little further on and I found our second pair of lost sunglasses. Someone else had obviously found them before me, as this pair was sitting atop a signpost. Anastacia's again? Er, no – not nearly loud enough – these were more like Jarvis Cocker.

It is usually me that has a bladder capacity problem, but that morning Chris was the one who first sought shelter behind a tree. Leaving me sitting on a log she exited stage left and after an interval of a couple of minutes she emerged from the undergrowth, barely had she done so when an elderly couple of walkers entered stage right: timing is everything! The couple muttered 'hellos' and cast a curious glance at Chris who was struggling to put her rucksack on, before heading off down the muddy path.

"Phew, that was a close thing," she gasped, fastening the waist strap and preparing to set off. "Think I got away with it though."

"Actually, I think they suspected what you'd been up to. Pretty obvious really – you've got a bit of fern sticking out the back of your shorts."

Down the muddy path we slid, emerging at a gate onto a lane. The couple were nowhere in sight and I decided to take the opportunity of some wayside shrubbery to make a quick toilet stop myself. But the shrubbery was the stinging, prickling variety and as I pratted about in the undergrowth trying to avoid the nettles and brambles my aim, such as it is for a woman, was decidedly off.

"Oh, great!" I gasped, stumbling back towards the lane and hastily rearranging my clothing.

"What's up?" asked Chris.

"I've peed in me boot!"

"Pardon?"

"I've got my foot all wet," I repeated in louder tones.

As I emerged from the undergrowth shaking a wet foot the couple stood up from a hidden bench just twenty yards down the road. They must have thought all we did was wee! We got ahead of them just a little while later, they had taken a wrong turning and were wandering about aimlessly in a field, but they soon caught us up to overtake us in silent embarrassment, striding out with their woolly red socks, heavy leather three season boots, map, compass and G.P.S. Chris and I exchanged silent glances and grinned; yes, we might pee in the woods but at least we had not got lost. For once.

We soon passed a fancy house, looking impregnable behind its ornamental railing. It was just a shame the intricate wrought iron gate was not closed. Had it been closed, not only would it have prevented unwanted visitors getting in, it might have stopped a huge, vociferous, wrinkle-faced dog from getting out and chasing us. Chris whimpered in panic. I turned, wishing to see what I was about to be dinner for. In the past we have been chased by a dog as mean as Anne Robinson but this one certainly could not be likened to her. Here was one mutt much in need of a face-lift, or three. It was one of those pedigree mutts people pay a fortune for and then have to spend half their time cleaning the numerous folds of skin, folds deep enough to hide food, drool, slippers, next door's cat and small children.

We left the lane after only a short distance, following the acorn signs of the National Trail to enter a few fields where the path echoed the meandering course of the River Trothy. Our route took us by the site of a ruined Cistercian abbey, so decimated by Henry VIII and the subsequent harvesting of its stonework that not even the foundations remained. We stared at the field of grass, straining to pick out any variation in colour or pattern that might indicate where the abbey had once stood but it was impossible to tell. The field's herd of long horn cattle watched us with bovine curiosity as they ripped up mouthfuls of grass with their pink and black tongues. What did they make of us, standing in a field, pointing at nothing when we could be eating grass instead?

The drizzle of earlier had cleared and the blue sky was patterned with white clouds as we emerged back onto the lane for a short distance of road walking. These short stretches of lane linking up off road walking were to be a characteristic of Offa's Dyke Path, something we had not come across with the coastal national trails we had walked. On the coast, roads were crossed but rarely followed, but on Offa's Dyke the lanes and roads were links in the chain of footpaths and bridleways that make up the long distance trail. By the time we reached Prestatyn many of the miles under our feet had been on lanes and roads.

Back in the grassy fields once more, we soon found an ideal spot for lunch. Sitting on an elevated bank above the stream we shrugged off our rucksacks and set out our picnic lunch. Overhanging willows dipped their branches into the stream, alders stood half rooted in the water, balsam grew on the far bank, flies buzzed and the occasional minnow broke the surface of the glassy water. Tree creepers, a delightful yet plain-looking bird, walked up and down the tree trunks, searching out insects in the fissured bark; long tailed tits flittered between the branches and two green woodpeckers flew across the field, all provided avian interest as we ate. Our packed lunch was as filling as the breakfast. We munched our way steadily through two filling farmhouse cheddar and onion chutney wholemeal sandwiches apiece. The packet of Farmhouse Biscuits, made in a little factory only a mile from where I live, were left unopened, although we did manage a plum and some cherries.

After lunch we followed the riverside path, passing a grotty farmhouse. A washing machine had been dumped in the field near the house, the field was awash with slurry, and rusting hulks of abandoned farm machinery and old cars lay in a pile, surrounded by a forest of rampant nettles. It was a depressing sight and made me wonder, not for the first time, how anyone could live in such beautiful surroundings and spoil them with such careless disrespect.

A few more fields and we left the river behind to emerge at the churchyard of an isolated and medieval church with a totally unpronounceable Welsh name. The guidebook kindly translated it: St. Michael's of the Fiery Meteor. The name conjured images of a stern rector, standing in his pulpit, preaching a damning sermon of fire and brimstone to a congregation of quaking villagers. The guidebook made a plea for donations towards its upkeep, hmm, the writer had not made a plea for donations to HAPPA, a bit of favouritism there I think. We didn't donate, nor did we go in: the door was firmly locked, but to ensure possible donations were not lost a coin slot was provided in the door. Sorry, we don't want you wandering round our church but we don't mind taking your money.

A steep climb through grassy fields brought us puffing and panting to a stile in the hedge and our first toad of the walk. Actually it could have been a frog; well to be truthful it could have been a mouse or even a bat. It was only on close examination that we were able to say with any degree of confidence that the desiccated, black corpse impaled on a spiky thorn was indeed a toad. How it had got four feet into the air to impale itself on the thorn we could only guess at.

Climbing the stile we emerged onto a quiet 'B' road and began heading in the direction of an opulent house marked on the map as The Grange. Views opened up ahead of Sugar Loaf and Skirrid as we crested the hill. Here the farmer had been making efforts to conserve the countryside instead of dumping old domestic appliances all over it. New hedgerows had been planted and fenced off from grazing animals and in the middle of one field, isolated in its ancient splendour stood a huge, old oak tree. It must have seen a lot of walkers pass by.

We descended towards Llantilio Crosseny, a little village with an impressive church dating from the 1200s, through a vast expanse of apple orchards. The regimented rows of trees, with their small budding fruits, were for once empty of squirrels. The landscape would look totally different in spring when the trees were covered in blossom. At a gate we joined yet another road, a sign on the gate proclaimed ownership of the orchard. Next time I drink a glass of

Bulmers cider I will be able to picture where it originated.

The lane led us down towards the village, passing a few isolated houses along the way. Children played with a boisterous, wrinkle-free dog in the garden of one cottage, making enough noise between them to scare off any wildlife and waken the deadest of corpses.

"Ah! The peace and quiet of the countryside," I muttered.

"Pardon?" asked Chris.

It was as we were passing the cottage that I happened to look down at the bank bordering the lane. A piece of fur caught my attention and as I bent to look closer I realised I was staring at a bank vole. I grabbed Chris' arm, dragging her to a halt and pointed silently at the vole who was sitting outside his burrow, oblivious to our gawping presence. I carefully got my camera out of the pocket of my shorts and struggled to silently get it out of the case and switch it on. The digital 'ping' as the camera came to life seemed deafening but the vole barely moved. I knelt down slowly, pointing the camera at the little mammal, my knees crunched loudly but still the vole didn't bolt down his hole. I took several photos before he suddenly sprang to life and shot into his burrow but he reappeared almost immediately and resumed his position, sitting in the sun. More photos and then a sudden roar as a car headed up the lane. Chris and I jumped with concern as the vole, frightened by the noise, ran down the bank towards the road. This really was one very stupid little creature! I shot a hand out to block his path and he curled up against it. Chris and I froze, staring in amazement. When the car had passed the vole uncurled himself, turned and ran back to his hole.

We were hopeful of more small mammal sightings as we walked across the next two fields full of ripening wheat, following a straight path of bare, dried earth that cut through the middle of the fields. However, if there were any harvest mice lurking in the stiff, golden stems they stayed well hidden: exhibiting a much stronger sense of self-preservation than Mr Bank Vole.

The next fields were full of cows not crops, the friendly Friesians drooling green saliva as they chewed the grass. Some nearby dried up ponds were not, as we initially thought, the source of a revolting smell. That distinction went to the curious looking fungi sprouting in a perfect fairy ring in the grass nearby. From the field a long rutted lane led us up to White Castle, a well-preserved late twelfth century stronghold. Together with the castles at Skenfrith and Grosmont, White Castle made up the Trilateral – the three castles protecting the Norman route into Wales from Monmouth. In the late afternoon sunshine White Castle was an impressive sight; moated and with most of its walls still intact it was easy to see how it would have dominated the landscape during the period of medieval strife between the English and the Welsh.

Rudolf Hess, Hitler's deputy, apparently visited the castle during his enforced 'stay' in Britain. Nice of the powers that be to let the dear man have a little pleasure to relieve his imprisonment, wasn't it? With time to spare and an attraction on our route that was actually open, a rarity in our walking experience, we were determined to take time out to look around the castle.

"Hello," said Chris to the lady in the little ticket kiosk. "I don't suppose you give a discount for Youth Hostel Association members?"

"No, sorry," replied the woman with a surprised expression.

"Oh! It's just that quite a few places do," explained Chris. "What about a discount for walkers, as opposed to people who've arrived in a car?" She added, nodding towards the overcrowded and rather small car park.

"Er, no."

"What about a discount for people wearing silly hats?" I asked, jerking my head in Chris' direction.

"Sorry, no discounts at all," replied the woman, who must by that time have been wondering if we had been out in the sun too long.

So we paid the full price and went through the entrance £2 the lighter in pocket and purse. Not a bad price to pay to wander through a medieval castle in the footsteps of past knights and men of arms, oh and someone from one of the cruellest regimes in modern history.

I left Chris sitting on a bench, examining her toe which she reported was hurting, to climb the spiral staircase up to the battlements. The views across the borders, back into England and on into Wales, were stunning. The green English hills rising up behind Monmouth were covered in trees; the Black Mountains of Wales appeared purple with blooming heather. Chris was a tiny spec on the grassy enclosure of the inner castle. When I returned to earth, Chris was just replacing her socks. The cause of her discomfort was a toenail, digging into the adjoining toe: she was bleeding all over her hand knitted silk socks. Later in the week she abandoned the silk socks entirely, swapping to conventional walking socks which were easier to wash and faster drying.

With socks back on and lots of photos taken, we left the castle and descended through grassy fields towards Llanvetherine to join the B4521. Somewhere to the right was our B&B, on a mixed working farm. We followed the road until we reached a long drive down to the farmhouse. A sprawl of old stone buildings and a whitewashed farmhouse faced us across a neat lawn with a few flowerbeds and a collection of collies, cats and chickens. Unsure which of the two doors we should knock on, we hesitated at the garden gate. Seeing our confusion, one of the collies came towards us and herded us towards the door on the right, scattering cats and chickens along the way. So this was what it felt like to be a sheep! The farmer's wife came to the door and soon we were being shown back across the garden and into a door in the other wing of the building. Quite elderly and rather unsteady on her knees, a condition I sympathised with at the end of a long day, she led us slowly up to our room on the first floor. After brief instructions on where to find the bathroom, she decided we could have our evening meal at 6.30 p.m. and left us.

We had only an hour to make and drink tea, bath ourselves and wash our clothes. Normally that would have been long enough, on some walking holidays we have managed a fifteen minute turn around when it meant catching the one and only pub before it stopped serving food, but that was without the limitations of sharing a bathroom with two other people. Whilst I put the kettle on, Chris rushed to the bathroom, when she returned I rushed to the bathroom. But not quickly enough: one of the other guests had rushed there before me! I gulped tea and hoped the other guest would hurry. When the snick of the bathroom door announced the completion of his ablutions I was out the bedroom and rushing down the corridor – only ten minutes till dinnertime!

As we were preparing to go down to the dining room, a group of four weary walkers, all aged about twenty, appeared. We listened and watched from our open bedroom window as a little drama unfolded, it set the scene for an evening of 'Fawlty Towers' farmhouse style. The young walkers were very polite, asking if it would be okay if they camped, apparently the lady at White Castle had recommended the farm to them. The farmer's wife was very willing to let them camp, asking only £1 a night each and even giving them a roll of toilet paper.

"But there is one slight problem," said the young man who had obviously been elected spokesperson. "We've got a dog with us."

"Oh! That's okay, providing he's well behaved."

"Well, he's not our dog," explained the boy. "He's a stray sheepdog. We found him wandering around further along the path. Oh, and one of your lambs is stuck in a hedge."

"Oh, those silly lambs! Where was it?" asked the farmer's wife. "I'll send Trevor. TREVOR!"

The stray dog was put in a barn and Trevor was sent off to rescue the lamb. The happy campers were shown round to the back of the farmhouse, now carrying a roll of loo paper and a bucket. And we headed down for our meal. As we sat down to eat our starter of egg mayonnaise, with two huge bread rolls, Trevor, having rescued the lamb, could be heard on the telephone in another room, phoning everyone he could think of in an effort to track down the owner of the lost sheepdog. We ate our main course of chicken in Italian sauce with mixed vegetables, to the accompaniment of Chopsticks being murdered by another guest on the piano in an adjoining room. As dessert was being served a car scrunched up, disgorging more guests. The farmer's wife disappeared with our dirty plates just before a foreign visitor appeared in the doorway. He shifted from one foot to the other, grinned manically and muttered something unintelligible, which may or may not have been in English. By a combination of pointing, charades and talking very loudly because he was foreign (and therefore deaf as opposed to just not very good at English) we finally convinced him he should go to the main door of the farmhouse. I was reminded of an incident over breakfast in a Swiss hotel earlier that summer, when Roger had asked the waitress a question, in English, about her working hours. When she asked him to speak slowly his automatic response was to speak louder. 'Roger, she's Swiss, not deaf!' I had groaned. As we were finishing our fruit salad the farmer's wife was showing the foreign visitor and his two female companions around. We could hear her upstairs shouting that there was the bathroom and breakfast was served at eight thirty. Another guest appeared coming down the stairs and into the dining room, he looked like an escapee from a Welsh Male Voice choir.

"Hello! You must be the walkers," he beamed. "I'm the lazy devil."

The piano player and family then came through the dining room, seeming surprised to see us. Then the farmer's wife appeared again, this time carrying a large tray of cheese and biscuits. The animals must have been feeling left out of all this and decided to put on a show of their own. We watched through the dining room window as the sheepdog was chased from the food trough by a kitten. The kitten adopted the failsafe feline method of puffing its fur out, to make itself look larger. Then two chickens raced onto the scene and frightened off the kitten. Next came a proud cockerel, who dipped his head in typical rooster fashion, seeming to point out a stray pellet of food on the ground to his accompanying lady friend. As the hen bent down to pick up the pellet the cockerel mounted her with astonishing speed. Before she even knew it, it was all over and the cockerel had rushed off to have a go at the pig – in a domineering as opposed to a sexual sense – who was minding his own business and having a gentle scratch against a nearby gatepost.

Chapter Five

The stray dog howled for much of the night, at one point Trevor went out to try to shut it up, which seemed to work for ooh, at least two minutes. However the keening for its lost home soon resumed with renewed vigour and continued throughout the night. But despite several awakenings, when the howling reached new pitches, we both slept restfully and woke late, rushing through the bathroom ritual in order not to be late for breakfast. The breakfast was equally as good and as vast as the evening meal had been. But had we thought the evening meal chaotic, breakfast was in a different league. The dining room was full: ourselves, the family with two piano playing children, the 'lazy devil' and his lady friend and the three foreigners. Not only did the farmer's wife enlist the help of her husband but her two daughters-in-law and two of her grandchildren also acted as serving staff, transporting a constant stream of fried breakfasts, pots of tea and racks of toast in one direction and taking the dirty crockery back into the depths of the farmhouse in the other direction.

With the campers packing up, the foreigners trying to pay and the stray dog howling in the barn, we walked back down the drive to the main road where we picked up the footpath. Sloping field paths gentled our legs along, warming them up for the climbing to come. That morning our way would take us up onto Hatterall Hill, on the eastern edge of the Black Mountains, climbing from 285 feet to 2037 feet.

Grey squirrels rained spent hazelnuts down upon us and the yaffling cry of two green woodpeckers broke the silence of the morning as we followed an old track. Then a steep field path brought us to Llangattock Lingoed with its thirteenth century church and the romantically named Hunter's Moon Inn.

"That's the pub which appeared in the film 'Arthur's Dyke," commented Chris, as we left the churchyard and came to a small road. "It's not actually on the path."

We had watched the British made comedy a few months ago during our planning of the walk and had thoroughly enjoyed it. Now we were busy trying to identify places in the film, not all of which were proving to be entirely accurate. Never mind, poetic licence and all that. The film had served to fuel our enthusiasm for the walk and could only have been positive marketing for this much overlooked and beautiful area of Britain.

Then it was through the village and up and down on a roller coaster of field paths once more, before crossing a tiny stream shrouded by alders and hazels. We climbed a col between two green valleys, looking back to the village on the hill. At the top of the hill we crossed a lane and ironically, as is often the case on walks, we then descended, to the main road bisecting the valley at Pandy, losing height only to have to climb again towards Hatterall Ridge. Walking up through the field towards us was a long line of walkers, most kept their heads down and ignored us, only a few cheery ones exchanged greetings with us as they past. At the bottom of the hill we walked through a field thick with thistles, butterflies swarming on the purple flower heads. We then spent several minutes trying to cross the busy main road. The fruit and veg man from Monmouth was not at Pandy to meet us, never mind we still had some cherries and plums and a couple of apples to keep us going.

Fields and then an increasingly steep switch back road brought us out above the valley but we still had a large climb ahead of us. We began our ascent up to the top of Hatterall as the sun emerged fully from the clouds. The steep, grassy slopes seemed steeper than ever under the strengthening sun. We puffed, panted and perspired our way up the hillside, past trees, bracken and stonewalls. Flies buzzed in the bracken and grasshoppers quieted their chirruping at our approach, remaining silent until they judged us safely past. A spotted woodpecker took off from the path as we walked around a clump of bracken, at first I thought it was just a magpie but Chris, in the lead, had a better view, and as the bird gained height above the bracken I too could clearly see its distinctive red markings.

We climbed all afternoon, passing trig point after trig point, shunning the first one as a potential lunch spot because of the wild bees that seemed to have made their hive in the base of the pillar. So we moved further on, sitting instead on a heather tussock on the edge of the ridge to have our lunch with views across to the Malvern's in the distance. Flapjack and fruit were a healthy, light and energy giving lunch. As we slowly gained height along the ridge of the heather covered moors the views behind became expansive. We could clearly see the blue grey line of the Bristol Channel and the dark green hills of Exmoor and the Somerset coastline. On top of the ridge, with no shade and the dry gritty path beneath our feet, the sun seemed hotter than ever. We were no longer following the line of the dyke, this part of the National Trail was a route devised to link differing points of the dyke whilst following an interesting and scenic line. With just the heather moorland, a purple expanse of fragrant smelling flowers carpeting the ridge top, there was less wildlife to be seen. No squirrels for once, instead we passed sheep and wild ponies, a few meadow pipits flew overhead and for a while we watched a Merlin as it hunted on the thermals. But the skies were silent, for there were no skylarks here; it seemed strange as we had been used to seeing them and hearing their song during all our walks along the coast paths and on the moorlands of home. Skylarks are supposed to be in decline, their numbers long threatened by changing agricultural practices but it was only here, on Offa's Dyke Path, that we really became aware of their absence for the first time.

Most of the time we could not see beyond the ridge to the west, as the land rose up away from the path but occasionally the path drew nearer to the western edge of the ridge and we would stop and look down into the valley below, admiring the view and marvelling at the perspective. Buildings and animals in the valley bottom seemed tiny, the thin lines of river and road threaded along the valley, it was like looking down on a world in miniature. The ruins of St Llanthony priory were just visible in the patchwork of varying green shades of the hedges, fields and trees. This was one ruined abbey that could not be blamed on Henry VIII; Owain Glyndwr had burnt it to the ground over a century before Henry decided the Catholic Church was getting in the way of his divorce.

At a quarter past four we began our descent down to the valley in the west, the Welsh side of the border, leaving the path to find the Youth Hostel at Capel y Ffin. For much of the way along Hatterall Ridge we had been right on the border, running as it does along the crest of the ridge, the same line that the footpath followed. So for several hours we had walked along unsure whether we were in England or Wales or a bit of both with each footfall.

We had a knee crunching descent, first through boggy ground, then deep bracken, until finally we entered a small wood following a path that eventually crossed a stream to join a road. We had a two and a half mile walk along the single track, but surprisingly busy, road to reach the hostel. Conveniently located accommodation it was not but we had had little choice with the way we had broken the route down, no B&Bs existed on the top of the ridge! At the village of Capel Y Ffin itself, we used the phone box to ring the hostel, still quite a way down the road. We wanted to order our evening meal before it became too late to do so, and knew if we waited until we reached the hostel it would indeed be too late.

As the phone in the hostel was answered Chris began to speak, then hesitated, then repeated herself in loud, slow tones.

"Foreign assistant with poor English?" I asked when she finally hung up, this was often the case in youth hostels.

"No, bad line," explained Chris.

Isn't it wonderful how modern day technology can have us talking via satellite to people on the other side of the world, but trying using a land line to telephone somewhere a mile down a valley road and you hit problems?

The thoughts of arriving late and missing tea spurred us on our way along the lane. I am sure we covered the mile to the hostel in Roger Bannister class speeds. The last mile of our sixteen-mile day was definitely the fastest! The hostel was, as is often the case, up a steep drive, in an elevated position above the road, the last hill of the day. Preparations for the evening meal were well underway as we arrived, the hostel manager and her assistant busily dividing their time between reception and cooking duties. The smells of several different main courses wafted out from the kitchen, making our stomachs rumble; breakfast and lunch were long in the past.

The hostel was busy with an eclectic mix of people from cyclists doing the End to End, (how I wanted to say 'I've done that' to them), to single parent families from Liverpool, a group of teenage girls there on a riding holiday and a group of four Germans. Our room was above the combined dining room and lounge, and was reached by a narrow staircase built into the wall at the side of the fireplace. The old wooden floor creaked as we crossed it to claim the only two remaining bunk beds. Noise from the room below drifted through the loose fitting floorboards and we expected to be in for a disturbed night.

Threat of closure hung over Capel y Ffin hostel. Costly renovations were needed to improve the very basic shower and toilet facilities, which were quite possibly the worst I have come across in any hostel, with only one shower for females and just two toilets in the main building. We devised a system of team work to overcome the problem of the miniscule shower cubicle: passing shampoo, conditioner, shower gel, towels and finally clean clothes over the gap above the door, whilst whoever was doing the 'passing' also washed the dirty clothes, before we swapped roles and locations.

The Youth Hostel Association is currently trying to reinvent itself, hoping to draw in new members. The traditional values of providing cheap accommodation for walkers and cyclists have been superseded to some extent by the need to turn a profit. New measures such as rent-a-hostel, do-it-for-real and activity breaks being just some of the ways the YHA is trying to attract new visitors. All this is well and good, but many of the less viable hostels, the smaller ones, many in isolated places that are frequented mainly by walkers and cyclists staying for one night, are under threat of closure as they become less economically viable. Capel y Ffin was just one of three hostels facing potential closure that summer and a petition was available in reception for visitors to sign who wished to log their objection to its demise. Fund raising was also taking place, with staff currently hoping to raise money to install individual lights on each bunk; although how such a small and rather minor improvement would convince the big bosses of YHA to review the hostel's closure beat me.

All the more ironic is the YHA's current initiative to encourage privately owned B&Bs to link up with the YHA to provide hostellers with accommodation along Offa's Dyke Path. We had contacted several of the B&Bs who had joined the scheme but none of them gave a discount for YHA members and most had no washing or drying facilities. We failed to see what the advantages were. Whilst the YHA is promoting this B&B initiative, they had in the past few years closed several hostels along OD path, Maeshafn being the last to close only a few months previously. This closure was particularly sad as the building had been purposely designed and built for the Youth Hostel Association by Clough Williams-Ellis, architect of Portmeirion. Maeshafn was the first purpose built youth hostel in Wales and from the outside looked like a Swiss chalet. Inside, the building was designed to resemble a ship's cabin; originally the bunks were in the form of hammocks, later being replaced by unusual three tier bunk beds. Of the few remaining hostels on the path Clun Mill was too far away to be convenient and Llangollen had only been taking bookings for groups of ten or more when we wished to stay. Very useful for our group of two! A new hostel had been opened in the converted buildings of the old cottage hospital at Kington, providing excellent accommodation but sadly it was self-catering only. Of our eighteen nights' accommodation along the path, only three of those nights were in youth hostels. We had originally joined the YHA only two years previously, when we decided to walk the Pembrokeshire Coast Path. That particular path was so isolated in parts that the only way we could find any accommodation for many of the nights was to stay in youth hostels. Our experiences at the hostels had been good and walking the Pembrokeshire National Trail without otherwise resorting to camping, would have been difficult if not impossible. Therefore it was particularly depressing that Offa's Dyke Path was so poorly served by hostels.

We shared a refectory style table with two families for our evening meal. The soup, stuffed chicken breast for Chris, sausages and mash for me and then homemade banoffee pie for dessert were delicious; the company, one monosyllabic family and one very chatty small child were not so good.

There was a gentle breeze blowing as we retired to the courtyard to write postcards, catch up on diaries and watch the sun go down. Chris had bought lots of postcards and I had bought just two. It was not until I had finished writing my diary for that evening that Chris suddenly groaned and began looking somewhat sheepish.

"I seem to have written your postcards," she apologised.

She had become so carried away with them that of the two postcards I had bought, both had been written, only one – not mine – remained blank.

"Yes, sorry about that," she continued. "Never mind, I'll pop into reception and buy you another." And she duly did.

"We could put them in the letterbox by the door," she said, on returning with the replacement postcards.

"Is that a post box?" I asked. "It's not red. I thought it was the mail box for the hostel!"

With all the postcards eventually written we shoved them in the post box. The postcards did arrive at their destinations so Chris must have been right.

Chapter Six

We need not have worried that noises drifting up from the lounge below would keep us awake. The hostellers all seemed to go to bed quite early. But the old bunk beds squeaked alarmingly with every inhalation, and in a dorm room of six sleepers there were a lot of inhalations, never mind turnings and shufflings and the thunderous snorings of one old woman.

It was a night of broken sleep but still not as disrupted as one night we had spent in a full dorm room at Land's End youth hostel the year before. That evening we had shared a room with an elderly lady (another professional snorer), a garrulous surfer from London called Sally and two Dutch girls in their late teens. It was a real mixed bag of females from various backgrounds but with the talkative, outgoing Sally in the room drawing everyone together, it was one of the most memorable of all our youth hostel stays. At three o'clock in the morning it suddenly got all the more memorable but for all the wrong reasons. There was a scream and then a terrific thud and the sound of running feet that woke everyone in the room. For the next few seconds there was total silence broken only by the sound of rustling bedclothes and twanging springs as five people sat up in bed and stared ineffectually around the pitch-black room.

And then Sally's voice came saying, "Turn on the light, someone!"

A torch came on, then another and after a few seconds someone climbed out of their bunk and switched on the main light. One of the Dutch girls stood in the corner of the room, tears streaming down her face and with one arm cradling the other to her chest. Her friend rushed to her and a broken conversation ensued, with the rest of us listening in concerned incomprehension.

"What's happened? Is she alright?" Sally finally demanded.

The second Dutch girl explained her friend had had a nightmare in which she was being chased and had quite literally jumped out of bed to get away from her imaginary pursuer. As the girl was in the top bunk, it was quite a jump and she had landed on her elbow. Insisting she was okay the girl went back to bed, but x-rays the following day showed she had broken her arm.

That morning at Capel y Ffin we shared a table with the two teenage cyclists completing the End to End. They pigged out on a full English breakfast, and from personal experience I knew they would need it. Chris and I had both opted for the lighter continental breakfast, although whether it was any less calorific was debateable. A large chunk of mature Welsh cheddar and the two butter-rich croissants were hardly 'diet' but were wholly delicious.

The road walk back to the village was slower than the day before. We left the road at a different point to follow a bridle path that crossed the stream and ran along an old green lane. The stream was supposed to be home to otters but as with all other streams and rivers I have been told are the habitats of otters, this one too proved, for us at least, to be totally lacking in otters.

Soon we had rejoined the steep bracken invaded path leading to the top of the ridge. Up and up we seemed to go for miles although, in reality I doubt it was more than one mile but it was an ascent of almost 1000 feet. With perspiration running down our bodies, we stopped for some of the remaining Monmouth cherries, sitting down at the side of the path to eat and to take the bits of bracken out of our boots. It was much hotter than the day before and with no shade on the top of the ridge we slopped on sunscreen and hats.

The path was a broad eroded swathe through the diminishing heather. Loose rocks, scree and dried up mud scarred an ever-widening line across the ridge. It was like walking through a moonscape. We passed a couple of trig points until we finally reached the summit plateau, the highest point on Offa's Dyke Path at 2306 feet above sea level. It seemed an ideal spot for lunch. Wild bees stopped feeding on the heather to investigate our hostel provided packed lunches. We sat on the English side of the ridge top border to eat tuna mayonnaise sandwiches, crisps, cake and fruit, and a few more cherries, and then some flapjack, and then some dried apricots.

"I wish we had some chocolate, just to finish off," I commented wistfully.

"Never mind, have some more apricots."

"Thanks but I think I've exceeded my sulphur dioxide quotient for today."

Few people were out on the hill that day, the weekend walkers of the day before were all back at work – and we weren't! What a great feeling. Only one couple passed us as we ate our long lunch.

The official route of the path skirts past Hay Bluff, the huge, steep incline at the end of Hatterall Ridge. But we did not wish to descend on the northeastern side and miss the spectacular views from the top of the bluff. We had not come so far along the ridge (the length being equivalent of one day's walking) to miss it. With hang gliders setting up their equipment on the plateau behind the bluff, and others already soaring on the thermals above and still others staggering up from the car park at the bottom, weighted down by the huge rucksacks that contained their gliders, we stood on the edge watching the aerial acrobatics and drinking in the views before us. Into Wales the nearby ridges of the Black Mountains marched away to the west, beyond them the Brecon Beacons.

From the top of Hay Bluff to Hay on Wye, five miles away on the path, there was a height differential of 2000 feet. We descended on the almost sheer path, the patchwork of tiny fields seeming to come up to meet us, as hang gliders cast silent swooping shadows on the ground below us. As the path finally levelled out, giving our trembling thighs and aching knees a rest, we passed a herd of wild ponies before finally reaching the road and the rough car park on the common, where a flock of cars had surrounded the ice cream van. Ice cream! But with such a huge lunch, did we really have room for ice cream? Oh course we bloody did!

Sitting on the short-cropped grass, near the ancient (and to us invisible) stone circle, dribbling ice cream and raspberry sauce down our chins and all over our shorts, we admired the view and listened, unwillingly, to the loud and one-sided conversation of a yob on his mobile phone. He was talking at one of his mates about his recently-ex girl friend. The split had obviously not been an amicable one. But from his attitude, his incredibly colourful language – and we're not talking Welsh here – and his graphic descriptions of his until-recent sex life, his ex girl friend was probably better off without him.

"She's going with f****** Jason now," he ranted, between greedy drags on his cigarette. "Well she can watch Jason f****** w****** instead of me. He'll dump the f****** whinging bitch soon enough!"

"What a colourful life some people have," I remarked dryly. "Just a shame they feel the need to share it with half of England."

"Wales," corrected Chris.

"Wales?"

"Pardon?"

"Wales?"

"What about it?"

"Are we back in Wales now?"

"Yes, I think so."

"Oh, confusing all this border crossing stuff, isn't it?" I muttered. "So is Hay on Wye in Wales then?"

"Yes, well partly."

"Which part?"

"The biggest part," Chris answered, hesitantly adding: "I think."

A few more colourful expletives broke into our conversation at that point, ending with the words: "Yeah, see ya later, yer tosser." We watched as the yob threw his cigarette butt into a patch of gorse, scrambled to his feet and leapt onto his mountain bike before cycling away across the grass, scattering frightened sheep as he went.

Ice cream finished and sensibilities offended, we clambered back to our feet, heaved on our rucksacks and set off across the mile long common. Our first shade of the day came as we ducked into the sunken lane that seemed to have a close affinity to a streambed. But soon we were onto drier field paths where thick hazel hedges provided a full larder for the energetic squirrels. The sound of waterfalls, burbling streams and bird song rang through the trees as we drew nearer to Cusop Dingle, a shady but all too brief patch of woodland walking. Four male hikers passed us as we paused for a drink in the shade of the woods. They all marched past, setting a cracking pace, no time to stop for a chat! The poor guy at the back of the group hurried along, trying to keep up with his companions and read a map at the same time. Then we were back into open fields once more, with their hedges, fences and kissing gates before finally entering Hay on Wye.

My mobile started to vibrate and the music for the Pink Panther whispered out from my rucksack. Chris hurried to retrieve the phone before Roger could ring off, or worse, leave a message on my answer phone that I would then have to pay to listen to.

"Hello!" I sighed into the phone.

"Hiya, just thought I'd ring you, seen as you've not been in touch!" said Roger sarcastically.

"There's not been a signal for the last couple of days."

"You've not rung for nearly a week!" he replied.

"I've only been away for five days, and you rang me three days ago!" I snapped back. "I suppose you're ringing to tell me you've found our wheelie bin."

"No, I was ringing to tell you I've priced up our Christmas holiday to Switzerland."

"Ooh, good! Is it affordable?"

"Well, it's affordable but I think it's a bit expensive to go back to the same place and the same hotel as we did in July. It isn't going to be any different."

"Oh, doh! Like snow! That might be a leetle bit different."

He might have priced it up but the destination of our Christmas holiday was to be an ongoing argument for the entire autumn. By the end of November we had still not decided where to go and I was becoming sorely tempted to just book Switzerland and then tell him. For all that that particular phone call achieved we might as well have had a talk about wheelie bins. In the end I was to get my way, and Switzerland at Christmas was even more magical than it had been in the summer.

Our B&B was almost out of Hay on Wye, in a lovely old cottage beyond the bridge over the broad river. There was no one at home when we arrived; a note tacked to the door invited us to go in, told us where our room was and to make ourselves at home. The bedroom, bright, clean and with a lovely en suite bathroom, was very warm and we threw open the window as wide as it would go and propped the bedroom door open to try to get some air circulating. Sparrows nesting in the eaves flew in terror as we hung our freshly washed smalls at the open window. Chickens in the garden below clucked, possibly in fright, at the site of two sets of underwear and shirts, just hope it didn't put them off laying!

By the time we crossed back over the river and into the main part of the town, we found most of the shops had closed for the day. We wandered the streets, checking out the available eating establishments that ranged from traditional pubs, a few takeaways, some trendy eateries and wholefood restaurants. Hay on Wye is famed worldwide for its bookshops. The first bookshop to be opened in the town was located in the old castle. It was opened in 1961 by Richard Booth nicknamed 'the emperor of the book towns of the world'; the title being well deserved as it was the efforts of this one man that was to transform Hay into a town of over one million books. As well as its books, Hay is now well known for the various festivals it holds every year, festivals which include Literature, Jazz and, more bizarrely, the Open Universe Conker Championships.

"'Open Universe'?" I quoted from the leaflet that described this bizarre sounding competition. "Does Hay on Wye get visiting Martians flying in with their thirty-niners, hoping to win the coveted title? What's Martian for 'oh heck, my string's snapped!'?"

Long accustomed to my ramblings Chris wisely chose to ignore me.

It would not be unfair to say that bookshops dominate Hay. There were other shops: outdoor clothing, shoe shops, newsagents (selling books) and a few others, even a chemist; but the majority of the shops had slowly been transformed into bookshops as other businesses went into decline. Clues from the remains of the old shop fronts suggest that bookshops have replaced butchers, greengrocers, fishmongers, haberdashers and so on. We struggled to find any greengrocers, hopeful of being able to stock up on some delicious fresh fruit the next morning. Whilst the demise of the traditional shops to the growth of the bookshops was a shame, it did at least make a change from the supermarkets driving out the smaller specialist shops. In so many towns and villages across the country nowadays the supermarket giants have squeezed out the little shops with their personal service, friendly staff and good quality produce. Now we have a selection of food from around the world, fruit and veg without season, fruit and veg without taste, meat and diary products produced without compassion or a responsibility for the environment. Yes, I can buy organic produce in supermarkets but the supermarkets have such buying power and such demands as to what a potato should look like, the ideal shape of a tomato, the straightness of a cucumber, the texture of an apple skin, that the organic growers are forced to destroyed a high percentage of their produce because it does not come up to the ludicrous standards demanded by the supermarkets. As long as it tastes good who cares what a tomato looks like? Give me flavour over uniformity any day! And yes, I can get my entire weekly shopping under one roof in the supermarket but when I buy my meat and green groceries at farmers' markets the difference in taste, variety, quality and choice is enormous. It is more expensive but then I would rather pay for good quality food and the knowledge that the animals and the environment in which the food is produced are being cared for in a responsible and environmentally friendly manner. So Hay might have lost its traditional food shops but at least the town remained vibrant, there were no empty premises, no boarded up shops and no steel shutters unlike so many other towns, villages and cities across the country.

This area of Britain is a rich agricultural region and so it should have been no surprise to find, of all things, an organic takeaway. Extreme Organix specialised in kebabs, burgers and curries, sourcing the lamb, beef and pork from their own organic farm. It was an easy decision to opt for an organic evening meal, especially when we saw there was seating available inside. The only hard decision was what to choose from the extensive menu. Beef, chicken or pork burger? Lamb loin, pork loin, chicken or beef kebab? Breakfast? Pizzas? Lamb, chicken or beef curry? What type of curry? Was the burger with cheese? Coleslaw? Salad? Peppers? Mushrooms? The choice and the menu were endless. After ten minutes of 'humming and ahhing' we opted for lamb loin kebabs with roasted peppers, mushrooms and salad, choosing to share a portion of chips. All the vast choice of drinks was also organic, and locally produced apple juice seemed like a good option. The food here had travelled very few miles in comparison to that found in any supermarket. We waited with rumbling stomachs as the kebabs were cooked and brought to our table. They were huge; we really did not need the equally huge portion of organic chips. Extreme Organix has to be the best takeaway I have ever found. During the time we sat, eating our delicious organic food, a continuous flow of customers came in to place orders. The takeaway seemed to have discovered a niche market.

As we walked back through the town, down a curving street, passing dozens of bookshops, we reached the old market clock. I don't know what it is about these border market towns, but nearly all the ones we walked through seemed to have similar clock towers. We were to come across them at Kington, Knighton and Monmouth. Were the clock towers the local equivalent of my hometown's Knocker Uppers? A Knocker Upper was a chap who walked around first thing in the morning with a long pole, tapping on the bedroom windows of the houses to wake the mill workers in the days when cotton was king in not just Burnley but all the mill towns of Lancashire. I had always wondered who woke the Knocker Upper?

Just across the road from the market clock was a trendy restaurant called The Granary. It seemed to specialise in yummy wholefoods and calorific cakes.

A few people occupied some of the pavement tables, dining on delicious looking food.

"How about dessert?" I asked Chris with a gluttonous grin.

She didn't take much persuading and soon we were inside selecting a couple of desserts from the refrigerated display cabinet. We ate the desserts, apple cake for Chris and raspberry cheesecake with clotted cream for me, sitting outside at a wrought iron table. But it really was a case of having eyes bigger than our bellies, and we both struggled to do justice to the delicious desserts.

In need of a bit of exercise we followed the signs along the river on the Wye Valley Walk, hopeful of seeing an otter. Yes, well, I think we were more likely to see a mis-shaped tomato on sale in Asda.

Some local yobs had congregated under the bridge as we returned along the riverbank. They were busy dropping litter and scrawling graffiti on the tops of picnic benches, shouting and swearing and drinking lager and being generally awful. We climbed the steps away from the footpath and crossed the bridge. The garden of the B&B came right down to the river, ideal for the family of pet ducks. One of the ducklings had got an injured leg and was left far behind as the rest of the family left the river and made their way up the sloping garden. I watched his valiant, webfoot-dragging efforts as he squeak pathetically after his deserting family, doing his best to follow them. He made it eventually. Returning to our room we discovered the washing had dried. But the sparrows had taken their revenge on one of my socks! Fortunately that too had dried and I was able to flick off the crumbly white mess.

Chapter Seven

The room was hot all night, and it may have been that or it may have been that I had over-eaten, but whatever the case I had a night of very lucid dreams. In the first dream I was a new headmistress in a primary school, trying to control a delinquent small boy. The second dream I was a new principal in the college where I work, spending all my time arguing with the staff and throwing out the yobbish male students. The most disturbing dream came towards the end of the night, when I dreamt a friend of mine was cooking my breakfast bacon days before I wanted it.

An eclectic mix of stuffed animals and parts of animals, some of which were a little tasteless – actually, make that most of which – watched from the walls, the bookcases and the windowsills as we ate the best breakfast of the walk so far. Yoghurt, fruit and cereal, then a lovely cooked breakfast and finally thick slices of toast with homemade preserves filled us up for the walk ahead.

Loaded up with breakfast we set off along the western side of the Wye on a riverside path. Still no otters but we did see a heron, and wrens, blackbirds and sparrows flitted in the shrubbery as I stood searching the river in vain for otters.

"You won't see any otters if they rate a mention on the information board," said Chris, referring to a board we had found at the point where the path left the main road.

She was right, as usual, and this elusive British mammal was to remain, for me, just that. I continue to have an ambition to see a wild British otter. I've seen them in wildlife parks – cheating – doesn't count; and I've seen wild French otters (and lots of them) on the River Salune near Avranches. Maybe one day I'll be lucky.

Field paths took us to a farm where a herd of cattle with their calves had just been let into the field. They charged through the gate, coming straight at us, Chris tried to hide behind me.

"I presume your line of reasoning is if they can't see you cowering behind me, only I will be trampled to death?" I asked caustically.

The farm buildings were scruffy, the yard littered with rubbish and the sign posting poor. The thought occurred to both of us that perhaps the farmer was a little less than careful about maintaining footpaths and ensuring signs remained in place. Several other thoughts, increasingly uncharitable, also sprang to mind as we staggered across the rutted mud churned field, attempting to find the path. It was no surprise to realise we were lost and soon we found ourselves at the edge of the Wye. Turning, we followed a boundary hedge of hazel that bordered a trickling stream until we found the well-hidden footbridge. One more field, where balsam grew tall in the fringes, and we reached the main road. The guidebook recommended pausing to look back and admire the view of the river valley but the trees in full leaf obscured it.

Traffic roared past as we stumbled along the rutted grass verge before a narrow lane rising steeply on the left took us into the shady peace of a deciduous wood, marked on the maps as Betws Dingle. Dingle must be the local word for dell, and we were to encounter a lot of dingles along the walk. The path continued to climb, the trees changing as we entered a coniferous plantation. The sound of the trickling stream continued but the bird song fell away, the avians preferring the habitat of deciduous trees to the regimented conifers.

Once beyond the plantation we were on quiet lanes once more, which we followed for several miles. Views back to Hay Bluff now opened out and we paused, leaning against a five bar gate, to look back to Hay Bluff and the ridges of the Black Mountains.

"Look, you can see Lord Hereford's Knob," said Chris, pointing towards the line of mountains.

"Many have said the same."

The bird life in the quiet lanes was greater than in the coniferous plantation. And as we walked along we watched sparrows, chaffinches, robins and tits flitting in and out of the hawthorn hedges. Honeysuckle drooped its red and yellow flowers from the heights of the hedge, old man's beard crept through the leafy branches, foxgloves bobbed their purple bells, red campion, stitchwort and pennywort flowered lowered down on the banks, and bees, flies and butterflies flew about. Raspberries were nearly over, barely worth picking but the blackberries were just starting to ripen, some already big and black and juicy whilst others remained still in the hard, green and sour stage.

We diverted down a lane to view the little Betws Chapel, recommended by the author of the guidebook as having an interesting roof and screen. It was to be our first introduction to the curate Francis Kilvert, who had preached at various chapels in the area during the nineteenth century. A prolific diarist, he had been a little too frank for his relatives liking and after his death only three of the twenty or more diaries he had kept escaped being burnt.

The chapel, situated just off a footpath, was locked. I tried the door, Chris tried the door, I walked right around the tiny building, Chris walked right around the tiny building, we both tried the only door again, hoping by some divine miracle to find it unlocked after all. It remained firmly locked.

"Well, this is great!" declared Chris. "Anything the guidebook seems to think worthy of a mention either can't be seen or can't be entered."

"Well, now we're here how about a break?" I asked, my desire for sightseeing being replaced by my desire to shove food down my throat.

We sat down on the single step of the church to eat the last of the Monmouth cherries, and it was not long before we were indulging in a totally gross and very silly cherry stone spitting competition.

"Ah! Mine went further than yours," I gloated as a stone whizzed away across the grass.

"That's because you've got a bigger mouth!"

"Greater lung capacity, actually. More puff."

"If you say so."

"Is this environmentally friendly, do you think?" I asked, chomping another cherry and nearly choking on the stone.

"It only becomes environmentally unfriendly if you choke on a stone and I have to call for ambulance," replied Chris. "That would be a new slant on food miles."

"We could come back in years to come and find lots of cherry trees grown up in front of the church," I mused.

"Yes, and what's the betting it would still be locked?"

Although it was cloudier than the previous day the sun was still strong and sun lotion, hats and sunglasses were vital. We slathered ourselves in factor thirty before leaving the chapel. That year we were using sun lotion that was marketed as being for children. It came in a plastic bag with a screw cap, not dissimilar to certain brands of soft drinks. The reason we had chosen to buy that particular product was the convenient size and lightweight packaging. The only problem was that two varieties of this sun lotion were available and it had been pure luck that we had not bought the one that was coloured green. We looked daft enough, if the various curious glances we garnered were anything to go by, without being green!

From the chapel we returned to the metalled lane before eventually reaching a green lane. Coming towards us down the banked green lane were a family with two silent, teenage children. The father, obviously a keen walker, began chatting with us, wanting to know all about our walk. He seemed regretful that he was not able to walk more of the route, explaining that his children were not enthusiastic about walking long distances.

As the lane ended at a wide-open field we stopped for lunch, sitting down on some rocks in front of a patch of gorse bushes. The yellow flowers were in full bloom and the smell wafted on the breeze. I always think of coconut shampoo whenever I smell gorse; the two scents seem so similar to me. We had not bought anything for lunch at Hay on Wye, deciding to eat some of the flapjack and two of the many oranges we had accumulated from our packed lunches. I balanced an orange on my knee and cut into it with my penknife, forgetting just how sharp the small piece of

Swiss precision steel was. The blade cut through the juicy flesh as easily as the proverbial hot knife through butter, and it was only my lightning fast reactions, totally out of character for me, that prevented the blade slicing into my knee. Chris tutted with despair. Two oranges later and everything seemed to be covered in sticky orange juice: me, my knife, my legs, my knees and a large area of field. I used some of my precious water to attempt to wash off the stickiness, only partially succeeding.

Chris had taken her boots off and sat examining her sore toe. I heard a rustle in the gorse and turned, just in time, to see a small brown head with shiny black eyes peeping above the grass; the little body stretched upright revealing a white neck and chest – a weasel! He bobbed down and I flapped a frantic hand at Chris. Then he darted back up and I flapped a frantic hand at Chris again. I turned to see Chris oblivious to the wildlife and still studiously examining her toe.

"What?" was her response to my urgent hiss.

"A weasel!" I whispered, motioning with my hand in the direction I had last seen the little creature.

We turned fully to watch for him but after several minutes of nothing happening, Chris went back to examining her toes. A chirrup in the gorse brought me to my knees and I crawled stealthily forward with my camera at the ready. Peering into the bushes I searched for the weasel but could not see him. As I leant ever closer to the bushes there was a sudden spitting, not unlike the sound an angry cat would make, that sent me shooting back in surprised fright – obviously just what the spit was designed to do! Not wishing to have an angry weasel attach his teeth to my inquisitive nose, I returned to sitting down on the rocks.

Not expecting Mr Weasel to reappear in the next few minutes, if ever, I removed my glasses and began applying more sun lotion. And that was when the little beggar ran across a large stone. It was just typical that it waited until Chris' attention was back on her feet and I could only see blurred things.

"Are you sure?" asked Chris, when I babbled excitedly at her. "After all, you've not got your glasses on!"

"Yes, yes," I hissed, putting my specs back on and ignoring the remaining blobs of white lotion that dotted my arms and face.

We waited in the growing heat of midday, hoping the weasel would reappear. After a few more minutes our patience was rewarded as he ran back across the stone and into the grass. We sat motionless hoping for more and soon he popped his head back up to look inquisitively at us. With camera grasped in sweaty palm, I took several shots at arms length, trying to get as close as possible and just hoping one of the images would be successful. The image on screen was too small to see; it was not until I returned home and downloaded the photos onto my computer that I knew

I had succeeded in taking one picture of the curious little weasel.

Eventually we left the weasel to his gorse bush, and set off again. We 'helloed' a man walking towards us, he replied rather bemusedly whilst giving me strange looks. Could it have been the white blobs of sunscreen? Or, more likely, the bits of grass and rabbit poo sticking, unheeded, to my knees?

We crested a hill and began descending through more fields, passing, as we descended, middens of forgotten muck, the tattered remains of plastic sheeting, discarded buckets, tangles of rusting wire and food sacks, before turning down a horribly muddy track just before a farmhouse. We had seen no litter at all that day, and suddenly here, at a farm, there were tonnes of it. I remembered with irony the frequently seen countryside slogan: 'Beautiful countryside, care of British farming'. In this particular case, as with many other farms I had seen, the words 'care of' should, I felt, be replaced by 'despite'. Now I know there are plenty of walkers who drop litter: that peculiar breed of person that wants to go out in the countryside but has no respect for it once they get there. Or the type of person who is quite happy to carry out a packed lunch but seems incapable of carrying back home the empty (and therefore much lighter) wrappers, cartons, packets and cans. The sort of irresponsible lout that drops litter like a deciduous tree drops leaves, discards sweet wrappers, crams empty crisp packets onto spikes of hawthorn and jams empty bottles into gaps in dry stonewalls. The kind of person who goes for an alfresco toilet stop and leaves not just a damp patch but a pile of soggy tissue behind. I despise these people. I despise all litterlouts but litter seems to me to be even more offensive when in rural areas. Why do these louts litter? What do they think happens to it? Do they even care? Probably not. And, quite rightly, farmers, landowners and country dwellers take exception to it. So I always feel particularly cross when faced with farmers, the so-called 'guardians of our countryside' who treat the land and the environment with the same lack of respect as the inconsiderate litterlout.

With boots coated in mud, which did make a nice change from sheep muck, we reached Newchurch. Just before we entered the village we passed a late fifteenth century great house that rated a mention in the guidebook for its cruck frame construction. Newchurch was a tiny hamlet with a little spired church. St Mary's church, with its grave of Emeline, was mentioned in Francis Kilvert's diary. Pinned to the gate was a notice, inviting Offa's Dyke walkers and visitors to take refreshment there. We needed no further invitation and hurried up the steps and into the churchyard. Amongst the gravestones, where beautiful wildflowers had been allowed to grow rampant, was a picnic bench. Gratefully we shed our rucksacks and hats and went inside the cool church to make a cup of tea, leaving a donation in the collecting box. A dog from a neighbouring farm came to check on us and seemingly satisfied with his findings he wandered off into the somnambulant afternoon. We sat, drinking tea, our legs burning in the sunshine and listened to the sounds of bees humming in the knapweed, grasses and daisies that brightened the lichen and moss covered gravestones.

Being responsible walkers, we returned to the church to dispose of our plastic cups, having finished the tea, and began reading some of the information leaflets and notices inside the church. In 1991 during a storm an 1100-year-old yew tree in the churchyard had been blow down. Two new yews had been planted at either side of the path but it would be many centuries before they achieved the size of the one they tragically replaced. In fact, perhaps leylandii might have been a better choice? A beautiful handrail had been fashioned from the fallen yew and mounted on the steps leading into the churchyard; so some part of the ancient tree still welcomed visitors to St Mary's.

The hill out of Newchurch seemed easier with a cup of tea inside us. We climbed Disgwylfa Hill with its sheep-cropped grass and tall stands of bracken. Just beyond the top of the hill we descended to a small marsh-fringed pond, where sheep paddled in the shallow water, nibbling the succulent shoots of the semi-submerged marginal plants. Hergest Ridge stretched across the horizon ahead of us; looking back, the Black Mountains had gone from sight: that was the last we saw of Lord Hereford's Knob.

Dropping down through the bracken on a gentle slope we joined a lane, passing through a quiet farmyard. As we walked by a small outbuilding a low growl reverberated from behind a closed, weathered wooden door. The growling changed to frantic barking and we hurried on, hoping the door was strong! Reaching a minor road where once the path had gone straight on, we had to execute a right then a left in quick succession to follow the realignment in order to avoid a new house that had been built on the site of an old barn. The house was surrounded by a high red brick wall, its entrance secured by gates and a cattle grid, signs warned of dogs and as we followed the new path round the perimeter the privacy was completed by a dense hedge of leylandii. But none of this stopped us looking back and having a good nosey from the top of the next low rise where we could see the blue paintwork, stone walls, artful and artificial stream and overly manicured lawns of the property.

"I don't understand sheep poo," said Chris suddenly as we ascended the hillside.

Were we in for another thought provoking, intellectual discussion, I wondered? "What is there not to understand?"

"Well, sometimes it comes in big blobs and other times it's little balls. And yet they eat the same stuff," she mused, watching as two nearby sheep conveniently illustrated her point.

People often ask us what we talk about for a fortnight when we are on a walking holiday. If only they knew!

We dropped towards the village of Gladestry, looking across to Hergest Ridge, with Chris muttering about

Mike 'Tubular Bells' Oldfield and trying to identify his old house. She pointedly refused to hum the tune and I was left wondering: had I ever heard it? Could I remember it?

"But why won't you hum it?" I pestered.

"I can't hum it," she replied.

"Well, whistle it then!"

"It's just not possible!"

"You know how to whistle don't you? Just put your lips together and blow," I instructed, doing a terrible impression of Lauren Bacall and collapsing into fits of giggles.

"You'd know why I can't whistle it if you heard it," she snapped. "It's impossible!"

Back home I searched through our CD collection, hoping Roger might have a copy of Hergest Ridge on one of his albums. He didn't. Eventually a colleague downloaded it at work and I was able to hear it for the first time.

"No wonder you said you couldn't hum or whistle it," I apologised to Chris.

Descending the last field before the lane and surrounded by grazing sheep, we suddenly became aware of a most un-sheep-like noise. It seemed to be two animals rutting – not sheep, not cows, not squirrels, rabbits, bank voles, weasels or lovebirds. Er more well, more human! We looked at one another, then looked around us. Was there someone in the deep ditches on either side of this narrow field? Was there anyone under the low hanging branches of the nearby trees? We looked at the sheep, they looked back. We all held our breaths and looked around. Wherever the lovers were, if indeed that is what we had heard, they too must have been holding their breath, amongst other things.

We soon joined the lane and reached the village, which for its size, seemed to have a good choice of accommodation. We were booked into the unfortunately named Dyke House, located beyond the church in the former rectory. Before going there Chris wanted to visit the village shop for postcards. We found the miniscule post office come grocers come newsagent opposite the pub and went inside. The window was full of notices and adverts for clubs, activities, meetings, B&Bs and organic farms. The shop sold everything from foreign currency, organic runner beans and herbs grown by the school children to locally produced postcards; it was a gem of a shop. A small blond haired boy of about seven years followed us into the shop, saying hello as he entered. We replied and then looked around for the shopkeeper. The boy darted between us and around the counter.

"Can I help you?" he asked. Very helpful and really polite he served us, took the money and wished us goodbye.

We walked through the churchyard on our way to the B&B, calling into the church for a look around. It too, offered help yourself refreshments, asking those partaking to put a payment in the offertory box. We didn't partake. But someone had. Not, however, of the refreshments. Unfortunately someone who only took had visited the church just two days before. A hand written note by a pillar explained the offertory box had been stolen. Here, of all places, in the middle of nowhere, a quiet rural village church had become victim to selfish dishonesty.

Our B&B, beyond the towering yews, was a welcome refuge. Run by a double of the Principal in the college where we work, it was a beautiful house. Overcoming our initial shock at suddenly coming face to face with our boss, we followed the owner up the staircase to our twin room at the front of the house.

"Come down for a pot of tea when you're ready," instructed the owner, even sounding like our boss.

We hastily took off our boots and socks, to discover with horror that we had both trodden in liberal amounts of stinking, pungent sheep muck. When we went downstairs for the tea we took the boots with us, leaving them outside, where they stayed all night. And as we went down the stairs we carefully checked for any muck that might have come off our boots, much to our relief there was none.

The lady's husband was just coming in from the front garden, carrying a soil encrusted gardening fork. He greeted us warmly, resting the fork on an old Persian rug, and began chatting to us about the walk and the weather.

"Peter," exclaimed his wife, coming from the kitchen carrying a tray of tea, "please take that fork outside. I don't want soil all over the floor!"

"Yes, sorry dear," he replied amicably, before continuing to chat, lifting the fork off the rug as he did so.

Thank goodness our boots had not shed any sheep muck!

Sitting in the lounge, eating biscuits and drinking tea, we puzzled over the military past of the owners. It was like playing a combination of 'What's my line?' and 'Through the keyhole' but without the irritating celebrity contestants. The clues were dotted around the lounge, the dining room, the hall and even the toilet; clues such as old trunks, maps of Hong Kong, medals, trophies, photos and other artefacts from all over the world. It was one of the pleasures of staying in B&Bs, being a part, if only for one night, of someone else's home.

Our clean clothes hung at the bedroom window to dry and our boots sat outside the porch to stink quietly as, clean ourselves, we set off for a walk round the village and an evening meal at the pub. Most of the houses in the village were quite old, a mixture of cottages dating back several hundred years, a few larger Victorian and Edwardian houses and, beyond the church and the old rectory, a few new houses that had been designed to fit in, with half timbered walls and mellow tiled roofs. Opposite these was a contemporary bungalow that seemed hideous by comparison. The only pub in the quiet village also provided accommodation and one family, consisting of grandmother, mother and young daughter, was just coming down the stairs as we took our drinks and a menu to a couple of chairs by the fire. The menu was limited to just a half dozen choices but all sounded tempting and we both opted for the beef and ale pie. It was proving to be a popular choice; the family had also ordered the pie.

"Which table will you be sitting at?" asked the barman, as I placed our order.

"Oh, the one over there," I said, pointing to a table in a corner of the dining area. There was plenty of choice at that time and it looked as if the pub would remain quite empty.

We could hear the barman calling our order through to the kitchen and soon a waitress appeared with sets of cutlery and condiments.

"Table number three, for the two ladies," said the barman to the waitress, and she duly set the table.

"Think I might nip to the loo before the food arrives," I said, leaving Chris to her postcards and following a sign for the ladies that pointed through the dining room.

At the far end of the dining room I found the toilets locked and a second notice pointing me back to the bar. Back in the bar, and receiving odd glances from the barman, the waitress, Chris and the family of three, I set off through the tap room, this time following another sign for toilets. Tripping up a step and nearly bumping into a young woman, I found the toilets. A man was just coming out as I tried to get in. A little further down the corridor I found the ladies.

Feeling rather foolish I returned to the bar, which had now filled up somewhat. Another family with two children, were just settling themselves at a table and two young women were ordering yet more steak and ale pies. We sat sipping our drinks by the fire and discussing our plans for the next day; we were due to meet two friends, Julie and Mo, on Hergest Ridge and spend the day walking and visiting some gardens at nearby Kington, before they left to drive back to their homes in the Midlands. They were bringing with them a parcel of clean clothes and some farm shop bacon and yoghurt for our forthcoming breakfast and some more sunblock.

The two young women had sat down at the table set for us but it was of no consequence, or so we thought. That is until the waitress arrived, carrying two plates of steak and ale pie.

"For the two ladies," called the bar man, busily pulling pints. "Table three."

"I think that might be our food," I muttered to Chris. We watched as the waitress served our meal to the two young women.

"Oh! That was quick," exclaimed one of the young women.

As we could hardly say, 'oi, that's our pie!' especially as we had not moved onto the table in time, we decided to wait for their pie. The family of three had also noticed the mix up and the grandmother kindly informed the barman, who turned bright red and apologised profusely. The two women, hearing this, also turned bright red and apologised profusely. It was all becoming quite entertaining and got even sillier when the grandmother and mother's pies arrived and were served to us.

Chapter Eight

Funny how when you're having a late breakfast you manage to oversleep! It was ten minutes past eight when I woke up, realising with frantic haste that breakfast was only twenty minutes away and I hadn't even had a cup of tea yet! Chris was already up, showered, packed and brewed up as I rushed off to have a shower before returning and gulping down my cup of tea. Then we hurried down to breakfast in the opulently furnished dining room. An antique portrait hung from the wall and a candle-laden candelabrum hung from the ceiling. Tablemats adorned the polished wooden table and homemade preserves stood with antique silver serving spoons. An engraved silver saltcellar and its accompanying dainty serving spoon sat next to a matching silver pepper pot. Only the IKEA cutlery seemed out of place. Homemade toasted bread accompanied the homemade preserves, the best strawberry jam I have ever tasted. It was another lovely B&B that we were sad to leave.

But leave we had to do. We walked through the village and up the hill onto Hergest Ridge.

"I think this one might be Mike Oldfield's house," muttered Chris, as we walked up the track towards the ridge. "Or it could be this one," she added as we reached another house.

At the end of the track we came out onto open moorland and diverted away from Offa's Dyke Path to walk back to the end of the ridge overlooking the tiny village. Gladestry was laid out below us like a model. Sheep nibbled the short scrubby grass and wheatears flew amongst the bracken. Having slathered ourselves liberally with sun block, it was the cloudiest day so far, but was still warm and at times the heat seemed oppressively thundery. From the end of the ridge there were good views back to Hay Bluff and the Black Mountains, whilst in front of us we could see the 'blue remembered hills' of Shropshire.

We were not sure what time Julie and Mo would be arriving, but knowing they intended walking up the ridge from the Kington end to rendezvous with us somewhere on the top, we observed every new figure appearing on the horizon with studied concern. Suddenly a figure emerged over the crest of the ridge. Grasping the binoculars I focused on the distant spec. Was it Julie? Fair haired and wearing trousers and a T-shirt it looked like Julie; behind it, the short figure had to be Mo. Seeing us, the first figure waved.

"It's them!" I waved frantically back.

Distantly, through the binoculars, the figure returned my wave enthusiastically then sat down to await our arrival.

"They're very early," said Chris.

"Don't tell me I've just waved at a total stranger," I said.

"I don't think it's them. They were going to stop at the farm shop in Pembridge on their way. The timing's all wrong."

Offa's Dyke Path struck off the main path and, being purists, we followed it, the seated figure disappearing from sight behind the waving bracken. Nearing the top of the ridge a link path branched off towards the other path.

"Better just check it wasn't them!" I insisted.

We walked onto the other path and back towards where we had seen the figure. The person was sitting about fifty yards from us, long bushy blond hair, green T-shirt and muscular arms. It was a man. Not Julie. The second figure, a rough collie cross, was sprawled on the ground next to his master. Not Mo. Most definitely not Mo! As we watched, the man started doing sit ups and stretching his arms. We hurried off, back onto the official path before he saw us.

"I told you it wasn't them!" said Chris.

"Well why did he wave at us?" I asked. "I mean it wasn't just a little flap of the hand, it was a full blown 'hello, I'm over here' sort of wave; one you might use to flag down a rescue helicopter. Made me look a right fool!"

"Yes, and you don't need any help with that, do you?" laughed Chris.

The ridge was a broad expanse of diverging paths running between forests of golden bracken. A glacial erratic and an old racecourse merited a mention in the guidebook but, true to form, we saw neither. A herd of ponies, with a total of eight delightful leggy foals, had congregated around a small pond and were drinking noisily. I had a Doctor Doolittle moment with one of the mares, gently blowing down our noses at each other whilst she permitted me to stroke her neck and ears. Then I was called away by a pitiful 'help': Chris was standing on the path, her way blocked by one of the ponies.

"They've got bloomin' big teeth, you know," was her muttered excuse as I gently chivvied the mare away.

Arriving at the trig point we scanned the ridge for people. It had got quite busy and several couples came under our careful scrutiny before I spotted two likely looking suspects.

"There they are."

"They aren't looking," said Chris, focusing the binoculars on them. "I'll watch and when they look this wave I'll tell you to wave. Oh, that's odd, there seems to be someone else with them! Maybe Mo has brought her niece."

Eventually they saw us and all three began waving. With contact made we started walking towards one another. But when we met, Mo made no introductions for the woman and after a couple of minutes she said her goodbyes and left.

"Who's your friend?" laughed Chris.

"Aw, I don't know," replied Julie. "We met her as we were contemplating the thicket of monkey puzzle trees. One minute we were asking one another why the trees were there, next thing this mad woman is launching herself out of the undergrowth and talking to us. We couldn't seem to get rid of her. She was just tagging along with us and wouldn't stop talking. The Great Gob of Hergest Ridge!"

We all laughed.

"It's not funny," exclaimed Julie. "We told her we were meeting friends and tried to set off and next thing we know she was coming with us!"

We had walked in silence until meeting Julie and her squeaky boots, now every step was accompanied by a high-pitched sound that would not have been out of place in a rodent convention. We walked back out along the ridge, passing the pond and diverting to the trig point, before continuing as far as the viewpoint overlooking Hanter Hill and the noisy quarry beyond it. Sprawled across the path was the woman, busily writing postcards, her boots, rucksack and map scattered around her. On seeing us, she sprang to her feet and began chatting with Julie. The rest of us continued strolling along the path.

"We thought she'd adopted you," we laughed as Julie eventually caught us up.

"Did I call her the Great Gob?" asked Julie. "I think perhaps the Gob Leach of Hergest Ridge would be more apt. She latches on to you and won't shut up."

"It's just you she's taken a fancy to," pointed out Mo.

"Would you mind rephrasing that, please?" groaned Julie.

We stood in a line, admiring the views before us, purple heather-covered hills marching away to the northwest. Harebells and gorse flowered on the edges of the ridge, untouched by the ponies and sheep. Low flying fighter jets swooped in the valley below us and roared away into the distant mountains, the sound of their flight reaching us belatedly. Into the sudden silence the noisy quarry broke the stillness; the distant rumbling of the huge vehicles had been an almost subliminal accompaniment to our walk, but now a siren rang out, carrying clearly across the empty moorland. Was that the call to stop for lunch? No: it was warning of imminent blasting. There was a dull crumping sound, the siren changed and then ceased. And a bit more hillside had been reduced to road stone. We stood for some time, contemplating the destruction of the landscape in order to make roads to destroy more landscape, and as we stood there, lost in our thoughts a bird of prey flew past.

"What was that?" we all chorused.

"Buzzard?"

"No, that's a buzzard," said one of us, as a buzzard swooped high overhead, uttering its mewling cry.

The other bird had gone and none of us had been able to identify it. Probably a bald eagle or a vulture then!

We turned and began walking back along the ridge towards Kington, past the small copse of monkey puzzle trees that seemed so incongruously out of place up there. The descent from Hergest Ridge was along a bridle way before joining a lane leading to Hergest Croft Gardens. Dumping rucksacks in the boot of Julie's car and swapping walking boots for sandals we went into the Gardens for a pleasant afternoon of being tourists and, more to the point, for lunch.

"I wonder if your new friend has been to these gardens?" asked Chris, earning a withering glance from Julie.

As we sat on the terrace, waiting for our lunch orders to be fulfilled, the family of three from the pub at Gladestry appeared and sat at a nearby table. We exchanged hellos and joked about who might get our food, but as things turned out we all waited nearly an hour for our soups and sandwiches to be served. The kitchen seemed to be understaffed and very busy. The gardens were a wonderful way to relax and we spent several hours strolling around the leafy paths, exploring the ponds, the exotic plants and making the most of the shady benches.

We were staying in the youth hostel at Kington that night and not wishing to miss any of the path Chris and I walked to the hostel, leaving Julie and Mo to drive there with our rucksacks. Having checked in and unpacked, we opened our parcel that Mo had brought, swapping clean clothes for used ones and resealing the parcel for Mo to take home and post back to us, then we all wandered off to the self-catering kitchen to make a cup of tea. And who should be in there…

"Hello!" exclaimed a familiar voice, latching on to Julie like chewing gum to a carpet. "I didn't know you were staying here."

"We're not, our friends are," explained Julie, with decreasing patience.

We made tea and headed for the lounge, Julie only too happy to leave the kitchen. Kington is a new youth hostel, the previous one in the town having closed several years earlier. Like the rest of the hostel, the lounge was bright, clean and newly furnished. We sat chatting for an hour or so, until eventually stomachs started to rumble and by mutual agreement we went out for some food. There was quite a good choice of pubs and other eating establishments in the little market town; numerous of the red-bricked buildings down the high street offering takeaways, cafes and restaurants. We finally stopped at one of the pubs that had been recommended by the hostel warden, where we enjoyed a good meal.

We returned to the hostel along a path behind the shops and houses, a mistake in the failing light as the path seemed to be frequented by dog walkers who had yet to come across the 'bag it and bin it' concept. Sheep muck the previous night, would it be dog tonight? By some miraculous intervention we arrived back at the hostel with eight muck-free shoes.

"Oh, no," groaned Julie as we entered the hostel grounds.

Her new found friend was sitting outside chatting to a chap who was displaying all the symptoms of someone who finds himself somewhere he really does not want to be and unable to escape. Julie, quite unwittingly, provided that escape.

"Oh, hello!" exclaimed the woman, with obvious delight. "I thought you said you weren't staying here."

"We're not! I told you, we were just meeting our friends!" repeated Julie, suffering fools not at all gladly. "We're going now!"

"Oh, that's a shame. Well have a safe journey," gushed the woman.

"I think she likes you," winked Chris, as we headed for Julie's car.

As we waved them off and returned to the hostel, the over-friendly woman had latched on to a poor defenceless cyclist and, having cornered him by the maps in the hallway, was talking at him enthusiastically. Chris and I went into the kitchen to make some hot chocolate, a husband and wife were already in there, the man poring over maps, his wife making sandwiches for the following day. The woman asked us if we were walking the Dyke and we soon began chatting, but the lady had quite a bad stutter. However she was keen to talk to us about the walk having done most of it herself, telling us that the next two days for us would be particularly scenic. The conservation finished long after the sandwiches were made but it was nice to listen to someone telling us how nice things were going to be, instead of the usual gloomy predictions of steep hills, too many stiles and not enough signposts and benches!

As we left the kitchen after the hot chocolate, the Great Gob of Hergest was still chatting to the cyclist, his eyes had glazed over and his face was pale. We could not help but feel sorry for him.

Chapter Nine

Our two-bedded room was on the ground floor, with the window overlooking the kitchen window. After getting up that morning we checked to see who was in the kitchen before we went to make breakfast. We thought we had avoided Julie's chatty and persistent friend but she appeared in the kitchen just as I was cremating some bacon. With our backs to her we managed at first to avoid her. She collared every other hosteller in turn before finally latching on to us. To anyone else we would have been only too happy to chat about walking but we feared that once we started we would never get away. She seemed to have walked many long distance paths and she had also cycled the End to End. Normally I would not have missed any opportunity to talk to a fellow End to Ender. Normally. The stuttering lady and her husband entered the kitchen at that point and Julie's new friend turned her attentions to them. The husband, perhaps sensibly, remained monosyllabic with her and soon escaped into the dining room with a box of cereal, but his wife was dragged into conversation with her. The poor woman had no chance: she was given no opportunity to get a word out, even had she been able to.

With our breakfast eaten and our washing up done we beat as polite and hasty a retreat as possible.

"Where are your friends?" asked the Great Gob of Hergest Ridge, as we were half way through the door.

"She told you, they weren't staying here. They're back at work!" we shot back, grabbing our nearly forgotten milk and bolting for Prestatyn.

Kington had a narrow but busy main street and it was nice to note that many of the specialist shops were still in business – and only one bookshop! We bought postcards at a newsagent and nectarines at a greengrocer's shop before passing a little café where the cyclist from the hostel was safely having his breakfast in peace.

We left town along quiet streets, dropping down a narrow lane to cross a tiny stream. Then began a long but not unpleasant climb up through a collection of houses making up Bradnor Green and towards Bradnor Hill, where England's highest golf course sprawled in neat-greened precision across the hillside. Ever wary of flying golf balls after a very near miss on a footpath in Devon, we crossed with some haste and much turning of heads and peeling of eyes. After the hazards of the golf course came the interesting sight of a farmer shearing his sheep.

A raucous cry drew our attention as a bird flew, almost in slow motion, from one tree to another.

"Was it a woodpecker?" I asked.

Its plumage had seemed rather dark. With the binoculars I picked it out walking along the tree branch. It was a jay. Which just goes to show how much difference sunglasses can make!

Suddenly we were back on the dyke after being away from it for over fifty miles, and we marched along its top enjoying views in all directions. In many parts along its length steps have been taken to minimise erosion of this unique ancient monument, but try explaining that to the wildlife. Along other parts of the dyke badgers utilise the steep embankment for their setts. That particular part of the dyke above Kington was an obstacle course of rabbit holes and shallow scrapes, and we had to carefully watch each footfall for fear of stumbling down a hole. Having just recovered from a bursitis under my left Achilles tendon, I really did not want to do any more damage to my ankles.

Bursitis is an inflammation of a bursa, a fluid-filled sack which when not inflamed acts as cushioning between tendons, skin or muscles and the bones over which they pass. The bursitis had taken several weeks to heal fully. Ironically I had damaged it during a cycling holiday but not whilst cycling. At Spring Bank I had spent a week cycling from Bath, to London, to home in Lancashire, completing two sides of a triangle, a journey of just over six hundred miles. I had spent two nights at Earl's Court Youth Hostel, allowing myself a day of sightseeing in the capital. The injury had started after a day of walking through London in a pair of brand new boots, the same boots that I was cycling in. By the middle of the week, walking had become agony although cycling was bearable. Determined not to give in I completed my cycling holiday but after only one day back at work, in a job that is far from sedentary, I could hardly walk. A week off work and some physio, ice, anti inflammatories and lots of rest and I was able to return to work, but I could not wear any shoes that touched the back of my heel. I spent the next two months in sandals, hoping my ankle would be fully healed in time for the walk. It seemed to be, but I was not taking any chances, and wore an old pair of hiking boots and carried a penknife, prepared, should it be necessary, to do a little modification to the back of the boot if it did become a problem. The first day out of Chepstow, paranoid of any problems developing, I imagined pain where none existed; as the walk went on I began to relax and by the end was convinced the Bursitis was not going to recur.

The guidebook made a point of mentioning three yews located a little way to the east but we were unable to distinguish them from the other trees growing on the dyke. Were we at the right place? Was the guidebook wrong? The latter seemed likely when we later spotted three trees of varying sizes on the horizon, which looked very much like yews. The mystery was never solved.

The next couple of miles had to be one of the most scenic so far; not vast panoramas but rolling hillsides covered by woods, bracken and heather. The hills layered one behind the other, with the sky dotted with a variety of cloud formations. The earth of the dyke was carpeted with harebells, ladies bedstraw and trefoil. There was colour and interest through every dimension. As we walked round the curving slopes of Herrock Hill we disturbed a ewe and her grown lambs, which careered out of the bracken, hind legs going from under them as they hurtled away from us down the slope. Butterflies danced across the path and through the vegetation to alight on the flowers, and in the valley bottom a compacted herd of cows grazed a small triangle of field corner, cordoned by electric fencing that was invisible to us from that distance.

More woodland, and more squirrels, surrounded the path as we dropped down into the valley and reached a road. We followed the road until it crossed a clear, gurgling stream at Ditchyeld Bridge. Looking back we could see evidence of the line of the dyke in the form of a bracken-covered narrow ridge that ran down the lower slopes of the northern side of Herrock Hill. From the old bridge we climbed through woodland below Burfa Bank with its hill top fort, passing a restored sixteenth century timber framed house looking beautiful in its woodland setting.

We were making good time and could afford a leisurely lunch stop. The spot we chose was in a grassy field and we kicked off our boots, pulled off our socks, gassing lots of wildlife in the process, and sprawled in the long grass to eat fruit, biscuits and dried apricots. The inquisitive sheep, which had run in terror at our presence and our feet, slowly began to come nearer and nearer. When I rolled over onto my stomach and looked up I found I was facing a line of sheep all slowly advancing towards us; they looked like a police search line.

Setting off again it was not long before my mobile began to ring. It was Roger.

"Hello, it's me," echoed his distorted voice down the line.

"Hiya. Where are you? It sounds like you're in a cave," I replied.

"I'm just examining the washing machine."

His reply set off an entire church load of bells ringing. Why was Roger taking a more than passing interest in our washing machine? This was very worrying. Give me wheelie bins any day.

"That's nice for you," I remarked neutrally. "How are you?"

"Do you know there's a hole in it?"

"Yes dear. That's where you put the laundry."

"No," he replied slowly, his voice dripping with mock patience. "This hole is in the rubber."

"Oh, that! No, it's not a hole. It was but I patched it. I think it got torn by a zip. It's okay now. Doesn't leak," I told him, thinking: keep it simple and easy to understand.

"No, it was patched," replied Roger, attempting to keep the conversation on an equally simple level. "But I put my finger through it."

"WHAT?" I shrieked.

"Well, it's no good with a hole. Where's all the water going?"

"Are your feet getting wet when you stand in front of it? Is the bucket floating out from under the kitchen sink? Have the cats taken to wearing life jackets and Wellington boots?" I chortled, "Puss in boots – get it?"

Roger was not amused. He became even less so when I suggested he might like to buy a new washing machine. When I got home the same old washing machine was still sitting in our kitchen. Leaking? No. And the hole? A purposely-designed finger sized dimple in the rubber.

With that most interesting of domestic appliances forgotten and wheelie bins no longer the hot topic of the moment, we continued, following the line of the dyke above several fields of golden wheat waving in the gentle winds. We crossed a road, empty of traffic, and entered Granner Wood roughly paralleling the line of the dyke as it skirted below the top of Evenjobb Hill. As we entered Upper Dunn's Plantation, the dyke twisted away to the west and we continued northwards on the path climbing up to the aptly, if unoriginally, named Hilltop Plantation. Chris was leading the way along the path bordered on our left by a fence; suddenly I heard her excited squeal and hurried to catch her up. She had disturbed a red kite that had been perched atop one of the fence posts and it had taken flight, swooping away across the field, using the thermals to take it over the hedge and into the fields and woods beyond. I had arrived too late to see it.

The smell of smoke reached us as we entered Hilltop Plantation and both of us were somewhat concerned by this. Fearing burning timber, fleeing animals and smoke inhalation we were relieved to discover the source of the smoke was not a rampaging forest fire but a campfire. A rather foolish young couple were frying sausages over an open fire that was sited almost up against the trunk of a young sapling. Had they not heard of the Countryside Code? Whatever happened to 'guard against fire'? I felt like stomping their fire out. And nicking their sausages. They did smell very good!

We crossed another road to begin a descent to Discoed, down through fields where sheep grazed the long grass. One friendly, half grown lamb came inquisitively to the fence, sticking its nose through the wire and bleating at us. We stroked its ears and hand fed it grass that it ate noisily.

"Bye bye, Alan," I said to it as we began walking away.

"Alan?" repeated Chris. "Why Alan?"

"Well, we both know an Alan who makes a pretty similar noise when he eats his lunch."

"No, that lamb was much quieter!"

In the valley bottom we crossed another road and walked through a couple of fields to reach the River Lugg. A huge brown bull seemed to be alone in one of these fields, causing us both an anxious moment until we spotted a few black and white cows and calves further across the field. Why is it that bulls on their own are considered dangerous but the same bulls are deemed safe if they have a little female company? Can they only think of one thing at once? Is that the theory? The daft cows didn't stop to ask him. Neither did the Friesians.

The path by the river was shaded by huge oaks. The guidebook foretold of otters and I got excited for a brief second before realising that if otters were predicted then I was bound not to see any. It also mentioned dippers. We didn't see that lovely brown and white bird either. A streak of blue, skimming low over the dancing river caught our attention and we watched as a little kingfisher came to rest on a branch overhanging the far side of the narrow river. The bird paused for a few seconds, searching the waters below before taking off again downstream. By the remains of a fallen willow, we found a huge bloom of fungus. Almost three feet across, its dimensions were impressive and we stopped to take a photo, although the image was to give little indication of size.

We crossed the river a little further along on a wooden footbridge, heading across fields to reach yet another road. Two green woodpeckers flew out of the trees and away towards the river as we neared the road. There seemed to be countless green woodpeckers all along this National Trail. At the road we left the path for that day, heading back down to the river along another footpath further to the east to reach our B&B on the Presteigne road. Crossing the river for the second time we saw a spotted woodpecker but still no otters.

Heading east along the road we came to a gate leading into a field; a sign on the gate pointed walkers up towards the farmhouse B&B. The gate jammed against the grass as we struggled to open it and then we were in the field, climbing up alongside a hedge, disturbing fearful pheasants that bolted in a terrified and illogical zigzagging run as we approached the cluster of farm buildings at the top of the field. The farmyard seemed immaculate, no straw, no clucking hens, no animals, no muck; making us stop to wonder if this was really a working farm. An equally tidy farmhouse sat in an elevated position facing a large open barn. With trepidation we approached the door: what would tonight's accommodation be like? Just as I was raising a hand to knock on the door, a man appeared around the corner of the building.

"Oh, hello. You must be two of our walkers. Take a seat," he gestured towards to white plastic chairs nearby. "And take your boots off."

We smiled a reply and began taking off our boots whilst the man removed his own Wellingtons and went inside to get his wife. She came out, clutching a duster and hastily shoving her feet into a pair of clogs.

"Hello, take your boots off. Oh, you have done," she said, seeming somewhat surprised. "Now what are your names?"

"Chris and Julia," I replied, trying to hide my filthy, smelly socks by curling my toes up under the chair.

"No, I meant your surnames."

We told her and watched her face cloud with consternation.

"Ah, yes, look you, we've got a bit of a problem. Anyway, come through to the front and I'll make you a pot of tea."

Exchanging worried glances, we followed her into a dark lobby where we were instructed to leave our boots and rucksacks. Doing as we were bid we then followed her through a pristine hallway and out the front door onto an equally neat front patio. Instructed to take a seat, we sat down in garden chairs and waited while she went back inside to put the kettle on. She returned a few minutes later with a tray of tea and a single page calendar of the sort the milkman usually leaves by your silver top on New Year's Eve.

"Now, look you, we have a bit of a problem," reiterated the farmer's wife.

"Oh," we chorused, wondering what disaster was about to unfold.

"Yes, we're double booked. Now don't worry. Look you, it's not a problem. I did try phoning you but the only number I've got," she said, peering myopically at a tiny bit of scrawl on her year-to-view calendar, "doesn't seem to work."

She rhymed off a number that neither of us recognised. What was coming next?

"So, yes, we have a problem. But look you, don't worry. I have two other walkers booked into your room. But don't worry. What I think I will do is… Don't worry. I don't want you to worry."

Blimey! We must have looked very worried.

"What I think I'm going to do is let you stay, as you have arrived first, and find alternative accommodation for the other walkers. We've only two rooms you see, look you, and I already have a couple staying in my double. But don't worry." With that she disappeared.

"I'm not worried," said Chris, settling back with a china cup of steaming tea. "It's her problem, not ours."

We sat sipping the scalding tea, Chris not worrying and me quietly going frantic, which has been the usual case in the past when this has happened to us, as indeed it seems to do every year. A few minutes elapsed before the lady reappeared.

"All right for tea are you?" she asked. "Look you, I've been having a think. As you two are here I think I will take you onto another farm, further along the road, it is. That way when the two gentlemen arrive, if they are much later, which they might be, you never know, not sure where they are walking from you see... Er... Yes, when they arrive they can stay here. They might be late, you see."

"Oh!"

"Well, you finish your tea and then I'll get my husband to take you to the other farm. They do B&B, look you. So we're not just taking you anywhere. And it's not too far from the path, so that won't be a problem for you in the morning. But I don't want you to worry, now. We'll sort you out."

Before we had any chance to raise an objection, the woman disappeared.

"Great! Not too far from the path could be anywhere," I groaned.

So far the walk had gone to plan: no hitches, no dire B&Bs, no bad meals, no getting lost (well not too much), no injuries, wasp stings, lost socks, delayed trains, double bookings. Suddenly we were facing being taken to goodness knows where by a scatterbrain woman with an obsession about boots in the house and a total lack both of organisation and a decent diary. I drank another cup of tea and watched the farm cat walking up the drive. Did she ask it to take its paws off before allowing it in the house? The cat tiptoed over the cattle grid and settled down to sleep on the sharp, lumpy gravel – how could it possibly be comfortable? It must be the feline equivalent of a bed of nails.

The door flew open, interrupting my increasingly depressing reverie and the woman appeared, kicking off her slippers and shoving her feet into the clogs.

"Now, look you, I've had a think and it's not a problem." (What, her having a think?) "As you arrived first, I think what we're going to do is let you stay and when the two gentlemen arrive we can take them to the other farm. Is that alright?"

"Yes, that's fine," we both said with relief. Fine providing she didn't change her mind again.

"Look you, have you finished your tea?" she asked, examining both our cups and our feet. "Are your socks clean? Come on and I'll show you to your room."

Brushing my socks on the doormat and nearly tripping over the discarded clogs, I followed her and Chris up the stairs, the farmer's wife attempting to carry both our rucksacks at once: a challenge that would defeat most people. At the top of the stairs she stopped, possibly for a rest, possibly for a heart attack, either seemed feasible. We stopped too, looking round the broad upper landing, where the expensive carpet flooded into every bedroom and coloured sunlight filtered through the intricate stained glass windows above the head of the stairs.

"Now, look you, this is the bathroom, and this," she said steering us along the landing to a room at the front of the house, "is your bedroom."

With a heave of the rucksacks she ushered us into the room, which was equally neat and pristine as the rest of the house. Antique furniture filled the room, a huge sheepskin rug filled the floor and ornaments filled the dressing table and the windowsill.

"The toilet is down the hall, look you. And there's a torch there if you need it in the night," she added. Perhaps she had seen me eyeing up the chamber pot that was decorating the windowsill. "If you want a meal, there's lots of choice in Presteigne, it's about a mile down the road, look you. Go down our drive and turn right. You can't miss it."

The farmhouse was actually a very good B&B, but our arrival had been fraught to say the least. We both made use of the brand new bathroom, enjoying a relaxing bath and great shower before completing the usual laundry chores, dangling our wet washing in front of the open bedroom window and setting off in search of Presteigne. After twenty minutes we were still walking along the narrow, hedge-lined, verge-less and incredibly busy road. Presteigne was nowhere in sight.

"We are going the right way aren't we?" I asked Chris.

"Well she told us to turn right," replied Chris.

"She also told us not to worry, look you, and that we could stay, no we couldn't, yes we could, no we couldn't, yes we could, no we…"

"Okay, I get the point!"

Eventually, after over half an hour of walking we reached Presteigne. It was most definitely not a mile down the road! To say we were hungry was to understate the fact. Presteigne was little more than a village but it did have a good choice of pubs, takeaways and a rather trendy little restaurant that Chris had found an article about in the local information pages at the B&B. The restaurant had just opened for the evening and, yes, they had a table for two available. We sat down, ordered drinks and perused the menu. The restaurant specialised in locally grown produce and the menu was a mix of traditional and modern dishes. We opted for soup, then chicken kebabs with mixed salad and finally crème brulee for Chris and chocolate mousse for me.

The soup, a delicious curried coconut concoction arrived with freshly baked bread and pats of butter. I lifted the first spoonful to my mouth and whoosh! A small midge swooped in front of my nose and kamikaze-ed into my laden spoon. I fished it out with the corner of a napkin.

Soon the restaurant filled with other diners. A large eclectic group, with upper class English accents arrived and sat themselves down around a huge table. They were loud, brash and full of themselves. As our own conversation lagged we both found ourselves inadvertently listening to the conversation at the other table. I only caught half of the conversation but Chris was earwigging with barely controlled glee. Her hearing seemed to have miraculously recovered.

"What did they just say?" I whispered and Chris filled me in. "How come you can hear more than I can and your ears are bunged up?"

"Practise!"

Day had turned into dusk as we left Presteigne and began the long walk back along the road. Dusk rapidly changed to a red tinted twilight, and cars travelling along the road wore their headlights like blazing beacons. Pinned in the headlights, squeezing up into the hedge to avoid being swept under their racing wheels we had a white knuckle walk back to the B&B. Chris was wearing a bright yellow shirt and I volunteered her to walk in the lead, maybe then oncoming traffic would have some chance of seeing us before they ran us down. By the time we were walking back up the long drive the moon was out, a floodlit crescent in the darkening sky, and dusk had bleached the colour out of the landscape till the trees we walked under and the grass and the lane were mere shades of grey. Darker shapes flew above our heads: bats out for their nightly forage.

Back at the B&B, we wiped our feet on the doormat and went inside to find the farmer's wife. We found her in the lounge, knitting and watching television. As we entered she looked up and then immediately her eyes diverted to our feet. We were wearing sandals! In the house! I could see she was tempted to ask us to take them off but we sidetracked her by asking what time she would be serving breakfast. Having discussed times and menu options, we headed upstairs – still wearing our sandals!

We knew from past experience that staying on a farm does not necessarily guarantee a peaceful night's sleep. Usually the sound of lowing cattle, bleating sheep or, worse, humming generators can ruin what should be a quiet night. At the last farm it had been the howling of the lost dog. When we went to bed that evening there was a deep silence, ah the peace of the countryside! It was not to last. Some fifteen minutes after lights out a dog howled.

"Erm, that sound's kind of familiar," I mumbled.

"Pardon?"

"A dog howled. Didn't you hear it?"

"No."

Then the howl came again. And again. And again. And that time Chris did hear it. In fact, it didn't let up for most of the night. It even sounded the same as the lost dog. How bizarre.

Chapter Ten

The indecision continued at breakfast, when the landlady could not decide whether to fetch the tea or the toast first. But when it arrived the breakfast was very good. Always a bonus with me was the fresh fruit and yoghurt. Chris opted for eggs on toast, which seemed to leave me getting her sausage and bacon as well as my own.

"I think you've had my sausage," she told me, watching as I did battle with the steaming plateful.

"But I've had three."

"Yes, I heard her telling her husband that the new dog didn't want sausage."

"You mean I've had the dog's as well?"

"No! I think he had one of mine and you got the other!"

"Did you say it was a new dog?"

We looked at one another, both thinking the same thing. It was a new dog. It howled all night. Could it possibly be the same dog? Had the other farmers failed to find its owner and eventually sold it on? We did not like to ask and so it remained a mystery.

We had as much trouble leaving as we had arriving. The farmer's wife seemed to be trying to make up for the less than ideal welcome of the day before. She chatted pleasantly about our walk, admiring our boots, asking about our route finding and the distance we were walking. Eventually she shook our hands and finally let us go. It was only as we were standing outside the back door putting our rucksacks on that we realised we were not wearing our boots!

We returned to Dolley Green, crossing the river, not seeing any otters but passing a lovely old timbered house and its long barn before reaching the road. Just a few houses stood at either side of the road, all of them unremarkable. The only building of note was the curious corrugated iron church, which looked more like a Nissen hut than a place of worship.

We crossed the road to rejoin Offa's Dyke Path, heading uphill along an agricultural road, a rutted track of large stones and animal muck, which climbed up to Furrow Hill. As we climbed further views opened up of our earlier hilly conquests: Hergest, Herrock Hill and the Black Mountains. The guidebook mentioned rabbits and buzzards so, predictably, we saw none. Sheep dozed in the sunshine and swifts swooped overhead; the land sloping away to the west was covered in heather. The dyke was prominent along this part of the path and we trod its twisty route for several miles, passing a stream of other walkers coming towards us.

The guidebook mentioned a prominent copse of Wellingtonias that could be seen near Pilleth. And guess what? They were there! They hadn't flown off, run off, gone off, beggared off, switched off or any other off. Unlike the otters, the dipper, the buzzards... Apparently the Wellingtonias were planted in commemoration of the Battle of Pilleth that occurred in 1402 when Henry IV took a beating at the hands of Owain Glyndwr.

We made a detour to the monument of Sir Richard Green Price, bringer of the railway to his beloved Radnorshire. Hm, never yet found a monument to Doctor Beeching! The monument seemed strangely placed, located as it was in the middle of a field, a hundred yards from the path and a nearby road and nowhere near a railway.

Before the road I took advantage of a secluded gorse patch for a toilet stop. After nine days of walking we had yet to find any toilets on the route unless it was at the start or end of a day. It was with some concern that I emerged from the gorse, turned a corner and realised just how close to the road I actually was. I mentioned it to Chris who was waiting by a parked Land Rover.

"Yes, I thought that when this drove up and a man got out," she grinned. "But fortunately he went the other way."

We soon passed the workman and his companion, cutting the grass, nettles and bracken that crowded along the path. As we descended towards Knighton the clouds descended too but the threatened rain held off, although the temperature dropped, which was no bad thing with the climbs we had to come that afternoon. The path down to Knighton exhibited some of the largest remaining parts of the dyke. It was an impressive sight as we walked alongside the deep, tree lined ditch and high embankment.

We were making steady and for the most part easy progress. Gloucestershire, Monmouthshire, Herefordshire and Powys had all come and gone as we walked northwards, crossing and re-crossing the English Welsh border. But at Knighton we realised we were in another county: Shropshire had crept up on us and suddenly our progress seemed to have taken us quite far north.

Knighton is considered the halfway point on Offa's Dyke National Trail. The town is home to the Offa's Dyke visitor centre, and its name in Welsh means 'the town on the dyke': Tref y Clawdd. The English name means 'settlement of the knights' or 'town of the horsemen', the derivation from the English being easier for my non-Welsh-language brain to understand. It is the only town on the path that has evidence of the dyke in the town itself. And as with most of the border towns, Knighton has a long history of conflict and littered with the sites of battles, castles and other defensive structures.

Located in England, Knighton enjoys a quintessentially English culture, with its own town crier and festivals such as the May Fair. It is another busy borders market town, with yet another off-the-shelf clock tower. The author of our guidebook seemed to take exception to all these similar clock towers but it seemed to me to be no different from the buildings of today. Many buildings conform to a design typical of their time with almost regimental accord. For instance my old junior school, built in the early 1970s, is the standard design for schools of that era. Although what the architects were thinking, designing schools with flat roofs in rain-rich Lancashire, is a question I'm sure the teachers and headmaster asked themselves on a regular basis as they were running round with buckets and mops!

However, Knighton was proving far too much like Kington, not in appearance but in name; the two towns were constantly mixed up in our heads and we frequently said Knighton when we meant Kington and vice versa.

We reached Kington, sorry, Knighton at lunch time on that Friday afternoon, and the first building we came to was the toilets. Well, I didn't need them, did I? But Chris did, and she went inside whilst I hovered about outside guarding the rucksacks and looking strange, if the glances of passers by were anything to go by. Leaving the toilets, the car park and the inquisitive stares we passed through an archway and emerged on the high street.

"Oh! A chemist's," piped Chris, and proceeded to hurry across the road, dodging traffic in her haste.

"What do you want from the chemist's?" I asked, running to catch up. "Julie brought us more sun lotion."

"Pardon?"

"It's okay. You've just answered my question."

I hovered in the aisles, looking at all manner of mind-boggling products from analgesics, blood pressure monitors, corn plasters, gripe water and worming milk shakes, to desensitizer sprays! From remedies to still the beating heart to potions to calm the savage beast. But did they have any eardrops? By this point in our walk Chris was desperate to cure her gammy ear, which was not only causing her discomfort but was, she claimed, impairing her eavesdropping abilities: something I had not noticed! Fortunately the chemist had a good supply of eardrops and we were soon back on the high street and heading in search of much more exciting products of a digestible nature.

The ascending high street in Knighton had, as we had come to expect from these borders towns, a good selection of shops, and we climbed the curving high street hoping to find a bakers. All manner of shops lined the high street including a fantastic kitchenware shop and an ironmonger; the wonderful things I could have bought if only I had a big enough kitchen and a big enough rucksack! Sure enough, at the top of the hill and just below the clock tower, we reached a bakery. Our noses had been aware of the shop's presence long before we saw it. But having found the bakery we were unable to decide what we wanted to eat. Pie or pastry? Sweet or savoury? Hot or cold? Cream or jam? Chocolate or toffee coated? Bath buns and chocolate muffins finally won the much-deliberated competition and were paid for and shoved unceremoniously into the bulging tops of our rucksacks for later consumption. We did not want to eat them straight away; we had a hill to climb!

The Offa's Dyke Visitor Centre in Knighton occupied us for a while, examining the exhibits and looking at the informative displays, pushing the interactive buttons and, in Chris' case, buying dozens of postcards. The visitor centre toilets came in handy too! Somewhere in the field behind the visitor centre there was a monument, erected when the path was opened in July 1971. We wandered about in the field trying to find the dyke and the stone, and failing abysmally. In the end we gave up. Chris returned later in the year whilst on a family holiday in Herefordshire when, with the help of four other people, she finally managed to locate the elusive stone monument. Her verdict: very impressive but we had been looking in the wrong place! Still, she took a photograph of it, so I feel I can say I have seen it.

Following our fruitless search for the stone, Chris and I descended to the River Teme, which we followed for a short distance before crossing it on a footbridge parallel to the railway bridge. I looked for otters in the river: what a waste of time that was! A coke can, a football, two ducks and a broken umbrella were the highlights of my spotter's list for the River Teme.

Next came a steep climb up to the top of Panpunton Hill, four hundred feet above the valley floor. The path ran just to the west of the deciduous Kinsley Wood, and we followed it up through stands of bracken, our knees creaked, sweat flowed, breathing came in ragged gasps and rabbits fled at the sight of these two strange apparitions. We stopped for lunch at a commemorative bench ('there aren't many benches on the path'); but had it not been for the guidebook we would not have known whom it was commemorating, the back of it was missing! But our appreciation goes to Frank Noble of the Offa's Dyke Association, we sat on his bench and ate our lunch and admired the views. Below us in the valley the River Teme meandered into the distance. At the farther end of the valley, stretching between rolling wooded hillsides, was the Knucklas Viaduct. As we watched, a train, tinier than a model railway, trundled over the arched spans.

It was looking decidedly grey as we sat having lunch on Frank's bench, a situation much improved by changing my sunglasses for normal spectacles. If only all grey clouds could be banished so easily! The wind was brisk on the hilltop and lunch was a hasty affair as we soon began to shiver. Hats threatened to blow off and my flaking chocolate bar was blown away, something that never happened in those sexy advertisements for the chocolate where waif-like women, who looked like they had never been near a bit of chocolate in their lives, daintily ate the product whilst reclining in a bath or gallivanting in a wild flower meadow. You didn't hear them swear when a bit of chocolate dropped down their fronts or blew away across the grass!

Cakes eaten, chocolate blown away and smeared in bits across my shirt, we continued on our way. In some parts the path closely followed the line of the dyke but mainly it ran along the contours of the hillside. Sheep and the occasional small herd of cattle grazed the slopes below us. Beyond a switchback of ups and downs we passed a small coniferous plantation before reaching a trig point. This part of the beautiful Shropshire hills seemed a remote place; we had the land to ourselves and were to see virtually no one for the remainder of the day.

From the trig point we began to descend, a dry dusty track that wound through low clumps of yellow flowering gorse. The path was uneven, rutted and narrow.

"You go first to break my fall," quipped Chris, standing aside to let me pass.

But it was I who slipped, my boots skidding from under me on the arid, dusty ground. I instinctively shot my arms out to regain my balance, grabbing at anything to stop myself falling: not such a wise thing to do considering the surrounding vegetation. My right hand slammed into a spiky gorse bush. Skidding to a halt I examined my hand. Blood covered two fingers, making the injury appear much worse than it was. I had been walking with my hands by my sides for some time, causing the blood to pool in my fingertips, and the two tiny punctures from the gorse had drawn more blood than the mishap warranted. A lick and a wipe on my shirt and the wounds were invisible but they certainly prickled.

We stumbled out onto a wider path at Selley Hall Farm where the ground levelled out and a few feeding troughs lay scattered by a gate. Chris, drawing level with me, kicked up a fresh dollop of sheep muck. Not enough that I should be covered in blood and melted chocolate, the sheep poo landed on my calf and attempts to flick it off just resulted in spreading it to my fingers.

We crossed a narrow lane where a small mammal squeaked piercingly from the undergrowth. Next came two tiny becks, crossed courtesy of footbridges built by the Royal Engineers, then a second farm and another long ascent. We followed a rutted, gravel strewn farm track, the official footpath that kept us off the dyke itself but which was hard on the feet, it was unpleasant walking. We continued on this track, ugly in comparison to the normal state of Offa's Dyke footpath, for two miles as it climbed to the top of the hill and ran along the ridge, with the dyke first on the left, then the right. The views to our left were extensive but these were marred for me by the ugly, wide track on which we were forced to walk. After what seemed like miles we emerged on a road where a group of elderly walkers were just getting refreshments from the back of their car. A cup of tea would be nice, please!

We walked along the road for approximately one mile, sharing Offa's Dyke Path with the local route of the Jack Mytton Way. Gateposts bore the National Trail acorn emblem as well as the logo for the Jack Mytton Way. Not sure just who Jack Mytton was we studied the logo and were able to deduce he was a huntsman. The dead animal theme continued as the narrow country road was marked at both ends by dead badgers in extreme states of decay. The smell was nauseating.

The lane had been recently resurfaced with that useless form of surfacing: tar and chippings, guaranteed to mark your car, fill the hedges and last no time at all. Already the new road surface was showing signs of disintegration where cattle had been moved down the road, depositing their deposits, as they went. As the muck had dried over the last week of hot, sunny weather it had contracted and started to lift the think layer of chippings, pulling it away from the tar underneath. Perhaps the highways department should consider abandoning sticky tar in favour of a more adhesive substance such as cow muck!

A loud rumbling signified heavy traffic on the road ahead and as we reached the cross roads to turn right we saw the cause. A tractor was turning slowly into a farmyard. Its towing cargo of huge round bales of hay threatened to topple as both sides of the trailer brushed hedges and fences. The roadway was littered with a confetti of straw. The farmhouse itself had initiative owners, offering not only accommodation and camping but also teas and refreshments. At any other time we would have welcomed the stop but with only a mile to go we knew that once we sat down our knees would seize up and walking that last mile would be difficult. So we pushed on, down hill all the way now on this fourteen mile day, through fields, following the dyke, passing old farmhouses on the way down to the valley bottom and the River Clun. Across the river, with no otters to be seen, passing near an old timbered farmhouse, then across another field and we were out on the lane at the little village of Newcastle, somewhere along this lane was the Bed and Breakfast place we had booked.

"It's here!" Chris exclaimed, pointing to a house just a few yards along the road.

"Can't be! We've not gone miles along the road before turning round and realising we don't know where it is, like we usually do."

"No, this is definitely it," Chris assured me.

While we stood on the lane, joking about how easily we had found the B&B, the door opened and a cheerful lady, clad in sweat pants, T-shirt and a flour-dusted apron, came out to greet us. Our accommodation was in a separate building just across the drive from the main house. Soon we were enjoying a pot of tea and delicious caramel shortbread in the garden and listening to a robin singing in the shrubbery.

Newcastle is not a large village and we had arranged to have an evening meal at the B&B. Excellent decision! It was quite possibly the best meal we had yet had. Sitting opposite each other at an old oak table, we munched our way through three delicious courses, trying at the same time to absorb as much of our surroundings as possible. The house was a converted barn, converted that is with originality and taste; wood and stone complimented the simple but smart furnishings and the lady herself clearly enjoyed having people stay with her.

The B&Bs so far, with the exception of the one at Chepstow, had been very good. Was this, we wondered, representative of the ones on Offa's Dyke Path, or had we just been very lucky? We would have our answer before Prestatyn.

Originally we had booked accommodation for that night in the youth hostel at Clun Mill. It was only on further investigation that we realised, belatedly, that the hostel was three miles from the path. As we did not relish the prospect of a seventeen mile day and a longer distance for the following day too, we had decided to cancel the booking and find a more conveniently located B&B on the path at Newcastle. Our decision had proved an excellent one for the food alone! Replete with delicious home cooking, much of which was also homegrown, we went out for a walk along the lane, and to find a post box!

As we strolled along the lane, bliss without our rucksacks and in the cool of dusk, Chris' mobile phone chirruped in its distressed budgerigar fashion. Chris had received a text from Clare, who at that time was living, studying and working in Germany. She read it and began to laugh.

"She wants to know if we can find an Internet café and email her some photos!"

"Internet café!" I laughed.

We considered ourselves lucky to find an ice cream van, let alone cafes, with or without modems! We did find a post box and Chris deposited a hefty batch of postcards into the care of Royal Mail. Then, having reached the end of the village, we turned and began walking back to the B&B, keeping a sharp lookout for Internet cafes along the way.

That night Chris filled her ears with eardrops and cotton wool and went to sleep even deafer than on previous nights. It was a pity she had not got the eardrops and cotton wool sooner, she might have had a more peaceful night at Capel y Ffin with the snoring woman! If nothing else the cotton wool prevented her from hearing my blundering trip to the bathroom in the middle of the night, when, unwilling to turn the light on and disturb her I crept about in the dark, bumping into furniture and crashing into a door before finally tripping over a rug and slamming into the shower cubicle. After that a noisy flush and gurgling pipes seemed quite quiet.

Chapter Eleven

Breakfast was every bit as good as the evening meal, with fresh fruit and yoghurt to begin, followed by all the usual including free range eggs, award winning sausage, home grown tomatoes and homemade jams. When we were presented with the packed lunches they added significantly to the weight of our rucksacks. At nine o'clock we set off from what many entries in the visitors' book had described as the best B&B on the path, and we had to agree.

It was a morning of hills, starting with the first just above the B&B. We puffed and panted our way to the top, closely paralleling the dyke. This must have been a particularly arduous stretch for the builders! As the contours wriggled around Graig Hill, the dyke and our path cut across them, up and down. A small stand of larches added their voice to the prevalent noise of bleating sheep, as a wind began to pick up, blowing through the branches with an eerie sighing sound. Grey clouds were blowing across the countryside and it looked as if our fortuitous run of fine weather was about to end. A steep descent along a rutted trail brought us crashing down to a minor road. We had just watched a fleecy drama play itself out as a worried ewe called frantically for her lamb. It seemed that she would not find it, but then a faint answering cry came from the far end of the field and a woolly equivalent of 'When I'm calling ewe, ewe, ewe...' and the pair were reunited. Terribly moving!

We crossed the deserted lane and began climbing again, passing a remote cottage with lots of bird tables and feeders, all of which were empty both of food and, not surprisingly, birds. Hedges and trees closed in on both sides, the hawthorn and blackberry joining with larger shrubs and trees to form a green tunnel around us. The path led us up, through a dark wood of coppiced hazel where spent filberts crunched under our feet and the occasional squirrel and blackbird took fright at our noisy approach.

"Something long and grey just went down that hole!" exclaimed Chris, pointing towards a hole half hidden by nettles.

"A drainpipe!" I said. "They are long and grey."

Chris gave me one of her withering looks and we carried on, passing a rabbit that was rather long and looked a bit grey as it sat outside the entrance to a burrow.

Near Hergan we encountered a curious anomaly in the dyke. The part of the dyke we had been following suddenly ended and some yards away to the west the dyke started again. It was nothing like previous gaps we had seen that had been cut through in recent times by farmers, and it was too wide to have been built as a traffic gap when the dyke was constructed. Instead it appeared that the two sections of dyke simply failed to meet up: a probable case of bad planning on the part of two different teams of dyke builders? Or had they been hitting the ale? Ooh, I bet they got in bother! Heads will roll, and indeed they might well have done!

Just beyond the gap we spotted a bird of prey sitting atop a telegraph pole. My stealthy attempts to creep up on the red kite using the dyke as cover, in order to take a photo, failed abysmally. I managed to take one shot that showed a brown blob sitting on top of a brown pole. I certainly would not win any awards for wildlife photography or covert operations.

The lowering clouds released their deluge at mid morning, cutting down visibility and forcing us to pause to hurriedly pull on full waterproof regalia: over-trousers, waterproof socks and cagoules. So sudden was the cloud burst that we were wet through before we could get the waterproofs out of our rucksacks. We walked on, steaming gently inside the rustling clothing, with rain running down our faces and dripping off our noses and covering our glasses in a film of moisture.

A succession of shorter ups and downs followed, lost to memory in a blurred curtain of westerly driving rain. We kept our heads down, watched our feet and trudged on. We passed four other walkers in quick succession: two lone men and then a couple. The couple both wore bright red capes that flapped crazily, threatening to propel both walkers across the hillsides like a pair of demented bats.

The dyke began a steep and muddy descent through more larch woodland, the fallen needles carpeting the wet path making it treacherous underfoot. Our walking poles proved vital in breaking our descent and saving our knees from too much pounding. Near the bottom of the hill, as a rickety caravan came in sight, the larches were replaced by more recently planted spruce and fir, some of which had been fenced off to protect them from the deer whose hoof prints we had seen on the woodland track. We waded through long, wet vegetation to a stile, slippery with rain and lichen, and crossed a road where a pre-war traffic sign still warned of a 1 in 8 gradient.

Just along the road from the stile was a small church. This was St John's and together with a nearby farm and the caravan this was Churchtown. The church also served Mainstone, a small hamlet about one mile away; just as well as the congregation would have been virtually non-existent otherwise. The church looked inviting, well to be honest a bus shelter would have looked inviting to us at that moment, cold and wet as we were, and we entered the well-tended graveyard, passing a huge old yew before taking sanctuary in the porch. Much to our surprise and joy the door was unlocked and we dried out as we admired the stained glass and the roof full of squeaking bats, whose droppings kept the members of the cleaning rota busy.

We sat in the porch for three months, eating all our food and hoping for the weather to clear but it was not to be, hunger finally drove us out sometime in November. Okay, perhaps I exaggerate a little. Notices, prayers and a lost glove were pinned up inside the porch and we spent several minutes reading about forthcoming jumble sales, whist drives and coffee mornings in this remote rural parish. There was a list of previous incumbents, old names from other centuries up to the present day. It was all refreshingly pastoral and a pleasant change from something I had read recently about the Church of England trying to become more politically correct in this increasingly nanny state of ours. For instance the word 'Christmas' had been banned from some services in case it offended non Christians; parents could no longer video their child's nativity play in case they were actually paedophiles and about to sell the video of little Mary and Joseph wearing tea towels and dressing gown cords on their heads over the internet. Modern churches around the country were 'getting with it' introducing their own Mission Statements, Aims and Objectives and Values. Out of curiosity I did an Internet search on 'church mission statement' and was left with my mind well and truly boggled by the number of pages that the search engine threw up for me. The common mission statement appeared to be 'to love and serve God and one another'. Did that really need to be stated? Whilst the mission statements for some of the churches in America were so long they could have been mistaken for a book of the Old Testament! The cynic in me half expected at least one church to have as it's mission statement: 'to bring in as many people as possible with promises of eternal salvation, free bread and wine, and thus raise enough money to fix the roof'. And what about aims and objectives? What about values? Aim to get more people in church with the objective of more bodies making the cold, lofty interior feel a bit warmer. Vales? New roof: £40,000; new heating system: £15,000; new cassock for the new vicar who can't squeeze into his predecessor's cassock: £120.

With a few apricots inside us and a bit of flapjack but no water – funny how you never need to drink and yet always need the loo when you are walking in the rain – we put our dripping rucksacks onto our dripping backs and left the dry sanctuary of the porch. A steep climb took us above the church to the top of Edenhope Hill, over 1300 feet above sea level. Chris took advantage of the height and a rare mobile phone signal to telephone her mum and wish her a happy birthday. I took advantage of the stop to photograph the view, suddenly clear of low clouds, of Corndon Hill, its lumpy profile clearly visible on the northeastern horizon.

With electronic gadgetry safely back inside waterproofs we headed down the grassy slope, now walking parallel to the dyke. But wet, grassy slopes, especially very steep, wet, grassy slopes are not the easiest of things to walk on, especially when carrying a heavy rucksack, and half way down I found the ground rushing up to meet me. I lay in the grass and the sheep poo, contemplating an ant's eye view of the dyke, before getting up and getting going again. An audience of bemused sheep and a giggling Chris watched my extra careful descent.

At the bottom of the hill we reached a narrow valley where sheep sheltered from the persistent rain under a few gnarled old hawthorns. The ground at the base of the trees was bare of vegetation where the sheep must regularly congregate, and on the low hanging branches and wrinkled bark wisps of grey fleece had collected in soggy clumps of wool. A solid bridge crossed an amazingly dry streambed and carried us into the aptly named Nut Wood. Guess what? Hazelnuts!

As we climbed out of the valley, higher and higher into the woodland, we had interesting perspectives down into the branches of the oak trees. The branches of trees are another world of ecosystems, where tiny creatures live in the flora growing on the tree. Lichen, mosses and liverworts covered the fissured bark, home to a vast range of invertebrates which in turn provide food for other invertebrates, mammals and birds. Beneath the tree canopy and higher up the wooded slopes ragwort and foxgloves grew at the feet of the increasing numbers of larch trees.

Out into the field at the top of the slope we took shelter under another gnarled old hawthorn, huddling as close to the trunk as the thorny overhanging branches would permit, sitting on an unpleasant mixture of wet grass, crushed hawthorn berries and bare, sticky soil that soon covered our over-trousers. We ate our packed lunches in this makeshift shelter, peering out from beneath our dripping hoods as the rain continued to fall in the form of fine drizzle. With the sandwiches, crisps and cake consumed I struggled to pierce my carton of orange with the flimsy straw, my fingers, which were cold and wet, making the task far more difficult than normal. Taking a sip I then rested the carton in my lap and started to eat my apple. I had nearly finished the apple and was just contemplating why it is that I always seem to bite into the core every time I eat an apple, when I realised my carton of juice was draining into my lap. Unnoticed, the carton had slipped and the straw was acting as a siphon. Oh well, at least I had my over-trousers on; an orange stain on the front of my shorts would have taken some explaining!

With stomachs full of food and rucksacks full of mud and moss from where we had rested them against the tree, we set off into the wet afternoon. Corndon Hill seemed suddenly closer as we reached the old drove road and began a steady descent to the Montgomery Plains. Once again we were walking on top of the dyke and huge ash trees threw a canopy of shelter across the path.

As we were standing admiring the grey, cloud shrouded view and taking full advantage of the cover provided by the ash trees, a man came into view, trudging up the hill towards us. He stopped to say hello and comment on the weather, dripping water from his face and clothing and squelching in his boots just as we were.

Further down the hill I took another tumble, jarring my knee and denting my pride as I went down in a sliding dive any rugby player would have been proud of.

"Are you okay?" asked Chris, barely stifling her laughter as I staggered to my feet with extra sheep poo attached to my legs.

I was soon rewarded with easier walking as we joined a road. There was much less chance of slipping, although there was a greatly increased chance of being flattened by some of the cars that hurtled along the narrow, banked lane. The high banks were replaced by hedges and fences as we reached a stile into a field. At either side of the road two fields contained separated bullocks and heifers. They had all congregated by the fences and stared, cow-eyed at one another across the dividing tarmac. It reminded me of my all girls secondary school: when pupils from the nearby all boys secondary school trespassed onto the playing fields our headmistress used to usher all 'her girls' inside away from their corrupting influence. We never knew whether to be amused by her excessive concern or frustrated by it. I sure the boys had no doubt about their feelings.

It was not long before we were safely back on the dyke and away from the traffic as we crossed a field to approach Mellington Hall. Once a Victorian Industrialist's grand pile in the country, probably built on the backs of hundreds of near destitute factory workers, it was now a fancy hotel with accompanying campsite. Choosing a secluded patch of trees I decided to have a W.C. stop before we got too near to civilisation. Chris followed my example. But it was not until we were putting our rucksacks back on (it being necessary to remove them for wet weather wees are always so much more difficult!) that Chris noticed a caravan overlooked our chosen spot. And as it was a wet day the happy campers had decided to stay indoors, watching the weather and the walkers streaming past outside!

"They won't have seen us," I said, trying to believe my own spin.

"No?" replied Chris. "So why are they all looking this way?"

The dyke, inside its thick woodland canopy, skirted the campsite where pristine static caravans in complementing shades of green and grey sat in serried ranks on the regulation greens and gravelled hard standings, separated from the path and the dyke and the wet, muddy walkers by a fence that shouted privacy and issued dire warnings to would-be trespassers. Badgers and rabbits had made their homes in the sides of the dyke and for that reason alone it would have been a nice place to camp; how many of the happy campers even realised the dyke was just beyond the fence, how many watched for badgers in the evenings?

We walked on through the empty woodland, wet vegetation pulling at our legs and the muddy path sucking at our boots. The woodland might have been empty of humans but there were plenty of birds and soon we heard the now familiar call of green woodpeckers, catching a glimpse of two as they flew through the trees. The footpath came out onto the drive into the campsite and soon we reached the imposing gatehouse of the old hall. The building arched over the road, once one house it was now divided, with each side being separate homes. One side looked well loved and cared for but the other half was beginning to take on a neglected, rundown air. Passing under the arch of the building we walked out onto the road, crossing a stream that marked our exit from Powys and our entry into Shropshire, again.

"When did we leave Shropshire?"

"Don't know."

"When did we enter Powys?"

"Don't know that either!"

"Confusing, all this border crossing, isn't it?"

Our route passed the equally neglected Blue Bell Inn at Brompton Crossroads; it was no longer doing much trade by all appearances. We waited several minutes for a safe gap in traffic before we could cross the main road, entering fields on the other side where we began to carefully watch for a footpath leaving the main path that would lead us to our B&B. Our accommodation for that evening was in a sixteenth century farmhouse, full of character, oak beams, low ceilings and mullion windows. After a couple of fields and a tangled farmyard we found the signpost for the footpath but then lost the footpath as it ran across a field of deep grass, ending up instead on a farm drive. Much to our embarrassment the farmer drove past us, no doubt wondering where we had come from and what we were doing on his private drive. It was only later that we discovered our B&B had created a specific footpath from Offa's Dyke Path and carefully signed it, had we continued a little further along the National Trail we would have found it. In the last ten minutes of our walk that day the rain stopped and the sun broke through the clouds, now why couldn't it have done that sooner? It looked as if we were in for a lovely summer's evening.

Leaving the drive and we turned right along the road, our B&B was just a little further along, and soon we were standing in wet socks on carpeted floors as our host showed us where to leave our sodden boots and dripping waterproofs to dry out. My boots were particularly soggy, not benefiting from a waterproof membrane as Chris' did. With a very welcome pot of tea and a couple of packets-worth of ginger nuts inside us, the next difficult task for us was figuring out how to work the temperamental shower: a task we both struggled with! I was just resigning myself to the thought that I was in for a cold shower when I realised I had turned the dial the wrong way.

The landlady had offered us a lift to nearby Montgomery for an evening meal but told us we would have to wait for some other walkers to arrive.

"What sort of vehicle do they have that her husband can take seven at a time?" I asked Chris afterwards.

"You idiot!" exclaimed Chris. "I thought I was the one suffering loss of hearing. She said he likes to go at seven because the pub gets busy later on, not take seven!"

"Oh."

The two other walkers, a married couple, arrived twenty minutes before seven o'clock. We could hear them in their neighbouring room, rushing through the shower and sorting out their luggage. They were walking Offa's Dyke Path too, but had organised their walk through a particular company that specialised in arranging walking holidays. Their accommodation, luggage transfer, mileage breakdown and journeys to and from Chepstow and Prestatyn had all been organised for them. But while the luggage transfer seemed like a good idea we could not help question the logic of some of their daily mileages. That particular day had been for them a gruelling slog all the way from Knighton, no wonder they arrived late and exhausted. We learned much about their experiences on the path as we shared the lift to Montgomery. From Leeds, they were a pleasant, chatty couple and it was interesting to compare notes and share experiences.

As soon as we arrived in Montgomery the couple headed off to the pub, but Chris and I decided to take advantage of the dry weather and remaining daylight to have a quick exploration of the town. Montgomery is an old town, another of the settlements of strategic importance along the borders. Its name derives from Roger de Montgomery, Earl of Shrewsbury and crony of William the Conqueror, who was given lands in the area following William's successful invasion. The town was granted a charter in 1227 and until the coming of the railways the weekly cattle market was held in the town, now it is held in more accessible Welshpool a few miles further north. For all its early history the town owes much of its appearance to the Georgian period, and the distinctive architecture dominates the pretty square. The town was witness to conflict not only between the Welsh and the English, its castle, built by our old friend Roger, being besieged during the English civil war. The victorious Parliamentary forces destroyed the castle, and now its crumbling remains can be seen from Offa's Dyke Path. The castle might be in ruins but the town hall and the county jail and the beautiful thirteenth century church of St Nicholas all remain intact.

St Nicholas was one of the most ornate churches we found on the walk. We visited the church, hoping to see the infamous Robber's Grave, where apparently no grass grows as a sign of the innocence of its occupant John Davies who, still protesting his innocence, was taken to the gallows in 1821 for allegedly stealing a watch and five pence. We missed the grave but we could not fail to miss the impressive carved tomb inside the church of Richard Herbert and his wife. Richard fought on the Yorkshire side during the War of the Roses, leading an army of 18,000

Welshmen against the Lancastrian forces; he was captured after defeat at the Battle of Edgecote and beheaded the next day.

The pub was really a hotel, the bar of which was already crowded with people, locals and visitors alike judging from the mixture of accents. We found ourselves seated at an adjoining table to the Leeds walkers, and their company made for an enjoyable evening of comparing notes on the walk and the accommodation and people along the route. Much revived after a couple of glasses of red wine, the woman chatted merrily away.

"You've perked up," commented her husband, as she began telling us all about their son's latest girlfriend. "An hour ago you were dead."

"Oh, I needed that drink!" she exclaimed, continuing in a forthright Yorkshire way, "Why did Bloody Offa have to build his dyke over all those hills? Why didn't he go round 'em? Be a darling, babe, and go and get us a bottle of red to take back."

With our new friends and their bottle of wine we waited outside the pub for the farmer to arrive and take us back to the B&B. On getting there we found our boots had been stuffed with newspaper and piled around the Aga, sheep poo and all.

For me, one of the pleasures of a holiday in the countryside is how dark it is at night. Living in a town surrounded by the glare of sodium lamps it is never truly dark, unless someone has a mishap with the nearby substation that is, so I relish the inky blackness of a night spent away from street lights. When we went to bed that evening, sure enough there was no light pollution to spoil the night, not from outside at least. I turned out the light and lay, staring at the ceiling but out of the corner of my eye I saw a faint light begin to move across the wall to my right. I turned my head but the light had gone. Not another haunted house? No, I was imagining things. Then the light came again, moving slowly towards the head of my bed.

"Did you see that?" I whispered.

"What?" came Chris' sleepy reply.

"A light, moving across this wall."

"It would be a car's headlights as it went past on the road."

"There was no car. I didn't hear a car. Did you hear a car?" I gabbled.

"I can't say that I was paying any attention," sighed Chris. "I was trying to get to sleep."

"So you didn't see the light?"

"I have my eyes shut. I do that when I go to bed. I find it helps me fall asleep. You should try it some time."

I tried it. Briefly. But perversely I was no longer tired. So I opened my eyes again and began to stare around the room, trying to pick out the shapes of furniture. A car drove by on the road, noisy in the silence, casting a strong beam of light that travelled across the walls and ceiling before fading with the accompanying sound of the car.

"You see!" I whispered. "The first light was nothing like that."

"Have you still got your eyes open?" Chris mumbled.

"Yes. Did you not see the light that time?"

"Nooo. I still have my eyes shut. I'm still trying to get to sleep. Why are you lying there with your eyes open?"

"I don't know," I shrugged. "I just am."

"Well, how can you go to sleep?"

"Well, my eyes will close when I go to sleep, won't they? I'm not a snake."

"You're an idiot."

"It might have been another ghost!" I exclaimed, the thought coming to me suddenly.

"Like I said…"

Nothing else happened for a while, no cars passed on the road. No more lights played on the wall. I know, because I kept my eyes open. Then out of the corner of my eye, I noticed on the wall to my left another faint glow. This time I stared at it, squinting to focus, it seemed to be barely moving, remaining hovering in one place.

"Hmm," I squeaked in a high pitched whisper. "Chris!"

"What now?" Chris replied wearily.

"There, quick, to your left! There's another light, a faint glow, it's not moving."

"For goodness sake! Will you shut your eyes and go to sleep!"

"But the light! What is it? Where's it coming from? Do you think this place is haunted? I know you don't believe me about St Briavel's but you never know."

I groped about on the bedside table until my trembling fingers located my spectacles and carefully put them on. The light jumped into sharp focus: a single narrow line of yellow light, not hovering but sitting on the wall about four feet from the floor.

"What are you doing now?" asked Chris impatiently. "How can you expect to go to sleep with your eyes open? I've never known anyone go to bed and keep their eyes open."

"I'm looking at the light. It seems to be coming through the wall!"

I heard Chris moving in her bed, then the sound of her fumbling for her own glasses and putting them on.

"Julia! The bloody light is coming through the wall, you idiot. It must be the light on the stairs shining through a gap in the wattle and daub wall. Now can you please shut your eyes and go to sleep? You were beginning to freak me out!"

"I was beginning to freak myself out," I admitted sheepishly, placing my specs back on the table and settling down under the duvet.

"Have you closed your eyes now?"

"Er, no."

"Well, please do. I feel so sorry for Roger sometimes," she sighed.

Chapter Twelve

It was a shame that our breakfast did not coincide with that of the married couple as it would have been nice to chat further, although had it done so we might never have got away. We met them on the stairs, we going up as they were coming down to a later breakfast. The woman's ankle was troubling her, the medicinal effects of the red wine no longer in evidence.

Dressed for damp boots but not damp weather: waterproof socks but no cagoule, I followed Chris downstairs just in time to hear her discussing my previous literary offerings with the landlady. As the landlady moved off into the kitchen Chris collared me.

"Quick, go and give her an advert," she said, referring to one of several A4 advertisements I had brought with me on the walk to leave with hostels and B&Bs.

"Why, what have you said?" I asked, somewhat startled.

"She asked me which of us was the writer!"

Wow! Fame at last! But how did she know? I put the question to Chris.

"She read about you somewhere on a website, but she can't remember which one."

Clutching an advert, I hurried after the lady and found her in the kitchen. Having given her the advert we began chatting. The farm had started offering accommodation when Offa's Dyke National Trail was first opened, and had been serving thousands of walkers full English breakfasts for over thirty years.

"You must have met some very interesting people," I commented.

"It's been a lifeline sometimes, helping to supplement the farming, especially during the lean times like after the Foot and Mouth outbreak the other year," she replied, warming to her subject. "We've really enjoyed it. There're not many guests I wouldn't welcome back either. Just one group I can think of, some Spaniards who had been shooting the little birds as they were walking. I couldn't tolerate that."

Like many of the B&Bs, this farmhouse had a collection of bird feeders, and the shooting of the birds to her, like us, was an abhorrent, callous act and totally incomprehensible. It seems strange to me that there are always a few people who derive some sick pleasure in destroying life rather than admiring it. The wildlife on the walk was, for both Chris and I, one of the highlights: why walk otherwise?

We set off on one of our longest days: fifteen miles to the next night's accommodation at Welshpool. The rain held off all morning despite a low, grey sky, which this time had nothing to do with my choice of eyewear! The sunglasses remained safely in the rucksack. Someone else's sunglasses proved to be less safe; we found yet another pair of lost sunglasses as we climbed a stile. Not Anastacia or Jarvis Cocker this time, more like Dame Edna Everage. I could only conclude there was a strange mix of absentminded and visually challenged walkers on the path!

For most of the morning we followed close to the line of the dyke along the path that cut an almost straight line southeast to northwest across the Montgomery Plain. The level walking carried us through ever-changing fields of grass, wheat, maize and occasionally stubble. The long grass was wet underfoot, and brushed damply against our calves as we walked. In one field, skirting the edge of towering stands of maize that rustled in the breeze, we came across a field mouse. He sat cringing on the path, looking wet and very scared but making no attempt to flee. We moved him carefully off the path, covering him with a long, green maize leaf; we did not expect him to survive very long but at least he stood less chance of being stepped on. A little further on we came to a few bee hives that we walked carefully around at a safe distance, listening to the low hum of the drones in the hive and the workers flying in and out.

The path and the dyke continued to run a true course across the level plain. It was almost like following the line of a Roman road, something that we would do later in the day after the path turned towards the northeast a few miles beyond Montgomery. Sometimes the path was to the west of the dyke, sometimes it crossed onto its eastern side, but never on that part of the walk did the path run along the top of the dyke. From the path to the west of the dyke we could see across to Montgomery and its nearby castle ruins elevated on a rise behind the town. Through a dense tunnel of hazel and ivy we walked, disturbing wrens and blackbirds who both sounded their distinctive alarm cries before flying away. As we joined first a main road and then began a slow, almost indiscernible ascent through fields we saw we were surrounded by distant hills that bordered the edge of the Montgomery Plain. Some of the hills to the south we had walked down, and over to the east was Corndon Hill and beyond it the Stiper Stones and the Long Mynd.

One of the fields we walked through had been ploughed right up to the edge, making walking difficult as the sticky soil clung to our wet boots. There was no field margin left for us to walk on and no habitat for invertebrates and their predators. As we gladly left the field we came to a water trough, a huge black plastic vat that could easily have housed a family of Japanese at their communal ablutions. There were no Orientals but a very dead rook floated face down in the water.

Crossing another road near Forden we had our first climb of the day, a gentle little hill for once that brought with it more views towards Welshpool and the mountains beyond. According to our map a Mote and Bailey lay hidden in a field somewhere to our right but like many ancient monuments marked on our maps we failed to see it, at least the dyke was easier to spot most of the time!

The dyke, and our footpath, at Kingswood ran behind a line of houses; that must really have cheesed Offa off – those Welsh daring to build some neat little semis right up to his boundary. But I was rather impressed by the thought of someone's garden being bordered by such a fabulous ancient monument, much more exciting than a railway line, or a back street, or a canal, or a main road. Whilst I had been thinking about having a dyke at the bottom of the garden, (made an interesting change from fairies), Chris had been routing about under a nearby hedge like a wild boar in search of truffles. She crawled out covered in cobwebs and bits of hawthorn blossom, clutching a jewel encrusted, honed steel sword. Okay, so a little imagination may have crept in there. It was grey plastic with some coloured beads glued onto the handle!

"Look what I've found!" she declared, scrambling onto a nearby stile, brandishing the sword and snarling and scowling.

She looked very scary but in an escaped lunatic rather than a valiant knight kind of way. Goodness knows what King Offa would have thought. I felt like fleeing from her myself, especially as the chance of other walkers coming across us was very real. With lots of persuasion and skills I am sure any hostage negotiator would have been proud of, I finally persuaded her to surrender her weapon and return it, Excalibur-like, to whence it came. Although I must admit that what really seemed to spur her into action was less the sound of my coaxing voice and more the noisy cries of children heading towards us down the path.

Through Kingswood we began a long gradual ascent, first on a deeply banked lane, the line of the Roman road; the dyke at that point actually forming part of the banking. Frequent gateways provided frequent view points for us to stop and admire, whilst leaning our hot arms on the cool metal rails and resting our aching legs. Across the valley Powys Castle and its near neighbour, Welshpool, had come into view. The red gritstone castle, strategically positioned on the hillside on the western edge of the valley, giving it commanding views towards England, was built as a home for the Welsh Princes of Powys around the beginning of the twelfth century. Today it is owned by the National Trust and leased to the Earl of Powys who continues to live there as his family have done for over seven hundred years. The castle grounds boast beautiful Italianate terraces and gardens, fine collections of paintings and furniture and the Clive Museum displaying Indian artefacts, of one Clive of India's sons having married into the family in the late eighteenth century.

Welshpool was our destination for that day, still some miles away and so we moved on, leaving the lane to enter the cool, shady woodland which had once been part of the Leighton estate. The estate had been quite innovative for its day, with its own gas works used to light the estate buildings, a funicular railway and ponds and tanks for collecting water used to drive turbines. Intermingled with the natural deciduous woodland were many more exotic, non native species of tree planted by the estate, including monkey puzzle trees and ornamental redwoods. Squirrels leaped in the trees and somewhere a mouse squeaked. I froze, searching for the wildlife amongst the trees but the woodland seemed to be holding its breath with me. After a minute or so I gave up looking, the woodland relaxed with me, the wind sighing through the trees, rustling the top branches as if they too had been frozen. Further into the wood coniferous trees took over from deciduous ones, and plant growth in the shadowed cover of the densely planted conifers was virtually non existent due to the thick carpet of needles and the limited light. Under more open parts of the forest ride and where a few deciduous trees remained foxgloves, grasses, creepers, anemones and wood sorrel covered the ground.

We had been looking for a good place to stop for lunch for sometime but the ground was wet and any fallen logs were slimy with moss and lichen. Eventually we stopped near the first of several ponds constructed to store water for the estate. We finished the Chepstow flapjack, then went on to biscuits, apricots and half an apple each, all the time perching uncomfortably on a couple of stones right on the path. It was a less than ideal picnic spot. Ironically a little further on we found a far better site in a sunny glade on the edge of the woodland where a second pond had been made.

Leaving the wood we walked up a lane, soon entering a field that rose steeply to the top of Beacon Ring. In the clearing afternoon skies it was a hot climb. At the top the views from the site of the old hill fort were spectacular. We walked half way around the fort on its prominent embankment, passing a television repeater station and a sewage pumping works that were partially shielded from view by the trees.

"I bet that belongs to Severn Trent," joked Chris as we looked at the sign for the water works. "They pump the sewage up here, treat it and then let it flow down into Wales!"

A small mixed woodland grew inside the hill fort; we could hear children's voices and as we continued along the embankment we came across a family picnicking and playing. It was like something out of the Famous Five, all that was lacking were lashings of ginger beer.

Having gone up we now had to come down: one thousand feet, according to the guidebook, before we would reach the valley floor at Buttington. We began a descent that was to tire us more than the ascent, as the steepness in some parts pulled at our thigh muscles and jarred our knees as we struggled to find comfortable positions to place our feet on the steeply sloping ground. The first part was not too bad, across an empty field of lush pasture but soon the gradient increased, taking us down through sheep and later cattle grazed meadows, we seemed to go down much further than we had gone up that morning. We were grateful that we were not walking in the opposite direction as the hill would make for a strenuous ascent.

We reached Buttington at four o'clock, by now a very sunny, warm afternoon, so warm in fact that our boots had almost dried out completely. Where the old bridge crossed the River Severn just outside Welshpool we stopped for an apple, Chris sitting on a stile whilst I sprawled full length on the parapet. (Mum: when you read this don't worry! I wouldn't have fallen in the river: I was on the part of the bridge above the neighbouring field, so it was just a low drop into the grass.)

Fed up of being stared at by all the passing traffic (is it just us who get all the goggle-eyed admiring glances or does it happen to other walkers too?) we set off into Welshpool, leaving Offa's Dyke behind for the day as we headed for our B&B. Our accommodation was at the other side of the town and we decided to walk along the towpath rather than follow the main road. It was a good choice; instead of thundering traffic for company we had damselflies, dragonflies, ducks, swans, moorhens, water beetles and silvery schools of red-finned rudd.

As we reached the centre of town, most of the shops were already closed and Chris went into maniacal postcard-hunting mode. She tried the Spar, Woolworths, a newsagent, a petrol station, a supermarket, a chemist, a pub, a vet's surgery, an undertaker, well perhaps not all of those, but it was to no avail. Maybe Welshpool doesn't go in for postcards. Eventually we bumped into the Welshpool and Llanfair Light Railway. This narrow gauge line was opened in 1903 only to close just half a century later due to lack of passengers. Less than a decade after its closure it was reopened by a bunch of dedicated enthusiasts, and now both steam and diesel locomotives regularly make the sixteen mile trip from the terminus at Welshpool to Llanfair-Caereinion. Whilst I read the exhibits and watched a small black steam locomotive give its last toot of the day and puff off into its shed, Chris scoured the gift shop for postcards. I felt I knew the history of this preserved railway line backwards by the time she finally emerged from the shop, clutching a bagful of cards.

"You got some then?" I asked, stating the obvious.

"Yes," she replied, and stating the downright obvious continued: "but they've all got trains on."

"Fancy that."

Our B&B was a mile or so further along a lane, out in the countryside beyond the town. Because of the names of the owners and its location we were half expecting it to be run by a couple of dungaree-clad lesbians, with an odd assortment of farmyard animals and exotic fowl, and with a predilection for strange ethnic cardigans that could hide a multitude of stains and small parasites. So we were somewhat surprised to be greeted by a middle-aged chap in corduroys and a check shirt, who admitted us into a hallway full of cases of stuffed birds and animals. Personally I would have preferred to see them running about, although not necessarily in the hallway of a B&B. At first he seemed a bit aloof and standoffish and not at all the cheerful garrulous hosts we had been expecting, but his demeanour was, I think, more to do with a certain shyness than any intentional lack of interest. He showed us to our room with the oft repeated 'that's right then' and left us having made arrangements to order a taxi for us later in the evening. The B&B had already booked a table at a pub in Welshpool for us, as previously arranged, promising the pub did outstanding food. As it turned out the promise proved to be 'that's right then'; although we never did discover why the names of the B&B owners in the Offa's Dyke Association Accommodation Guide were both female: maybe he was their slave!

The room had a choice of four beds; we took two by the window and set about airing our boots and my foul-smelling waterproof socks. The boots went on the window ledge and the socks were suspended outside, killing off most of the moss and lichen within a two-metre radius. We then did all the usual: shower, laundry, unpacking and making a pot of tea, before finally we were ready and waiting for the taxi.

A white Peugeot scrunched up the long gravel drive and Chris leaned out of the window, almost gagging on the fumes coming off my socks, before announcing the taxi had arrived. This one-man operated taxi company was run by a slightly bumbling but friendly old guy. Taxi drivers where I come from all seem to have CDs dangling and flashing from their rear-view mirrors, dents in their vehicles, ropey tyres, even ropier M.O.T.s, fake Burberry caps and track suits. Never before had I met such a well mannered taxi driver as this one – from opening doors for us to his fob watch – he was a real gent. He deposited us at a pub not far from the railway where Chris had sought and bought her postcards.

The pub was busy with locals and we were directed to a table in a corner of the tiny dining room. The menu was extensive, which made my choices all the more difficult, and all the food was sourced locally, with the pub priding itself on using Welsh meats. When we came to leave a few hours later, it was beginning to get dark. Having phoned the taxi we sat at one of the outside benches and waited. A young girl in her early teens walked into view on the other side of the road and began staring in our direction. We were by then quite accustomed to receiving stares and strange glances but that was usually when we were perspiring under heavy rucksacks and looking bedraggled and exhausted, or when Chris was wearing her daft hat; it did not usually happen when we were clean, tidy and rucksack-less. Feeling like a bug under an entomologist's magnifying lens I turned away and began examining my fingers.

"She just waved at us," whispered Chris.

"Oh, great!" I muttered. "She's probably part of some teenage girl gang, sent to suss us out before the rest of them appear in their pink tank tops and white tracksuit bottoms and start happy slapping us and trying to steal our mobiles."

"Do you really think they'd be interested in *our* mobiles?" asked Chris. "They won't be trendy enough for them!"

"Mine can do colour photos!" I objected indignantly.

"Yes, but you've never figured out how to send them, have you?"

"No, I think I need to ask a teenager about that."

"Well, you might get a chance in the next few minutes," Chris reassured me. "In any case, they won't be interested in a phone that doesn't have inbuilt video facilities, WAP, MP3 player…"

"Okay, I get the picture. My phone is out of date. But at least I don't have to keep saying 'pardon' into it, unlike some people!"

"That's nothing to do with my phone!" exclaimed Chris. "My ears are still a bit blocked that's all… PARDON?"

"I didn't say anything," I replied confused.

"I know you didn't, but she did," Chris indicated the girl who was now crossing the road towards us.

"Oh, quick hide your mobile!" I mumbled, shoving my archaic piece of technology further into the pocket of my trousers.

"Have you seen some boys?" asked the girl as she reached the pavement and walked towards where we were sitting. "Our dinner's ready and we can't find my brother."

"No, sorry," replied Chris.

"Okay, thanks," said the girl and turned to wander off up the road.

"Their dinner's ready?" I repeated. "At nine thirty in the evening? What sort of time is that to be feeding your kids? No wonder her brother's lost with parents like that. And did you see her jeans? Far too long, they looked a right mess. What is it with the current fashion to wear jeans that barely cover their hip bones but are so long that four inches are trailing under their shoes and getting all wet and frayed and dirty? I'd refuse to wash them if I was their mother. I tried some hipster jeans on once, you know. My purse has a bigger zip than the jeans did, my knickers were showing inches above the waistband, and if I had worn them with shorter knickers I would have had to shave! Do teenage girls not grow pubic hair any more? It is no longer a secondary sexual characteristic? Has that been superseded by enlarged texting thumbs? What is the world coming to?"

"It's strange," mused Chris. "But I don't remember seeing you on that programme."

"What programme? What are you on about?"

"Grumpy Old Women."

Chapter Thirteen

It was the first B&B with stuffed wildlife and the first with fried bread; funny how even an English breakfast can vary so much from one guest house to another. The chap was dashing about serving the guests with lots of 'that's right then' and hot toast: butter-meltingly hot toast. Always a bonus in my view: the ability to serve hot toast. Not many places manage it though, much to my continual disappointment. When we were ready to settle our bill and leave, the chap was still dashing about and having seen no one else we were beginning to think he was running the place single-handed.

Just to get back to the path at Buttington we had a three and a half mile walk down through Welshpool, a much busier place than it had been the evening before. It was Monday morning and cattle market day; scores of Land Rovers towed livestock boxes through the town to the cattle market beyond the canal. Woolly backsides and furry hides poked through the slats in the sides of the boxes, what fate awaited these sheep and cattle? Having enjoyed a delicious lasagne made with local Welsh Black beef the evening before, I guiltily preferred not to think about it.

We had a bit of shopping to do and walked down the high street looking for the nearest baker's shop. We found a bakery and stocked up on essential supplies of cakes, and then went in search of that next most essential supply, essential for Chris that is, postcards.

W.H. Smith was open but they did not have any. So next we tried the visitor centre. That proved to be much more useful and Chris happily stocked up like a squirrel hording nuts for the winter. Coming over all reckless I even bought a couple of postcards myself.

Welshpool is an old town, the cattle market alone dating from the thirteenth century. The streets, clogged with the modern day excesses of the internal combustion engine, seemed almost too small to cope as cars, lorries and farm vehicles jostled for position and waited in impatient, polluting lines at the bottle neck traffic lights. The modern shop fronts of national chain newsagents, chemists and electrical shops seemed incongruous next to the Georgian facades and the beautiful black and white timbered buildings of earlier medieval times. Perhaps the most noteworthy building in the town is the old Cockpit. The building, which houses a hexagonal pit where cock-fights took place, was built in the early seventeen hundreds and remained in use until cock-fighting was banned in 1849. After that its uses varied until, inevitably, it fell into disrepair. In 1978 it was restored and now visitors can wander inside the high-windowed structure.

We rejoined the towpath to take us to Buttington, a pleasant stroll in the sunshine. At one point Chris spotted the Leeds couple and we waved to one another across the curving stretch of the canal. They sensibly stayed on the canal as it bypassed Buttington, thus cutting off a bit of Offa's Dyke Path, before joining it a little further on. We foolishly had not noticed this more pleasant link and returned to Buttington along a noisy road to rejoin the path where we had left it the previous afternoon. We walked across a cow-trampled field, hard going underfoot, following the path which would eventually lead us back to the canal. Before reaching the canal this stretch of path cut a straight line across the fields, periodically meeting the sweeping curves of the River Severn. I searched in vain for otters, would I never learn?

"Any otters?" I asked Chris.

"Nope."

"Water voles? I'd settle for a water vole, they are quite rare nowadays, the mink are eating them all apparently."

"Nope."

"Brown rat? Frog? Tadpole? Waterboatman? Daphnia? Duck? Dragonfly? Fish? There must be some fish! Drowned crow? Anything?"

I didn't seem a darned thing. Not animal. The banks were deep cut, with the nesting holes of sand martins pocking the earth walls. Willows and aromatic Himalayan balsam grew on top of the banks. Sheep grazed the surrounding fields. But there was no aquatic fauna and not even any birds; it seemed the sand martins had flown the nest.

We rejoined the canal after risking life, limb and lunch crossing the busy A483. This beautiful part of the Shropshire Union Canal has been restored in recent years, and although there were no otters here either there was plenty of duckweed and even a little pike lying silent and watchful in the still, clear water. The walk along the towpath was short-lived, soon the path took us back to cross the road again and follow field paths near the river. We were walking on top of a low ridge that ran in a curving line beside the river. Was this a scenic meandering bit of Offa's Dyke Path? Well yes, it did look similar with its rounded hump covered with grass but in fact it was several centuries younger than the dyke: we were walking atop flood defences.

The walking couple from Leeds were in our sight on the path ahead of us, walking with two other people. Before we could catch them up the foursome divided, the Leeds couple continuing and the other two women stopping. With a total lack of modesty one of the women scrambled down the riverbank, barely disappearing out of sight. There was only one possible explanation for her sudden diversion, and although we sympathised with her need we were a bit surprised by her brazenness. We carried on, overtaking the other woman waiting for her companion. Our cheerful 'hellos' were met with a curt nod of the head and a smile; perhaps she was embarrassed by her friend's actions. It was only later, having met them again and again and again, as we were to do over the next several days, that we learned she was German and her brazen companion was

English; the language barrier explained why one seemed to do all the talking and the other just listened and nodded and smiled.

We did not catch up with the Leeds couple. My protesting stomach forced an early lunch stop. Its bellowing rumbles were threatening to drown out all bird song. We sat on the edge of the flood defence, facing the Breidden Hills and shared out Bakewell slices, an orange and some apricots; not the Tesco apricots – they had run out a few days ago – we were now on to a packet of M&S apricots that Mo had brought us. Less sulphur dioxide and a lot more taste!

We had been careful where to sit – avoiding thistles – but not careful enough. A stream of gradually worsening expletives from Chris halted my orange slicing in mid juicy flow. True to form Chris had found an ants' nest. I seemed to be sitting in an ant-free zone and so, dragging discarded socks and boots she came to sit on the far side of me. All I was plagued by was a hoverfly and a seven spot ladybird; it is very strange, this weird affinity Chris has with ants. A sudden itch on my neck made me think perhaps I had not escaped the ants after all and I scratched furiously, transferring jam from the Bakewell tart onto my neck. Really – can you imagine what a mess I was like as a child?

The bumpy rise of Breidden Hills to the east of the plain dominated that flat section of the walk, overlooking the many meanders of the Severn as the river wound slowly southwest through the fertile plain. Criggion Quarry, extracting basalt, was a nasty eyesore than even as we watched destroyed another piece of this igneous hillside. The quarry, owned by Hanson Aggregates, produces road stone. The company has taken steps to become involved with the local community, not only is it an important employer in the area but it has sponsored local environmental conservation projects. While I cannot belittle any conservation measures, I am cynically bemused by the paradox of such sponsorship from a company whose business it is to destroy one environment for the creation of more roads that subsequently destroy other environments. I do not claim to have any answers but I am sure more road building is not one of them. Maybe it is time the Government stopped talking about integrated transport and actually did something constructive to make it a reality. In the meantime, Chris and I would continue to enjoy that often overlooked method of transport: legs.

Perched precariously to the north of the quarry, on an as yet un-quarried part of the hillside we could see a prominent monument, which the guidebook informed us was Admiral Rodney's Pillar. The monument was erected in 1781 to commemorate the Admiral's victories over the French and Spanish navies and had been financed by local landowners. Much of Britain's Royal Naval vessels, including those that later took part in the Battle of Trafalgar, were built of oak that had been grown in Montgomeryshire.

Lunch over, we set off again under warm but cloudy skies, the path meandering almost as much as the river as we made steady progress north. At a point where Offa's Dyke Path met another path the stile erectors had obviously lost their way, not unlike the dyke builders back near Hergan. Which of the two sets of two nearby stiles was for Offa's Dyke? The stile builders had given up and left both unsigned but it didn't matter. Once over the first stile we realised that the two routes merged.

The fields hereabouts were dotted with large ash trees and we soon spotted a tree creeper climbing up the deeply fissured trunk. Some sheep in the field kept a wary watch on us as we circled the tree, trying to keep the little brown bird in view. One of the sheep looked a little odd in the bum department and with the aid of binoculars we soon discovered the reason why: it had a prolapse.

"Poor thing," said Chris sympathetically.

In the next field we saw a cow with the same problem, but on a much bigger scale. Good grief! Was it catching? The cow seemed to be attracting a lot of flies and was obviously not a happy bunny; in contrast the sheep had seemed oblivious to her pink rear. We both winced in sympathy as the poor black, white and pink Friesian slowly swung her tail in a pitiful attempt to rid herself of the flies. She seemed to have anatomical similarities with a baboon rather than the rest of the herd.

Just before the next village we came to a field where an electric fence bordered the path, and we walked along to the left of the fence, between it and the hedge. However, at mid point in the field, the fence blocked our way, cutting across the path at a right angle. Chris carefully lifted the wire with her walking pole and limbo-ed under before holding the wire up for me. But, as I was half under myself, the wire slipped off the pole and fell on top of me, narrowly missing my nose. I was having a 'Green Mile' moment before I realised the wire was not live.

Having survived electrocution we reached a farm, presumably the farm responsible for illegally blocking the footpath with an electric fence. The guidebook had warned of a muddy farmyard, it rarely gets things wrong when it is referring to something unpleasant, but this was not just mud, what we encountered was slurry. The slurry had been left to run across the path right up to the hedge and into the ditch. We were lucky, after the recent spell of dry weather most of the stinking slurry was dry enough to walk on. However, the path would be virtually impassable in wet weather. It seemed to be a deliberate act on the part of the farmer to deter walkers, particularly when combined with the electric fence. As we picked our way carefully across the slurry we passed a ramshackle collection of barns. Calves mooed plaintively from inside one of the barns whilst in a row of individual plastic crates several other calves were tethered by short chains.

We were thankful to reach the much pleasanter sight of a lorry yard, once the site of the old railway station, as we emerged into the small village of Four

Crosses. Divided by the busy main road and with a few houses, shops, a pub and a small post office, Four Crosses does not seem particularly spectacular. The sort of place you whiz through in a car on your way to somewhere else. But this sleepy little village, rudely awakened by the rumbling traffic on the A483 trunk road, was once an important location for ancient Britons to bury their dead. Due to disturbances caused by ploughing a series of ring-ditches were uncovered and subsequently excavated in the early 1980s. It is thought the ring-ditches date from as recently as the Early Bronze Age, 1800 BC. We did not see the ring-ditches but instead we saw a most welcome sign outside the recently renovated pub: 'Teas'.

With a mutual look of consent we crossed the road and entered the cool interior of the pub. It was like a scene from a Western when the gunslinger walks into town. As the door fell closed behind us, everyone in the pub, which consisted of a group of four locals sitting round a table, turned to look at us and a hush fell over the room. We nodded a greeting and swaggered over to the bar.

"Whisky, and make it a double!" snarled Chris, slamming her six-shooter down onto the bar. With gawps at us, and a frantic scraping of stools, the other drinkers rushed for the door.

Okay, so what she actually said was: "Could we have a pot of tea for two, please?" But we still got the stares and the other drinkers still headed for the door;

we tend to have that affect on people when we are walking.

As the landlady went off to put the kettle on, the landlord appeared and exhibiting fine salesmanship asked if we would like a piece of cake with our tea. It was not one of our most difficult decisions. We carried the tray of tea and cake into the garden at the rear of the pub, away from the noise and dust of the main road, and whom should we find sitting at a table with an identical pot of tea and plate of cake but the couple from Leeds! They were staying at the pub that evening, having walked a ridiculously short day of about seven flat miles. Their mileage breakdown seemed ludicrous when we considered how far they had walked two days previously, how little they had walked that day and how far they were walking the next day. Why not break their journey, as we were doing, at Llanymynech and thus have two consecutive days of more balanced mileages? When we returned home, we investigated the walking company that they had booked their holiday through, curious to see how the holiday was arranged, what the options of accommodation were like and how much the couple would have paid. Our findings made us adamant never to use such a company: the choice of accommodation was no different from organising it ourselves and for us, half the enjoyment is in the planning of our walking holidays, and yet the overall cost was more than double what we were paying; the only advantage we could see was luggage transfer, but most accommodation providers seemed to offer that anyway.

Once, Offa's Dyke Path had followed the road all the way to Llanymynech, and a horrible, dreary two miles it must have been. But with the restoration of the nearby Shropshire Union Canal, the path had been realigned. A short lane soon after the pub linked with the towpath and we followed it for approximately three hot but tranquil miles into Llanymynech. Little used by boats today, the canal, originally two separate ones: the Ellesmere and Montgomery Canals, had once been an important transport route for the limestone quarried in the surrounding area. Llanymynech had its own wharf where limestone was first broken by hand before being loaded onto the waiting barges; three barges a day left Llanymynech when the canal was at its peak.

From a cloudy morning the afternoon had turned hot and sultry. As we walked along the grassy towpath nothing seemed to stir in the balmy heat of late afternoon. With no pleasure craft to disturb the water, aquatic plants thrived. Duckweed threatened to drown out everything else in some parts, whilst in others pondweed and water lilies flourished. At the edges, bulrushes and reeds hemmed the banks, and crowding the towpath sweet smelling balsam, valerian, honeysuckle and meadowsweet grew tall. Wrens called in the hedgerow, and swans, cygnets, moorhens and ducks dabbled in the water.

Two ladies walking ahead of us down the path suddenly lost all control over their bull terrier, which raced towards us. It seemed undecided whether to attack or beg for a pat as it alternated between frantic tail wagging and threatening growling. After much coaxing its owner succeeded in bringing it to heel, at which point she very sensibly put it on a lead. It was the second animal to bare its teeth at us that afternoon, the first being a horse that had initially seemed happy for a pat but then chased us down a field to a stile. I had tried to fend it off whilst walking briskly away and Chris had jogged backwards, keeping a wary watch on the horse and making helpful if inaccurate comments such as 'it's snarling at us'.

We reached a picturesque aqueduct that carried the canal over the River Vyrnwy, its Welsh name being equally difficult to pronounce: Afon Efyrnwy. Next to the aqueduct an equally picturesque viaduct carried a road over the river. At nearby Wern, little more than a few houses near the canal, we came to a second large family of swans, this one with seven cygnets. Nearly fully grown but still in their drab, grey plumage, the cygnets fed by the water's edge, with their parents standing guard at either side of the group; fortunately for us they were on the other side of the canal. Having been chased by a swan on the banks of the River Helford in Cornwall, it is not something I wish to repeat: the swan had had the advantages of flight and no rucksack!

Just before Llanymynech we heard low mooing and as the hedges on the other side of the towpath disappeared we saw a small herd of cows with their young calves standing in the reed fringed margin of the water on the opposite side of the canal. As one of the cows inched across the field, contentedly grazing, the bull tagged along beside her. Every time she stopped he nudged her with his head and licked her shoulder. We stood voyeuristically watching this bovine equivalent of foreplay – well he could hardly give her a box of chocolates or a bunch of flowers…

"Here, want a daisy?"

"No thanks, I'm just enjoying this nice patch of clover."

"What about a Dairy Milk?"

"No, gives me indigestion. I can't ruminate on them."

Every so often he would glance across at us as if to say, "I'm not doing anything while you two pervs are watching." With dogged determinate he pursued her across the field. But he had not taken account of her calf that was tagging along behind and apparently in need of a drink. Somewhat confused and perhaps overcome by thirst the calf shoved his head under the bull's abdomen, searching in vain for a teat but finding something else. At which point we decided we had seen enough.

Llanymynech is another small village on the busy A483, the main route into mid Wales from the north and a road we had used several times before on our trips to Pembrokeshire. At the crossroads a sign pointed to Knockin, a few miles away.

"I wonder if there's a shop there." I pondered.

"Why? There's one just over the road, look," replied Chris.

"Think about it!"

You cannot get more on the border than Llanymynech, for the English Welsh border runs up the main street and cuts right through the Lion Hotel. Before the English and Welsh licensing laws fell into line it was possible to enjoy a drink in the English bar but not in the Welsh lounge. Long before the English and Welsh were quibbling over the border and whose round it was, the Romans were marching through Llanymynech on their way between Chester and Caerleon. And there are rumours of a lost Roman fort unearthed by a farmer whilst ploughing and quickly covered again before archaeologists could invade and disrupt his sowing. Although dating back through the centuries, much of the architecture in this small village is quite modern, a result of the prosperity that came with the mining and the canal and finally the railway.

Our bed that night was at the eighteenth century Cross Keys and only a short walk from the path where it left the canal towpath. Fortunately for our ears, our room was three floors up, away from the potentially noisy bar and juke box. Unfortunately for our legs, our room was three floors up, away from the dining room, where we later had an excellent meal of chicken for Chris and my favourite of liver and onions on a bed of mashed swede and potato. We both indulged in ice cream Sundaes for dessert.

Despite the main road location and that fact that we were staying in a pub, we expected to be in for a quiet night as the pub had been almost embarrassingly empty and traffic on the road quite light. However, even in a small community you still seem to get noisy teenagers staying out and shouting and kicking lager cans about until late at night. It took several bullets from Chris' six-shooter before I finally silenced them completely.

Chapter Fourteen

Light streaming through the thin curtains did not wake us. We were dragged from our slumbers by an explosion of sound that not only jangled our nerves but also seemed to shake the very walls of our room. To our sleep befuddled minds it seemed at first that we had awoken in a war zone: had an incoming mortar exploded outside? Then it came again, and again. These were no incendiaries, although they were the results of blasting: noisy quarry wagons bouncing emptily over the road on their deafening journey to the quarry at Criggion. The first lorry must have exploded past our window at five in the morning, and from that first detonation of sound there was a continual fusillade of these vehicles. Sleep was near impossible, snatching five minutes of returning slumber only to be awoken by another deafening, quaking blast as the next in a line of quarry wagons charged down the road. How did the residents cope? I resorted to earplugs but to absolutely no effect. Ear defenders of the type worn by anti aircraft gunners would have been more appropriate. And even with military strength ear protection I would still have been able to feel the walls, the floor, the bed, the room, the building shaking under the continual onslaught. Surrendering to the inevitable, we got up and put the kettle on, admitting defeat and shaking a hypothetical white flag to our enemy.

Chris was having problems with her G.P.S. as we set off that morning. Having made contact with the required number of satellites she was unable to make the sat nav register correctly. She pushed so many buttons that I think she might have started something apocalyptic!

Having enjoyed two days of relatively level walking, that morning began with a short stagger up a big hill. Ah, yes! Back to the climbs. We crossed the road, leaving England and walking back into Wales. By this time we had given up all attempts to count our border crossings. We had walked through rich farming country in the previous week and a half, now we were entering the mining area of the Shropshire Powys borders. For a short while we followed a lane, up past cottages with beautiful gardens, before entering the Wildlife Trust Nature Reserve of Llanymynech Hill. It was minerals from this hill that brought wealth to Llanymynech a few centuries ago, but long before that it is thought prehistoric man mined the hill for its minerals, and it is known that the Romans extracted silver and copper here, in 1965 a horde of Roman coins was found in the maze of underground workings. There is a local legend that tells of the blind fiddler of Llanymynech Hill, who has been lost for generations in the Ogof, the most extensive of the old mine workings, he wanders alone and fiddling in a desperate search to find his way out. I can't help thinking he should have ditched the fiddle and taken a ball of string with him instead.

Soon we reached the summit of the hill, where limestone bluffs from the disused quarry looked out across the flat lands of yesterday's walk. A hazy mist partially hid the Breidden Hills, and across the

Shropshire Plains we watched a big rain cloud coming our way. The old quarries had been re-colonised by nature with a little conserving help from the local Wildlife Trust, notice boards and some accompanying leaflets provided information about the work of the Trust and the nature reserve. Not everyone was quite as appreciative of this information as we were, judging by the scattering of torn up leaflets along the path and littering the undergrowth. Coppiced hazels, rare whitebeam, crab apple trees, orchids, wood sorrel and butterflies, slowworms and lizards inhabited the area, and there was plenty of evidence of rabbits and omnipresent squirrels. But for once we did not see any squirrels. Leaving the peaceful seclusion of the nature reserve we disturbed a green woodpecker, that yaffled and took flight as we reached the first green of a golf course. Emerging onto the green we carefully skirted the edge of the course.

"Fore!" bellowed a hidden male voice, and we both instinctively ducked.

This golf course, like so many things we encountered on our walk, is split by the border: three holes being in England and fifteen in Wales. The path and the dyke ran round the edge of the course, so much easier for both ourselves and Offa's workmen to avoid annoying the golfers that way. According to the guidebook we need only simply follow the dyke but this was easier read than done. In one place we found ourselves battling through a dense thicket where the path was almost overgrown with nettles and thick brambles; we could have turned and gone back but that would have meant the golfers seeing our retreat, so we fought on, trying to muffle our pained squeaks as the brambles and nettles made OXO grids of our bare legs.

On our right were the barren greens of the golf course, with a few stunted bushes and some sterile, lifeless bunkers, but to our left was dense mixed woodland where little light penetrated to the forest floor. A large bird suddenly launched itself from a branch, silently flying through the trees. We bobbed our heads and craned our necks trying to keep it in sight, hoping to identify it but the interweaving branches hid it from view, it might have been a buzzard but we could not be sure.

Climbing a stile, we entered the wood and soon came to a crossroad of footpaths, taking the left hand path to begin a descent deeper into the trees. On the path to our right we saw the two ladies from the previous day; they were joining Offa's Dyke Path from a different route, making us wonder where they had stayed overnight. We passed and in turn were overtaken by them several times that day.

At the bottom of the hill we crossed a field and then the much overgrown track of a disused railway line. The rails and sleepers were still intact but thick vegetation grew up almost obscuring the metal and wood. Another field and then a short track brought us to the tiny village of Porth-y-waen, surrounded by a triangle of obsolete railway lines. Once again we were walking on metalled roads, towards what was once a busy mining village, Nantmawr. A short way along this road we passed a line of houses. Two dogs barked at us as we went by, we saw them again later in the day being taken for a walk on the old Oswestry racecourse.

A level crossing took us by surprise but it was on another dismantled railway. A notice on the freshly painted gates of the level crossing explained that a preservation society was in the process of restoring the line. From the tiny settlement of Nantmawr we climbed steeply towards Moelydd Uchaf, firstly through fields and then through another nature reserve called Jones' Rough. As we reached the summit we heard a strange bird call and then another. Creeping carefully nearer to the source of the sound we spotted a grey partridge. For a bird little bigger than your average chicken it was capable of making a real racket. Our excitement at this latest wildlife discovery quite overcame us and we failed to take in the views that the guidebook raved about. It was some half a mile later before one of us remembered, asking the other if they had seen the views. A little further along and I heard a gentle knocking, not for once my knees or the percussive thump of the walking pole on the back of my rucksack but a spotted woodpecker. We quickly located him bashing away at a branch of an oak tree. The bird beat and then tugged at the bark, searching out insects. Food seemed like a good idea and we made a stop for apples, also taking the opportunity to apply sunscreen as the clouds had cleared revealing a bright, strong sun that soon turned ideal walking temperatures into uncomfortable walking temperatures.

At Trefonen we caught up with the two ladies and joined them in the mutual experience of getting totally lost. We all thought we knew where we should be going, but there did not seem to be a route. The ladies tried someone's garden, we tried backtracking, Chris tried careful scrutiny of the map, I tried hacking through a hedge. Combining forces we eventually located a signpost that was well hidden behind a bushy and much-in-need-of-a-good-prune shrub. Our newly discovered path ran between houses where competing lawnmowers drowned out any sound of bird song, but the cut grass smelt nice, so reminiscent of summer.

In the next field we stopped, desperate for lunch. Refreshments shown in the guidebook were sadly no longer there, the pub at Trefonen having been converted to a private house. We sat on a gnarled old tree stump, its weathered edges digging into our backsides and thighs, and ate melting chocolate, apricots and Welsh cakes. I seemed to be suffering from the heat and dehydration, feeling nauseous and unsure whether it was due to hunger or illness. The food did little to restore me and I was eager to be away and out of the sun.

"Are you drinking enough?" nagged Chris when I confessed to feeling unwell.

She was right – she's a mother, she's always right! No, was the answer and I rectified the matter with large gulps from my drinking siphon. If I was feeling sorry for myself it was nothing compared to what the woman who passed us only a minute later looked like. Together with her male companion she charged past us; they marched across the field in single file, stomping like a pair of Marines on exercise. Both were somewhat overweight and both were carrying huge packs. The red-faced, red-haired woman looked in danger of keeling over from exhaustion, heat stroke, heart attack or any and all of the above, at any moment. We watched with a kind of bemused, concerned amazement as they reached the stile at the edge of the field and levered themselves over it and into the lane. We half expected to find them later that day, prostrate and surrounded by ambulances, paramedics and St. Bernards toting barrels of brandy, but we never saw them again.

With little water left we set off again and, much to my relief, soon entered cooler shade of a wood. After a climb we came to a stone grotto in Candy Woods and gratefully slumped onto the rough seats, enjoying the shade. The dyke formed a huge ridge behind us, into which the grotto seemed to have been constructed. The sound of rustling leaves and bird song was broken by approaching boots and soon the two women came into view, climbing steadily up the leaf-strewn path. The first woman, the English one, asked us if that was the dyke, pointing to the stony bank at our back. We replied in the affirmative and she turned, looking down the path to her companion.

"Das ist der Dyke!" she called to her friend.

"I must tell Clare that," Chris decided, referring to Clare's bilingual skills. "Dyke must be the same in both languages."

"Or she could have been saying 'look we've bumped into these two lesbians again'," I commented wryly.

From our stony perch in the dyke it was a short climb to the long disused Oswestry racecourse. From the beginning of the eighteenth century the racecourse was a popular venue, drawing in race goers from around the country. By the mid nineteenth century it had closed, now all that remains are a few ruins marking the site of the grandstand, some old cottages and the partial remains of the figure of eight track that ran for one and a half miles over the hilltop plateau. The track was almost entirely obliterated by the grassy vegetation, the whole hilltop being covered in long grass, knapweed and thistles, and home to countless peacock butterflies.

Today the old racecourse is not only a feature on Offa's Dyke Path but is a popular spot with locals for walking and picnicking. Where the national trail joins the racecourse at the southern end it is marked by a carved stone monument of a two-headed horse. It was an ideal photo opportunity and I climbed onto the back of the horse whilst Chris took a picture. Back on terra firma, I took the camera off Chris and, with a bit of a shove from me, she levered herself up onto the carved horse. This was one equine she felt comfortable with. But the comfort was to be short lived. Her little legs were too little and as she tried to get off she found herself stuck with one leg dangling in mid air and the other wedged across the horse's back. The sight of her suspended provided yet another unmissable photo opportunity and also gave me a great laugh. When Chris stopped laughing too I set about pulling her off. Whilst Chris might have a similar stature to Frankie Dettori, she certainly does not share his stile of dismount.

We looked at the toposcope in the ruins of the old grandstand but while the toposcope was informative, the trees in full leaf hid the views that it pointed out. Another feature we failed to see was the public toilets. On the map they were marked near to the car park but on the ground they were non-existent, and with too many picnickers and dog walkers in the vicinity we hurried off to find a secluded bush.

We left the old racecourse, crossing a road and following another road that skirted Baker's Hill where the dyke ran its course although no public right of way existed. Instead we followed this road for a mile, sharing it with dog walkers, cars and a line of horse riders.

"The horses smell better than us," I whispered, breathing in the evocative smell of warm horse, straw and leather.

"That doesn't take much doing," sighed Chris. "The horses don't seem to have trodden in any dog dirt!"

"What? Oh!" I hurried onto the verge and began scrapping my boot across the grass.

At the equestrian centre at Carreg-y-big we left the road and rejoined the dyke, once again a steep embankment dotted with trees. From the rise we could look back to see the line of the dyke bisecting Baker's Hill. We passed a smallholding where dozens of ducks and geese quacked noisily from their pens and floated on their little communal pond.

Henry IV had made camp in Wales but had been driven back by the terrible weather. Furious, he had had the eyes of his prisoners gouged out. The worst we had suffered had been not weather, but flying ants on Hergest Ridge, it was a subject of our conversation as we reached the final hill of the day.

"At least we've not had any more flying ants," remarked Chris. "Julie really did not like them."

"I think the ants were marginally more popular with her than the Great Gob!" I laughed.

But Chris had spoken too soon. Literally seconds later we found ourselves covered in flying ants. We hurried along the path, beating frantically at them as we tried to outrun them. Then we began the last climb of the day skirting the western slopes of coniferous-topped Selattyn Hill and descending steeply to the tree lined road at Craignant.

The guidebook recommended a diversion to see the Offa's Dyke stone plinth mounted in an old wall. We diverted to the suitably unimpressive stone, stared in disappointment at the brief inscription, turned and walked back to where we had left the path.

"Where's the B&B?" I asked.

We were somewhere close but in the narrow, wooded valley, with the road winding out of sight in either direction it was impossible to pick out any houses. Chris got out her map and carefully examined the highlighted pink blob that denoted our B&B for that evening.

"Ah!" she said in an apologetic tone.

"What?" I groaned, fearing I was about to hear we had another two miles to go or, worse, had passed it an hour ago.

"Yes… It's actually back along the road, just past the plinth."

"Fine."

We turned to head back along the road, noticing as we did so that coming down the track to join the road were the Leeds couple. The camaraderie of walkers can be quite amazing, a bit like the depth of friendship exhibited by a couple of drunks! We greeted one another like long lost cousins and then stood chatting for some time, recounting experiences:

"Lot of dog dirt on the road back there!"

"That horse monument was a bit tricky to get off."

"Wish we'd stayed at Llanymynech."

"Long way to walk from Four Crosses with an iffy stomach."

We said our goodbyes and went our separate ways. They still had several miles to go to reach their accommodation near Bronygarth. It was to be the last time we saw them, as their mileage breakdown would mean they finished the walk one day before we did.

We found our B&B, a farmhouse, just on a bend in the narrow country road, and just inside Wales.

"Hello!" called a voice from the elevated garden above us. "You've missed my drive."

The friendly, elderly lady directed us back along the road, a road we were now becoming very familiar with, to the entrance to the farm drive and we soon joined her in the garden of a relatively modern house. The farm overlooked a narrow valley where a tiny stream gurgled through chicken and sheep grazed fields to pass out of sight under the road. Behind the house the ground rose steeply and on the other side of the valley a dark, brooding conifer plantation climbed the hillside. The lady had run the B&B and the farm with the aid of her son since the death of her husband many years previously and obviously benefited as much from the contact with her guests as from the additional income her visitors brought in. With no pubs, restaurants or shops nearby she had told us when we booked that we would need an evening meal. Unaccustomed to such assertiveness we had readily agreed. She was expecting three other guests that evening, a mother and her two daughters, who were also walking Offa's Dyke and, hoping to serve us all in one seating, she suggested we eat at seven o'clock. Whilst waiting for the other guests we had a long chat with the lady over a most welcome pot of tea. We learnt a lot about her family and her farm and about a recent burglary that she had suffered. We expressed surprise that somewhere so quiet should be subjected to crime but although it seemed like we were in the heart of the country, in fact we were only a few miles from Oswestry and all the social problems that now seem inherent in any urban area.

We felt much better after several cups of tea and went off to our room to unpack and do all the usual laundry and postcard writing chores. We were sharing the only bathroom with the owner and the other walkers, which can sometimes make things difficult, especially first thing in the morning when you've got a full bladder and there is a queue for the loo. But the advantage of using the family bathroom is that there are always toiletries provided. Standing under the shower I grabbed an interesting looking bottle of bright pink shower gel. It smelled of strawberries and there seemed to be strawberry seeds in it, it also proved rather glutinous and difficult to rinse off. This was shower gel and not jam, wasn't it?

At six forty-five the telephone rang, it was the other guests. They had just reached the old racecourse and were phoning to say they might be quite late. As there was little point waiting any longer we sat down to eat: homemade soup, cold meat salad and chocolate gateau.

At nine o'clock the dog began a frantic barking, heralding the arrival of the weary family. They staggered up the drive and threw themselves down on the lawn, exhaustedly removing muddy boots and socks. They ate their meal in silence at the dining table as we sat on the nearby sofa drinking a pot of tea. The mother made a little conversation but the two girls, in their early teens, seemed far too tired to do more than eat. Like us, they had walked from Llanymynech but had not set off until eleven o'clock. The next day they were going on to Llangollen, several miles further than us.

The tranquillity of that secluded farm was a sharp contrast to the pub on the main road at Llanymynech where the thundering quarry wagons had awoken us in the early morning. We had one of the most peaceful nights of the entire walk.

Chapter Fifteen

It was an awkward breakfast, sitting around the dining table with the silent family. The mum made some effort at conversation but the girls seemed even more monosyllabic than the previous night, seeming as tired that morning as when they had arrived. We could not but feel some sympathy for them. This walking holiday with their mother would surely put them off walking for life if they had any more tiring days like their last one.

Quite by chance we found ourselves setting off at the same time as the family but did not fall into step, a relief both to the girls and ourselves. I was determined not have to make difficult conversation with two miserable teenagers and marched down the road with Chris trotting behind desperately trying to catch up until I finally realised that the strange gasping noises were Chris' attempted requests for me to slow down.

It was generally a steady uphill climb from Craignant. At one point part of the path ran behind a house and along the edge of its garden, which had been neatly mown and the hedge-side nettles trimmed, a bit of gardening that we much appreciated. Reaching the top of the hill we started down again, I was beginning to develop a degree of sympathy with the Duke of York's men. At the bottom of the hill we reached a wooded glade with a brook sparkling over stones under a wooden bridge. This was Nanteris and the glade, nicknamed 'Dirty Dingle', had once been part of Offa's Dyke Path legend thanks to all the mud. The wooden steps down which we had descended and the bridge, put there courtesy of the Royal Engineers and the Offa's Dyke Development Officer, had overcome the problem of the quagmire. It was a beautiful, peaceful spot; four wrens hopped along one of the low branches growing across the stream and sunlight dappled through the leaves. It was difficult to imagine how such a picturesque corner had ever earned such a horrible nickname. Leaving the dingle we climbed again, Chirk Castle coming into view atop its woody mound.

Chirk Castle is yet another remnant of the border castles, built in the fourteenth century to control those troublesome Welsh. Like Powys Castle, it too is owned by the National Trust and has undergone considerable remodelling through the centuries, both inside and out. The medieval dungeon remains intact, so do the fifteen feet thick high sandstone walls and distinctive drum towers but much of the interior dates from later times, as do the beautiful gardens and landscaped parkland. Situated on top of the hill, with extensive views across the surrounding counties, the castle's size and solidity dominate the landscape today, as this imposing fortress was no doubt meant to do seven hundred years ago.

We finally dropped to the bridge over the River Ceiriog at Bronygarth after one and a half hours of walking. The family were now way behind us and we did not expect to see them again. Bronygarth had been the destination for the Leeds couple the previous day. They had set off three miles before Llanymynech, so adding an estimated five miles onto what had been for us an eleven and three quarter mile day. This only emphasised the illogical breakdown of their walk, and must have made their walk to Bronygarth seem very long indeed.

There were no otters on the river but I did find a dead dragonfly that was quite agreeable to posing for the camera. And, as it was dead, I had a chance to admire this voracious carnivore of the insect world. With its emerald green and black body and head and long lacy wings it was quite beautiful, but still not as good as seeing an otter.

With Chirk Castle now out of sight in the trees above us, we began climbing first a dusty lane and then a dusty track. At a small cottage, where ruffled brown-feathered chickens scratched in the dirt, my attention was caught by a sack of chicken feed in the open boot of a battered old Ford that was parked on the edge of the track. Chris likes to read plaques and notices be they on memorial benches or telegraph poles; I, on the other hand, have a tendency to read ingredients whether the list is printed on the side of a cereal packet or, in this case, a sack of chicken food. This food, for these free-ranging hens proudly proclaimed it contained 'natural yolk colorants'.

Why oh why, do we have to have bright orange egg yolks? Why does the food industry insist on brightening up our grub? If colorants were not put in food would the consumer not just accept it for what it is? Why do we as consumers expect emerald green mushy peas, or deep red strawberry yoghurt, or scarlet chicken tikka masala? Why? Because the food industry has brainwashed us into thinking that is the colour they should be, that food wouldn't be as tasty or nutritious if it didn't scream 'sunglasses' at us and make half the children in Britain hyperactive. Indian foods such as tikka masala are a good example. Authentic tikka masala does not contain colorant, its paler colour comes from the natural ingredients: herbs and spices. But it was thought that non-Asian consumers would not be tempted to try the food if it was not made to look more attractive, so now, not only mass produced Indian ready meals but many genuine Indian takeaway and restaurant meals have food colouring added. I was amazed the other day to discover, as I was opening a can of cat food, that that too contains colorant. As cats don't see colours in the same way we do, and rely on their sense of smell (and the cost of the food) to decide if something is worth eating or not, the addition of colorant to cat food can only be for the benefit of the pet owners. As the Americans would say: go figure!

Leaving the bright-orange-egg-yolk-producing, free-range chickens to scratch about in the dirt for a bit of natural, colorant-free food, we carried on up the path. Between the wooded slopes the track continued to rise steadily. Chris suddenly stopped me, grabbing my arm and pulling me to a halt just as I was about to stand on an injured or possibly fledgling woodpigeon, that sat huddled dopily at the edge of the track. More active was the brace of game birds that darted in the bracken as we entered a field, finally leaving the dusty track behind. Soon we reached the top of the hill, from the summit of which we had a new vista of Chirk Castle, and for the first time we were able to see the flat scenery of the Cheshire Plains, with Wrexham looking industrial and ugly in the near distance. It was impossible to pick out further landmarks as the heat haze made everything indistinct.

As we stood in the middle of the field on the sun-warmed grassy hilltop, my phone began its muffled ringing and gentle vibrations from deep inside my rucksack. By the time Chris had fought her way between packets of apricots and a bag of toiletries to reach the phone it had stopped ringing. Suspecting the unidentified caller might phone back I left the mobile in a pocket of my shorts and we carried on across the field. Sure enough, the mobile burst into life once more.

"Hello!" I gasped, pulling the phone out of my shorts and slapping it to my ear. There was a click and then silence. "Hello? Hellooo? They've hung up!"

"Same unknown number?" asked Chris.

"Yep, must be a wrong number. But they could at least apologise before they hang up. Ignorant sod. They could be putting me to all sorts of trouble to answer it. Interrupting anything." I stuffed the phone back into my pocket from where it immediately began to ring and vibrate again.

"Hello!" I barked impatiently.

"Ah!" squeaked a disembodied voice in my ear. "Er, sorry I think I've got the wrong number. I wanted to speak to Roger."

"Merrifield?" I asked in surprise.

"Yes. It's Peter. Is he there? Can I speak to him please?"

"Er, bit difficult actually – he's in Lancashire and I'm in Wales! Have you got his number?" I relayed Roger's mobile number and we disconnected. But I remained baffled as to why a colleague of Roger's should have my mobile number and not his. Had my pesky husband been using my mobile to phone people when his own had run out of credit? It seemed all too likely.

We joined a lane where, climbing onto the stile, we got a good view for the first time of the old lake that had been built in the gardens of the castle. The builders of the lake had not been sympathetic to the ancient monument, which went right through the site of the lake. That line of the dyke disappearing into the waters was the almost the last we saw of it; we were to cross its line just one last time near the A5. Our ways split that day and we walked the remainder of Offa's Dyke Path without the dyke.

It was road walking from then on until we joined a field path above the busy A5 near Froncysyllte. Soon we would be on the busy towpath of the Llangollen Canal and not wishing to be caught short on the upcoming civilised bit, where no public conveniences were marked on the map, I made the most of the field for a necessary stop. I ducked down next to a water trough by a hedge, imagining I was below the level of the road. But then a big lorry came along and I realised with extreme embarrassment that the driver and his mate, sitting high in the cab, had a bird's eye view of me! No doubt the sight of a full moon rising in the field was soon spread far and wide on the CB network.

Red of face but empty of bladder I joined Chris on a stone stile at the side of the road. We carefully crossed this busy road and turned down a track on the other side of the carriageway, clambering over a stile to enter a field of maize. One more field and we reached the Llangollen Canal.

The Llangollen Canal is a branch of the Shropshire Union Canal. Starting at Llantysilio Bridge it runs for forty-six miles to join the Shropshire Union Mainline at Hurlestone Junction. One of the planned purposes of the canal was to carry water from the River Dee at Llangollen to feed the mainline of the Shropshire Union Canal, and it is probably this that saved the branch from closure during the inter war years of the twentieth century when other branches of the Shropshire Union network succumbed due to lack of trade. Telford designed the crescent shaped Horseshoe Falls near Llangollen to divert water from the river to the canal.

The Llangollen Canal is now a popular venue for boating holidays, running as it does through beautiful countryside and having many interesting engineering features, such as lift bridges, tunnels, locks and the famous Pont Cysyllte Aqueduct. Other aqueducts on the Llangollen Canal are constructed of stone arches, but the one thousand feet long Pont Cysyllte Aqueduct consists of eighteen stone piers carrying the canal across the valley of the River Dee in a narrow cast iron trough. The aqueduct was designed and built between 1795 and 1805, by Thomas Telford. On the boat-side of the aqueduct there is a sheer drop with no railings to the valley floor over one hundred and twenty feet below. The narrow towpath on the other side of the trough is guarded by a chest high rail, much to the relief of anyone walking across, including us. On the northern side of the aqueduct, the canal turns west towards its terminus at Llangollen, originally it was intended that it should continue north to link up with Chester and Wrexham but this link was never built.

Thomas Telford was responsible for not just canals, but the building of the A5 that stretches from Holyhead on Anglesey to London. Born in 1757, the son of a Scottish shepherd, he grew up to become an apprentice stonemason. He soon moved to London and became appointed as master mason on the building of Somerset House, from where his career progressed to the renovation of various buildings and even the excavation of the Roman city of Uriconium at Wroxeter in Shropshire. By this time he was keen to try out the latest new material: cast iron, and his trials would eventually lead to the building of the Pont Cysyllte Aqueduct. He was appointed as assistant to the chief engineer of the Shrewsbury Canal, Josiah Clowes, but when Clowes died part way through the project, Telford took over his position. A major engineering feat of its day, the Shrewsbury Canal secured his name and Telford went on to design and build several other canals including the Llangollen Canal and the massive Caledonian Canal in Scotland.

As we walked along the newly surfaced towpath of the canal, all the tiny chippings seemed to be determined to find their way into our boots. We hobbled along like two footsore walkers, collecting strange glances from the many boaters and walkers passing by, mincing about and flicking our feet to attempt to shift the chippings to the ends of our boots. At one of several shady benches we stopped to empty our boots.

In the middle of August, boating holidays were at their peak with dozens of brightly coloured narrow boats chugging up and down the narrow waterway. The colourful narrow boats were decorated with paintings of canal scenes, flowers, swans and intricately executed logos from the various hire companies, and each boat was bedecked with pots of colourful geraniums blossoming in painted pots and watering cans. We overtook numerous slow moving craft and it seemed to me to be less of a leisurely holiday and more of a tedious and frustrating one as the barges crawled along, many being held up by others steered by complete incompetents.

"That man clashes with his boat," said Chris, pointing to a man wearing a bright pink T-shirt steering an orange boat.

"I don't suppose he thought about coordinating with his hire boat when he packed!"

After a bend in the canal, where boats were queuing, we arrived at the spectacular Pont Cysyllte Aqueduct. Offa's Dyke Path does not go over the aqueduct, following instead the road down to the old road bridge over the River Dee. However, crossing the aqueduct seemed like a must and we had decided to leave the National Trail to do so. Actually I think I had decided and Chris had gone along with my decision, reluctantly. She was, in fact, somewhat nervous about crossing the aqueduct. Okay, that's a slight understatement. Chris had been underwear-spoilingly petrified whenever she contemplated walking across it, which in the months, weeks and days leading up to our walk was something she did with increasing frequency.

"How high is it?" she panicked as we stood contemplating the aqueduct stretching out into space before us and watching other people inching their way across, clinging to the guard rail like Kate Winslet hanging on to the rail of the sinking Titanic.

"Not that high," I attempted to reassure her. "We've been on much higher cliffs on the coast paths, and none of them have had guard rails."

"But there's no rail on the waterside of the aqueduct!"

"Well, providing you don't go for an unplanned swim you'll be okay!"

"Suppose I fall in?"

"Why would you fall in?"

"Vertigo."

"Vertigo?" I repeated, desperately trying to think of something sensible to placate her. "Okay, supposing you fell in... which isn't likely to happen, is it? Not unless you overbalance. Or someone bumps into you."

"Julia..."

"Or somebody pushes you."

"Julia..."

"Or there's an earthquake as we're part way across. Or you trip over your own feet."

"Julia!"

"Or someone else's feet."

"Julia!"

"Or you go over on your ankle – course that would have to be your left ankle, if you went over on your right ankle you'd just slam into the guard rail and bounce back."

"Julia!"

"So if you did fall into the trough, you'd have to hit the bottom and bounce out and to the left and gain sufficient height in your bounce to carry you over the lip of the trough. Bit like trampolining really. It would be quite impressive to watch…"

"JULIA!"

"Hmm?"

"Will you shut up! That has not exactly reassured me, you know."

"I was just trying to take your mind off things with a little humour," I said aloofly.

"I should have known that the same woman who creeps up behind me in a field and does horse impersonations to scare the life out of me, would be absolutely no use at talking me across a one hundred and odd foot high bit of ironmongery."

"I think that's rather unfair," I said with mock hurt. "It was hilarious though."

As a boat drew alongside us to begin its own slow traverse of the aqueduct, Chris fell into step beside it. Once started on her journey she seemed quite happy to get on with it, not at all the quivering wreck I had been expecting who had earlier threatened to cross on all fours; although she did remove her hat, hanging on to it grimly until she was safely across. Other barges were sailing slowly over the aqueduct too, a long line of them, with others waiting patiently at the far end to take their turn crossing. On some of the narrow boats crossing the aqueduct the occupants sat perched on the roof, with nothing to stop them should they tumble off the side; it was a stomach-churning prospect!

Once back on firm land beyond the aqueduct and with Chris' Tilley hat back on her head, we turned our attention to lunch. The nearby car park serving the canal and its marina was heaving and the canal side full of holidaymakers picnicking and enjoying themselves. We looked around for a tearoom but there was none. A pub on the opposite side of the canal beckoned us and we scurried over the humpbacked bridge, battling with traffic, small children and large adults to reach the beer garden. The pub was named after Telford, which made Chris contemplate if Clare, studying for her Masters in Civil Engineering, might one day have a pub named in her honour. Soon we were seated at a shady table on the lawn, gulping juice and munching tuna sandwiches, watching the boats going by and tempers fraying in the hot midday sun.

"Watch out!" shrieked one man as his teenage son set a collision course with a moored barge.

"I've seen it!"

"Give him a chance, Graham, or he'll never get the hang of it," the mum snapped, rallying to her son's defence.

"I know what I'm doing dad!"

"Silly me! Course you do. You're a teenager," snarled the dad bitterly. "I must just ask you before you reach twenty and while you still know everything: what're Saturday's winning lottery numbers going to be?"

"What?" asked the son distractedly, as the barge moved threateningly close to the other narrow boat. "How should I know that?"

His father's reply was lost amongst the sound of a dull thump as the two boats made contact. A dog started barking in the moored boat and on the other the mum started wailing and the dad cursing.

"Now look what you've done!"

"That was your fault! You distracted me!"

"Ah! Happy family holidays!" sighed Chris. "It's so nice to be on a walking holiday where I don't have to worry about anyone else. Mind what you're doing!" she contradicted herself, as I set my glass rocking with an uncoordinated, panic-ridden elbow movement as a wasp buzzed by. "You big dope, you nearly knocked your drink over then!"

Next stop was for postcards and ice cream. We sat on a bench by the canal, eating our fast-melting ice creams and looking at the guidebook. We had reached our destination for the day, a planned short walk to give us time to take in the aqueduct and have a restful afternoon. As it was too early to go to the Bed and Breakfast, just a short walk from Pont Cysyllte, we decided to follow a footpath at the bottom of the hill, which the guidebook showed running along the river's edge to a country park. It should be a pleasant stroll and would, I hoped, give me an opportunity to look for the elusive Lutra lutra. We found the footpath without difficulty, following it until it crossed what smelled like an open sewer, before petering out in a minor landslip. Having little choice, we decided to turn back. So, another river, another otter-less walk.

As it was still only two o'clock we decided to get the bus to Llangollen, some four miles down the road. Not wishing to heave the weighty rucksacks about we decided to see if it would be okay for us to leave them at the B&B and we set off up the road away from the river until we found our accommodation. The owners were in and more than happy to let us dump the rucksacks, even offering to make us a pot of tea but we elected to forego this in order to have plenty of time in Llangollen. Still in our walking gear, but having changed sweaty boots for comfortable sandals, we caught the bus.

Llangollen, when we arrived, was crowded with holidaymakers. Coach parties of pensioners thronged around the postcard stands and the fudge shop getting in Chris' way but she stood her ground defending her selection of postcards with battle-hardened resilience. Loaded down with postcards and bags of fresh fruit from a nearby greengrocer's, we walked along the riverside path, the Victorian Promenade, which had been constructed in honour of Queen Victoria's Diamond Jubilee. Sitting under a shady tree overlooking the wide, shallow river as it rushed over rock shelves and through eddying whirlpools, we ate our nectarines and despaired over the intelligence, or lack of it, in some sections of humanity. Lager-swilling, beer-bellied men, many still in their teens, were jumping from a rocky ledge into the river, executing back flips (and themselves nearly) in the shallow water and kicking a football about. One woman was even jumping in fully clothed. As we walked back towards the town the football floated gently past us, soon followed by a blue sandal. Ducks eyed the flotsam curiously; we just eyed it with a kind of resigned despair.

Today Llangollen is a tourist hot spot in north Wales, attracting, as we were witness to, coach parties, families and young people from the nearby Merseyside conurbation. Sitting in the Dee valley, surrounded by spectacular upland scenery and on one of the major road routes into Snowdonia National Park, it is a busy, small town. For centuries it had been a prosperous market town, and when Telford built the A5 it opened up the area bringing in more trade. The Victorians were quick to discover the wonderful scenery and pure air and soon Llangollen was developing into a popular holiday destination, with the canal, which had originally been built to transport slate, soon providing pleasure cruises. The railway reached Llangollen in 1861 but like many branch lines it did not survive the 1960s, a landslide being a contributory factor in its eventual closure. Thanks to the efforts of willing enthusiasts the station and seven miles of renovated track are now viable once more.

Today the town is internationally renowned for its annual Eisteddfod held in July, attracting musical performers from around the world. The Eisteddfod was nominated for the Nobel Peace Prize in 2004 because of its ethos of promoting peace through music, something it has been doing for almost sixty years. The 2004 Nobel Peace Prize was actually won by Kenyan environmentalist and human rights campaigner Wangari Maathai; there were a record 194 nominations that year so the organisers of the Eisteddfod shouldn't feel too disappointed.

The history of Llangollen dates back over three thousand years with many findings of prehistoric settlements and hill forts in the area. During the Dark Ages, the Welsh King Arthur, subject of so many legends, ruled the region, fighting to defend it against Saxon invaders. Nearby Castell Dinas Bran is reputed to have been the one time hiding place of the Holy Grail. And much research has been undertaken to prove the theory that the now ruined Valle Crucis

Abbey, a little to the north of Llangollen, was the genuine Glastonbury.

We returned to the bridge, the water flowing silently around the stone piers where branches, weed, footballs and a sandal had collected, and walked across towards the old railway station. The bridge is known as one of the 'Seven Wonders of Wales' and consists of four arches of differing sizes and heights. It was built in the fourteenth century by the Bishop of St Asaph, then rebuilt during the Tudor period and finally widened in 1873. The other six Wonders of Wales include a peal of church bells at Gresford, Wrexham steeple, the yew trees at Overton, St Winefride's Wells, Snowdon 'without its people' and Pystyll Rhaedr – Devil's Waterfalls.

On the road opposite the end of the bridge a row of dilapidated shops sat facing the river. The tidiest of these seemed to have windows full of wildlife. Any otters? Thankfully no: it was a taxidermy shop, our third encounter with stuffed dead things.

The afternoon had passed quickly and we retraced our steps to the side road with its collection of bus stops that served as a bus station. We did not have long to wait, a bus soon pulled in and we clambered on brandishing our return tickets.

The driver examined the tickets with a cursory glance and said, "Penal."

Not sure what to make of that I held out the tickets again.

"Penal," he repeated.

I tried again. So did he.

"It's a valid ticket," I explained.

"Penal."

We were encountering the not unusual problem of communication: Lancashire accent meets Welsh accent. And then I realised that what his monosyllabic response actually meant was: 'your ticket is a non transferable one which can only be used on buses operated by Bryn Melin'. But it obviously takes a lot less effort and sociability on his part to mumble something that merely sounds vaguely like the name of the relevant bus company. We squeezed our way back off the bus past the crowd of impatient teenagers all clambering to get on. Standing on the pavement killing twenty minutes until the correct bus came along, we admired the concept of integrated transport and wished it existed in this country. Thirty minutes later the correct bus arrived ten minutes late.

Back at the B&B we showered and changed and had a pot of tea. It was not the best B&B on Offa's Dyke. The house smelt faintly of dog, although our room did not. The tiny en suite shower room had a Saniflow system installed that had me jumping with shock every time I flushed the loo thus activating the macerating system. The showerhead holder was broken and so we had to loop the hose over the shower unit and attempt to balance it in place or turn it off between latherings. The thin towels had seen better days: the one I have at home for drying my bicycle is much softer and thicker. But to make up for all that we had been offered a pot of tea on arrival and there was fresh milk in the room instead of those nasty little cartons of UHT milk.

Having done our laundry we did our usual 'how are we going to get this lot dry with no working radiators, no fan heater, no hairdryer?' routine; we eventually suspended everything on coat hangers hooked over the curtain rail in front of the open window and hoped for the best. Evening sunlight streamed into the bedroom casting sock, knicker, bra and shirt shaped shadows on the floor, picking out dancing dust motes in the air and shining onto a small green cricket on the carpet.

"Ah! There's a little cricket here," I said, picking up the tiny corpse and showing it to Chris who lifted her pen from her postcard long enough to examine the insect.

"Have you stood on it?" she asked.

"No, I don't think so."

"Well, it looks like someone has."

"Yeah, it is a bit two dimensional, isn't it?"

I put it in the litterbin and as I was doing so saw another one. I picked up the second, which was equally as dead as the first and put that too into the bin. Taking my cup of tea I sat down on my bed and saw a third dead, green cricket lying on the rug.

"Gooood grief!"

"What?" muttered Chris never breaking stride in her postcard writing.

"Three!"

"What – number of cups of tea you've drunk?"

"Oh, ah ah! No. Crickets." I put the third with its two friends and poured myself a fourth cup of tea as I was passing the teapot.

"How many crickets constitute a plague?" I pondered.

"More than three I should think."

"Well, we've got a plague on our hands then because I've just seen another one!"

We walked back up to the canal, crossing the aqueduct once again on our way to Telford's pub for an evening meal. I lingered on the aqueduct, hoping to get a good sunset photograph but we were a little too soon and my stomach was in no mood to wait. With my stomach growling noisily I hurried off after Chris, catching her up at the end of the aqueduct.

The pub, when we reached it, was only slightly less busy than it had been in the middle of the day and many people had opted to eat outside, as we did. Music from a nearby barge floated across the water and the sound of hammering rang from inside the same vessel, someone was working late renovating the old craft. Chris and I both opted for steak pie and when it arrived we were not disappointed; the serving of delicious homemade pie was huge and was accompanied by an equally huge serving of chips and peas. Neither of us had room for any of the tempting desserts.

We walked slowly back along the canal in the direction of the B&B. By the weir near a boatyard a duck was calling frantically to two of her offspring that had been swept over the small weir. The ducklings piped back but they were stuck below the short waterfall and unable to return. We watched their frantic efforts, unable to help without a net or a swim! With nowhere to go the ducklings would be safe until morning when the boatyard owner could get them out as we had seen him doing earlier in the day. It was obviously a common occurrence with these inquisitive ducklings.

We left the mallard family and continued along the towpath, crossing the aqueduct once more. Chris was becoming quite blasé about the experience now. The sun had set leaving the sky tinged with pink and the full moon in the east had taken on a rosy hue. Bats swooped over the canal hoovering up the hundred of annoying midges.

We left the canal at the next bend, crossing on the swing bridge to join the road leading to the B&B. A few houses, their lighted windows illuminating the narrow lane, lined the road and outside one a skip was overflowing with various household objects and building refuse. Curious as to what people throw away I peered over the edge of the skip: a cupboard door, an old ironing board, a teddy with one leg missing and a child's bicycle were tumbled haphazardly together on top of a pile of broken floorboards and pots of paint.

"There's a bike here, would be about the right size for you!" I called to Chris.

"What are you doing?" she asked, glancing round in embarrassment. "Come away before someone sees you!"

"You don't want the bike then? Strange things skips," I pondered hurrying to catch her up. "We hired one when we bought our first house and were doing a bit of renovation work…"

"You doing D.I.Y.?" repeated Chris.

"Yes, I know, amazing eh? It was only ripping out a few old cupboards and replacing the carpets. By the time we carried the stuff out to the skip there was no room for any of it! All the neighbours had filled it with their junk whilst we were inside. Cheeky sods! Carpets, doors, window frames, broken prams. You name it – it was in our skip! Talk about welcome to the neighbourhood."

"That wasn't the infamous bathroom carpet incident, was it?" asked Chris, grinning.

"No, that was at the house we're in now."

Roger had decided we needed a new carpet in the bathroom and overcome with a misplaced confidence in his own abilities had set about fitting one himself. I have to admit his idea was good but the method had lacked a little planning. He had decided to use the old carpet as a template. The only trouble was it was upside down. The new carpet was a perfect fit, providing we laid it rubber side up.

"I can laugh about it now," I said, shaking my head at the memory. "But at the time when he said 'try and see the funny side' I could quite happily have killed him, rolled his body up in the carpet and shoved him in a skip!"

Chapter Sixteen

A welcoming pot of tea and fresh milk in the room can earn any B&B extra points, but a mattress that has seen better days easily undoes any such good. I tossed and turned over the springs, sinking towards the floor and floundering in the depths of the saggy bed. By morning every bone in my back ached and I was stiff and bruised.

Breakfast in the musty smelling dining room, surrounded by overstuffed cushions, dusty curios and dried flower arrangements, was brief. The cornflakes and anaemic looking muesli sat on a heavy sideboard, and as no offer to help ourselves was forthcoming we meekly sat and sipped our orange juice for a minute until the cooked part of breakfast arrived, startling us by its early appearance. Well, Chris' cooked breakfast that is: scrambled eggs, which looked very good. My breakfast was still being cooked. A sound not dissimilar to Chinese firecrackers exploding in the kitchen suggested that the fat for my fried egg had got a tad too hot and I sat anticipating the sound of smoke detectors.

With packed lunches collected and our bill settled, we set off down the garden path, passing what I hoped were unsuccessful mole traps positioned around the lawn. The grass showed much recent activity of tunnelling but I could not help feel sorry for the little furry burrowers. Chris and I had seen a mole when walking in Pembrokeshire, attempting to dig himself into the safety of an earth bank. Considering how small this velvety little mammal is it is amazing to see how much soil they can shift. Now, I know moles aren't popular with gardeners and farmers, their surface tunnels can ruin lawns and damage crops and farm machinery and of course they eat earthworms, nearly two thirds of their own body weight a day in fact. But according to the Mammal Society they are not entirely deserving of their villainous reputation; the moles' deeper tunnels help to aerate the soil and apart from earthworms their diet consists of many invertebrate pests such as cockchafers and carrot fly which can have devastating effects on crops. Okay, so a mole tunnel can ruin your flowerbed, but so could your neighbour's child's football and people don't resort to putting down strychnine for them. Hmm, tempting thought though.

We followed the road, the official route of Offa's Dyke Path, down to the old bridge to cross the river, from where our route took a path up through a small wood to cross the canal on a narrow footbridge. Once across I continued to follow Chris as she led us confidently up a precipitous slope, scrambling on loose earth, grasping the slender trunks of saplings for purchase to reach the top of an old railway embankment. Every walking holiday we have ever undertaken would not be complete without Chris leading me along perilous paths; she has taken me through landslides in the southwest and climbed sheer cliffs in Pembrokeshire and now scrambling! Later that day we were due to cross a scree slope, hmm, I could hardly wait!

"Oh! Where's the path?" wondered Chris as we reached the top of the slope.

Down we slithered, back on to the very obvious path that Chris had somehow missed on the way up. Now back on the correct route, we crossed a main road to a lane that led us to Trevor Hall, a place not a person. Passing somewhere to the rear we climbed through woodland. Yet more squirrels breakfasted on yet more hazelnuts, and chaffinches and robins sang from the trees. Sunlight shone down through the branches in dazzling rays. Out of the wood we joined a single-track road and soon came to a bench with spectacular views across the valley to the mountains, Llangollen, the river and the slowly unfolding limestone escarpment of Eglwseg Mountain that we would soon walk across.

A young Australian, looking brown and fit, joined us, commenting on the wonderful views. We had seen him dossing down on a bench by the canal the evening before and were to see him often that day: overtaking each other several times as one of us stopped to take in the scenery. Throwing himself down on a boulder, the Aussie began snacking on his breakfast and we left him munching kangaroo jerky, Anzac biscuits and vegemite sandwiches, or it might have been bread and cheese. For a couple of miles we walked along the road that curved around the slopes of the limestone escarpment; noisy sheep grazed the grass on either side and a couple of burnt out cars reminded us that we were not too far from civilisation and all the uncivilised things associated with it. But if we could learn to ignore the rusting chunks of tangled metal, the shattered remnants of windscreens, the unravelled steel belts from the incinerated tyres, if we could concentrate on the natural environment instead then the views along this quiet road were truly some of the best on the entire walk and far beyond my expectations. The heather covered hillsides, the verdant valleys with their many shades of green, the tree covered slopes, the sheep-mown grass full of delicate flowers, the purple-headed thistles and the tops of the hills carpeted with purple flowers of heather and ling. And like the Australian, we too stopped many times to drink in the view. All along the road stonechats called in the hawthorn and bracken, and countless green woodpeckers yaffled between the trees. Ahead and to the left, Castell Dinas Bran sat isolated on its own prominent hilltop, which rose like a pyramid out of the surrounding valley.

A school group was just leaving one of the small lay-bys, kitted out with hard hats for a morning's supervised rock climbing. It was obviously a popular place for such activities as there were several minibuses parked there, bearing the logos of different schools and youth groups. We could imagine the youth hostel in Llangollen must be rather crowded and noisy for most of the summer with such groups.

Where a narrow road came up from Llangollen, we encountered the family from Craignant. They had just had a long climb up from the town, the two girls looked exhausted already, not a good sign as their day would finish at Clwyd Gate some sixteen miles later.

We stopped for a chat under the bright sun as they lolled silently in the shade. Their mum explained that they had tried to get a taxi up to rejoin the path but the taxi company had refused to take them. Feeling very sorry for the girls but a little amazed by the ambitiousness of their planned route, we left them to their own personal hell-walk.

Soon we left the road, taking the stony track, first through sheep pasture then over scree that ran under the impressive limestone escarpment of Eglwyseg Mountain, the longest limestone escarpment in England and Wales. The scenery was amazing: the deep, winding valleys to our left, ahead: the twisting path across the scree, and to our right the steep, rock-strewn slopes and the grey top of the limestone ridge standing stark against the cloudless blue sky. The scree slope was denuded of nearly all vegetation thanks to its ever shifting nature, occasionally we would find a small alpine plant grimly hanging on to life amidst the rocky desert. A few stunted rowans and hawthorns clung tenuously rooted in the stones, their twisted trunks, grey bark and small leaves testament to the poor, thin soil on the exposed slopes.

We stopped for lunch on a conveniently placed rocky seat, with the occasional baaing of sheep and the croaking cry of ravens as the only sound, apart from the creak of my knees as I straightened and flexed my legs.

"Will you please stop?"

"Stop what?" I asked straightening my right leg and hearing a particularly loud, wet-sounding creak come from the joint.

"Argh! That! That's what!" snapped Chris. "It's revolting. Doesn't it hurt?"

"I wouldn't do it if it hurt, would I?"

"I don't know," she sighed. "You're daft enough."

"It's just a little lubrication moving about you can hear. A drop of synovial fluid."

"No, it's just a lot of cartilage and bare bone grinding together! We should make the most of these walks while we can. In another few years we'll only be able to do wheelchair-friendly paths."

"Why? You're not that old."

"Not me – you. Half wit!"

"Full wit!" I shot straight back at her.

"Point proven!" she said, leaving me to figure out what I'd said.

We munched our sandwiches in silence for a while, I dare not open my mouth for fear of putting my foot in it, a feat which would have meant flexing my legs and making my knee pop. The German woman and her English companion passed us, then two Americans with their heads down, sticks swinging and legs marching. They seemed oblivious to the beauties around them – the scenery that is – Chris and I hardly qualified, we were hot and sweaty, with our hair plastered to our heads and food stains down my shirt, I blamed the greasy breakfast bacon. The Australian passed us, commenting on the scenery once again.

After lunch, we passed him; his rucksack abandoned at the edge of the path, he was scrambling down the boulder-strewn slope towards us, his hands full of large rocks.

"Strewth! This is ace! Totally unbelievable!" he enthused, holding out the rocks towards us. "Take a squizz at these!"

He chattered on about the fossils, showing us several impressive large specimens he had just found. Each of his rocks contained a large fossil. I had been looking for fossils on and off all morning and had found none. He had spent ten minutes up the scree slope and found half a dozen. An in-depth geology discussion between Chris and the Australian then followed, with the words 'amazing, wow, bonzer, cool and unreal' featuring frequently. I really wish Chris would broaden her vocabulary! Then the conversation turned to the walk in general and the scenery, but the Australian was as unimpressed with the burnt out cars as we had been.

"What sorta drongo would do something like that?" he asked rhetorically. "They must have kangaroos loose in the top paddock!"

"Yeah," we agreed, nodding and wondering what on earth he was on about. Even English can be a foreign language between English speaking nations.

He told us quite a lot about himself, it seemed he was walking his way through Europe, sleeping rough, eating little and enjoying every moment of it. His adventures made me quite envious. His skin was brown from hours outdoors: mine was brown from mud, his hair tangled and in need of a good cut: mine was the same but then it always is – fine and flyaway according to my shampoo bottle, and his face could have benefited from close contact with a sharp razor: likewise my legs. He had just walked through Germany and was carrying an old cannon ball he had found. Maybe Chris' idea of carrying several fossils was not as daft as I had first imagined. He clearly loved to linger over his walking, taking in as much of the scenery, history and culture as he could. We left him to his fossils, never expecting to see him again so enraptured was he by that part of the path, and we fully expected to finish the walk days before he did.

Chris' fear of the scree was well under control and we crossed the shifting limestone pebbles without incident. A sheep had been less fortunate, its carcass lay just below the path, the smell and the relatively intact corpse proving it was quite a recent casualty. It was easy to see how the sheep had fallen, as we watched a frantic lamb demonstrate just how unstable the scree was. The almost full-grown lamb raced across the slope towards its ewe, slipping and completely losing its rear end traction as it went: legs, bum and loose stones slithering down the hillside.

A narrow ribbon of road snaked up the valley bottom and we eventually met it at the oddly named World's End, where our footpath and the road converged to cross a stream at the head of the valley. Our route would take us up the road, out of the valley and onto the moors, where the road would eventually lead eastwards to Wrexham. At this point the road was unfenced: a single track with the occasional passing place; grass and heather encroached onto the edges of the road and crickets hopped onto the warm tarmac from the surrounding vegetation. Views down the valley were partially obscured by larch trees growing near the stream but we could look back towards the curving crags of Eglwyseg Mountain rising above the valley. The road climbed steeply at first and we passed two mountain bikers, the first was sprawled at the side of the road studying a map, the second came freewheeling down the hill towards us. The road levelled out somewhat as we left the trees and came out on top of the open moorland, colourful with yellow gorse and purple heather. A couple of cars past us and sheep nibbled the roadside vegetation in this blissfully quiet corner of northeast Wales.

Part way along the road we turned off onto a boardwalk, heading for a conifer plantation on the horizon. The boardwalk consisted of a line of railway sleepers laid side by side, running across the peat moorland, there to prevent excessive erosion of the fragile environment. The warmth retained in the old sleepers had attracted many lizards that lay basking in the sunshine. Very bold, or perhaps very foolish, they scarcely moved as we passed. Several had lost their tails; perhaps they had been too oblivious to the tramping boots of other walkers.

We were walking in full sun and becoming rather hot and thirsty, we really needed a break and a drink but in the middle of the heather moor there were no benches and few convenient places to sit down, neither of us fancied sinking down amidst a patch of heather. At the first available stones near the path, we stopped for a drink; we perched on the small rocks just inches from the ground, with our legs curled up uncomfortably around our ears. Growing amongst the heather were numerous clumps of bilberry and I sat harvesting the delicious little berries and shoving them in my mouth, getting purple stains everywhere – face, hands, clothing.

Soon we entered the large conifer plantation, a sustainable forest providing timber for paper and building and now home to a series of popular mountain bike courses. The hum of bees and the warmth of the sun were left behind as we passed into the trees. We walked along broad rides and narrow forest paths, stepping round muddy puddles and over exposed roots that twisted across the path. In parts the trees were so close together than no light penetrated to the forest floor below their gloomy trunks. In the open clearings and near the edges of the path where more light filtered down through the branches moss, ferns and grass covered the ground. A wonderful variety of fungi sprouted beneath the trees: large black ones, small white ones, brown ones and a few huge orange-domed ones with a strange inverted shape that reminded us of grapefruits cut in half.

The path levelled out and then began dropping down through the woodland, leading us eventually along a muddy path to a gate. Beyond the gate we left the wood behind, crossing through fields where horned rams sat idly watching us, before reaching the main road that carried heavy streams of traffic from Chester and Wrexham into north Wales. Through an overgrown path between houses we reached the smaller road to Llandegla, walking down the village street past houses, a school and a village shop that included the post office – a rarity in many villages these days. Chris headed inside for postcards and I tagged along behind, tempted by a bar of chocolate, which as things turned out I was not to eat for some time.

There were several guesthouses in Llandegla, unusual for such a small village. Faced with a choice of accommodation the deciding factor for us had not been the drying facilities, the price or the pictures on the websites. We had picked it for one reason only, a single sentence in the Offa's Dyke Association accommodation guide: 'cream tea on arrival'.

"Of course you realise we are just going to be disappointed," cautioned Chris. "Things are never as good as we imagine."

"Oh, here we go, the voice of doom," I tutted. "You need to think positively."

"I'm positive we're going to be disappointed."

"That's not the sort of positive thinking I meant, and you know it!"

"There won't be any cream tea on arrival, we'll be lucky to get a dry biscuit and a pot of supermarket own brand tea." Her prediction was right, but not for that particular evening, not for that particular guesthouse.

We found our B&B at the bottom of the village street, once it had been the village rectory, now it was a family home that had grown sideways, taking up what must once have been outbuildings that had been converted into integral accommodation. Filled with the usual trepidation we walked up the garden path, what would this guesthouse be like: good, bad or indifferent? We knocked on the door and waited for sounds from within. The sounds, when they came, were from without, running feet and a cheery 'hello' as the owner appeared at the side of the building and escorted us to a door at the rear of the house.

We must have died somewhere up on the scree slope that day; I don't remember it so at least our deaths must have been mercifully quick. We reached heaven, rather appropriately, at the Old Rectory. The welcome was warm and so were the homemade muffins, ginger cake and scones served with clotted cream and homegrown and homemade raspberry jam. We ate them, sitting at a cloth-covered picnic bench in the garden, washing them down with cup after cup of loose leaf tea from the huge teapot.

Near the picnic bench, the gnarled old apple tree dropped fruit periodically onto the gravel drive with heavy dull thuds. It was a wonder Isaac Newton had any sensible ideas at all after being hit on the head by an apple. Birds gorged themselves on the bird feeders as we did on the cakes. Bread put out for the birds looked fresh and far better than some we had had in our packed lunches and for our breakfasts. A blackcap fed from one of the bird tables and blue tits swooped between the branches and the feeding stations, carrying huge chunks of bread back to their fledglings in the nests.

Running feet heralded the arrival of one of the landlady's children; a small boy appeared, out of breath and with tousled blond hair. He grinned at us and said a polite 'hello' before disappearing through the kitchen door. Soon he reappeared, clutching a biscuit, and ran across the drive and out onto the lane, leaping over two abandoned bicycles that lay slewed on the drive. A little while later, as I was enjoying my second cream and jam-loaded scone, the family from Craignant, as we had come to refer to the mother and her two daughters, walked past on the footpath that ran directly by the side of the B&B. It was five thirty, they still had some way to go to Clwyd Gate, and we contemplated what time they would arrive that evening; one thing was certain, they would be very, very tired. As they passed the B&B in silence the girls were dragging their feet and trudging along with heads down and slumped shoulders.

Feeling like I could never eat again, we went upstairs to shower and change before going out to the pub for an evening meal. The pub, located at the nearby crossroads, just outside the village, was a busy place, full of locals and passing trade. The owners were very friendly and seeing our hopeless search for an empty table in the bar, opened up the dining room where we were soon tucking into some delicious Welsh lamb shanks. Feeling like we could never eat again we returned to the B&B a couple of hours later and to a light supper of fruit and biscuits provided in our room. I grazed my way across the top of a bunch of delicious red grapes, unable to stop myself as I waited for the kettle to boil.

It was a wonderful B&B, clean, homely, welcoming and full of all the things a tired walker needs. The shower room was supplied with good quality toiletries, the towels were fluffy, the beds were comfortable and the good quality tea, coffee, hot chocolate, biscuits and fruit in the room were the finishing touches. Was it a coincidence that the family running the B&B were walkers themselves and were quite new to the business? Other excellent B&Bs we had stayed in, not just on Offa's Dyke but on other long distance paths, were usually run by people in similar circumstances. The B&B at Newcastle was another good example. It often seemed that the ones run purely as a business by the same people for a number of years were not quiet as welcoming, not as innovative in their menus and often not as clean as we would wish for. We could not choose our favourite B&B on Offa's Dyke: Rectory House or Quarry House, in the end we decided it was a draw.

The bedroom was stocked not just with refreshments but also with a selection of magazines and two daily newspapers. I usually prefer to avoid newspapers, influenced no doubt by my Dad who always used to say the only thing you could believe in a newspaper was the date, but I sat down with a cup of tea and flicked through the more reputable of the two papers available. On one of the inside pages, competing with so-called celebratory antics at a film premier and George W. Bush's latest verbal faux pas was a colour photograph of Tony Blair in a pair of lurid green swimming trunks. 'Guess where he is and win a holiday there!' exclaimed the accompanying headline.

"Where do you think he is then?" I asked Chris, flapping the newspaper at her.

"Is he walking Offa's Dyke?" she asked.

"Have you seen anyone in green shorts? Because I haven't and I'm sure I would have remembered. Anyway, it would have ruined my holiday. Can you imagine – getting away from it all on a walking holiday and bumping into that twit and his silly wife? More frightening than having a ghost sitting on your bed."

"Well, at least he's real."

"The ghost was real! And a lot more use than that pair," I added.

"Here, stop thinking about silly spooks and have a look at the breakfast menu," said Chris.

Not sure if she was referring to the ghost or the Blairs I took the A4 list from her. As I read through the extensive breakfast menu which included all the usual cereal, fruit, yoghurt and several delicious variations on the theme, plus the usual cooked breakfast but with alternatives like omelette, boiled eggs, haddock, smoked salmon, muffins, chocolate croissants, brioche, pancakes and French toast with various fillings as just some of the interesting alternatives, I began to think it had been a mistake staying here for only one night. But that is the nature of a long distance walk: you've got to keep on going. How would our remaining two nights' accommodation compare? The guesthouses would have to be outstanding far beyond our expectations to come close to bettering the Old Rectory.

"Too much wonderful choice," I sighed, handing the menu back to Chris.

"Sod Prestatyn!" exclaimed Chris, glancing once more at the breakfast menu before throwing it down and reaching for another biscuit. "I'm staying here."

Chapter Seventeen

The breakfast menu was about as extensive as Sainsbury's stock list but with the added bonus of most things being homemade or homegrown. Having read the menu through several times the evening before, we were still unsure what to have for breakfast. Eventually we made our decision and the landlady went off to begin her preparations. She appeared a few minutes later with two glass dishes filled with our choices; Chris went for half a Gallia melon with strawberries and raspberries, I went for the fresh fruit, yoghurt and chopped nuts drizzled with honey which was delicious – and I don't even like honey! The French toast filled with strawberries, blueberries, bananas and cream, and the croissants that we managed to find room for afterwards, were equally delicious. We had no room left for toast and the range of tempting homemade preserves that adorned the dining table.

We had decided when we booked the B&B to order a packed lunch, as we would be passing through no towns or villages that day. Making that decision months in advance is a mere logistic but it is always pot luck what the packed lunch will turn out like. The lunch we had got from the B&B the day before had been okay, your typical white sliced, plastic effect loaf with your average unexciting filling of lettuce and cheese, an apple and a milk chocolate wafer bar. The packed lunch at the Old Rectory was, like all the other food there, outstanding, and was to be one of the experiences of the walk that we reminisced about again and again, as indeed was our entire stay in the Old Rectory. The evening before the landlady had asked us what we would like on our sandwiches.

"What are the options?" Chris had asked, expecting the usual choice of tuna, cheese or ham.

"Well, I've got some very nice Cornish brie, which I could give you with a bit of rocket, cranberry and grapes, or…"

"Yes, please!" interrupted Chris enthusiastically.

"Me too please!" I had added with equal keenness.

When the lady had gone, Chris had turned to me and said, "But you don't like Brie!"

"I know but it sounded so good." And indeed it proved to be.

We finished breakfast and went upstairs to pack. Did we really have to leave? Down in the kitchen I wrote out a cheque, which seemed barely enough to cover all the food we had eaten, whilst the lady bagged up our packed lunches.

"Here's one," she said, placing a brown paper bag on the counter next to me.

"One?" I squeaked. The one packed lunch looked large enough for a week.

"Yes, that's the sandwich. I've put the salad separately so it doesn't make everything go soggy. And then you've got a muffin, one of my raspberry scones and a homemade flapjack. Each."

"Wow! Thanks."

"And here's the other packed lunch," she said, heaving a second brown paper bag onto the counter. "There's also a packet of crisps and a drink."

Apart from the youth hostel packed lunches, these were the first to come with a drink, rather a key feature of a packed lunch I would have thought. Although we always carried water it was nice to have a carton of juice for a change.

Like all good B&Bs before it, we did not want to leave the Old Rectory. The rain of the evening before had gone but the long grass was wet underfoot and soon our boots were soaking as we walked down the field to cross the stream.

"Any otters?"

"Yeah, hundreds. Didn't you see them?"

The relatively flat field paths followed close to the stream, passing near to several strips of woodland. Soon we were approaching the Clwydian range of mountains stretching north towards the coast. Where we left a narrow road to skirt a conifer woodland by a track, I decided to make a toilet stop. However, the ground beneath the thick grass was uneven, the nettles were stinging and the shrubs were prickly. I floundered about trying to keep my balance and was totally distracted when a horsefly the size of Liechtenstein landed on my left knee. Not wanting to have a matching scab for the one left by the horsefly in Redbrook two weeks previously, I swatted at it and asked it to leave me in peace. That was a mistake as, distracted from my original task, I peed in me boot, as I had done two weeks previously near Monmouth! I staggered out of the shrubbery with vegetation in my knickers, thorns in my hair and urine soaking warmly into my boot and sock. I warned Chris not to go in, but she was determined and I have to say she did emerge looking better than I did – not difficult actually.

Then came miles of walking along the Clwydian range. Like the Black Mountains, I had not been looking forward to this bit of the path, imagining once again a bleak moorland landscape of windswept Pennine proportions. Instead, as with the Black Mountains, I was pleasantly surprised by the unexpected beauty of the landscape, with the purple heather and bilberries, yellow gorse, tiny basking lizards, extensive views in all directions, blue skies, scudding grey clouds and the criss-crossed pattern of jet streams of planes heading into and out of Liverpool and Manchester airports.

There are moels all along the Clwydian range, moels that is, not moles. The guy from the B&B at Pont Cysyllte would have been kept busy for years trying to get rid of these. The first moel we reached was Moel y Gelli, quickly followed by Moel y Plas, Moel Llech, Moel Llanfair, Moel Gyw, Moel Eithinen, Moel y Gaer, Moel Fammau, Moel Dywyll, Moel Llys-y-coed and Moel Arthur. We did not need a good grasp of the intricacies of the Welsh language to be able to translate moel. It was obvious from the map in our hands and the landscape surrounding us that a moel was a hill. (There's a joke in there somewhere about moel hills but I'm not going to lower myself). Sometimes the footpath went round the moels but at other times it took a steep route up towards the summits. The scenery was spectacular as we climbed one moel after another and totally unlike my expectations.

We joined an EEC funded agricultural road that the guidebook described as 'bringing the factory to the countryside' but it seemed no worse to us than some of the other tracks we had covered and there were no clocking in machines, no fire regulations or first aid posts that we could see, nor smoking chimneys, north light roofs or security huts.

We stopped for an early lunch overlooking the Vale of Clwyd and the town of Ruthin sprawled in the bottom of the valley. It was quite chilly on top of the hills and we put on cagoules before starting to eat our packed lunches. With the Gore-Tex blocking out the wind and the vast quantities of delicious food to eat, we lingered long over our lunch that day, sprawled on our backs in the grass, watching a distant herd of cows slowly grazing their way across the hillside.

"Do cows get tired walking up hills?" asked Chris, and one of our profound, philosophical discussions ensued.

"Well, they must be used to it, so probably not," I said thoughtfully.

"But we're used to it and I still get tired."

"In case you haven't noticed, we are carrying twenty pound rucksacks, those cows are not."

"But they have big udders."

"I'm not sure I like the direction this conversation is taking," I sighed, tilting my cap down to shield my eyes from the sun that was peeping out from behind a cloud. "Those cows have always got big udders but we don't always have rucksacks."

"They don't have big udders when they've been milked," observed Chris reasonably.

"Okay, so you think changing udder size and having four legs rather than two can make a difference to fatigue levels in the modern dairy cow?"

"Er, basically, yes."

"So if we walked on all fours we'd get more tired?"

"Do you not think so?"

"I think if we walked on all fours a few things would occur: we'd get back ache and we'd get indigestion, especially after a packed lunch like this one. Oh! And our rucksacks would slide down and whack us on the back of the head; most uncomfortable."

"Yes, but don't you think if we had twice as many legs we would get twice as tired?" persisted Chris.

"If you take this argument to its logical conclusion, it must be totally knackering to be a centipede!"

"If you're going to be silly, I shan't bother speaking to you."

"Good, in that case I might have a little snooze."

I had been joking about the little snooze and so it came as a shock to find myself being shaken awake by Chris an hour later.

"Are you going to stay here pushing out the zeds all day?" moaned a bored Chris. "You've been fast asleep for ages!"

"Got fed up of watching the cows have you?" I asked, struggling to sit up.

"Got fed up of listening to you snoring, more like!"

We dropped down to cross the main road at Clwyd Gate, meeting three young people walking in the same direction as ourselves. As we waited for traffic to clear the two guys left the girl, hurrying away up the road before she had a chance to cross and follow them. When she did eventually cross she then seemed to get lost in the car park of the Clwyd Gate Motel. At first we felt sorry for her but having had a particularly confusing conversation with her we began to sympathise with her two errant companions. Consulting her map and guidebook she wandered off in the wrong direction, ignoring our advice that the footpath continued a little further along the road; she seemed to be getting more lost with the map and guidebook than her friends were without them! By Bwlch Penbarra, a few miles further along the route, they had left her far behind and the poor befuddled soul was searching for non-existent toilets in the small car park.

After leaving the noise of the main road and following a dusty track I decided another toilet stop was called for. This time I can blame neither the vegetation nor the insect life for the resultant second soaking of my foot.

We left the track to climb an increasingly steep path that skirted a small conifer plantation, rising up to a col before climbing heather covered slopes to reach the site of one of dozens of hill forts along the Clwydian Mountains, this one at Foel Fenlli. Most of these Iron Age hill forts are very well preserved with their defensive ditches and banks still intact, amazing when you consider they would have been abandoned around the time of the Roman invasion in A.D. 43, even more amazing when you consider they were constructed without the aid of machinery, personal protective equipment and compensation specialists – who would you claim from if you dropped ye olde boulder on your foot?

Clouds mainly hid the sun, although it was still fine, when we began our descent to Bwlch Penbarra, where a narrow mountain road crossed the Clwydian range. The sound of the rumbling cattle grid echoed up the hillside with every car that passed and cars in the car park below seemed out of place surrounded by the wild moorland and conifer plantations.

Bwlch Penbarra was our pre-arranged pickup point for a lift to the guesthouse for that evening, and was to be our drop off point the next day. This arrangement had proved necessary as Offa's Dyke Path was far away from any civilisation along this part of its route. We had phoned that morning to confirm that our landlady had not forgotten about our lift and we had arranged to get in touch when we reached the car park. Having sat down, taken off our rucksacks and got out my mobile phone, I keyed in the number of the B&B. After a few rings an answer phone kicked in and I left a message. After fifteen minutes and no return call I tried again. And again the answer phone kicked in. Fifteen minutes later, and with growing concern, I tried again. It was approaching five o'clock; surely someone would be at home by now? The answer phone was suddenly interrupted by a real, genuine human telling me someone was on the way. Panic over. But we had had cause to panic: we had a similar experience when walking the Pembrokeshire Coast Path. On that occasion our pre-arranged lift never turned up, our phone calls went unanswered and there had been no answer phone on which to leave any message of the 'where the chuffing hell are you?' variety. Eventually we had found alternative accommodation nearby but it had been a less than relaxing end to the day.

Every car that rumbled over the cattle grid made us look up, hopeful that it would be our lift. Finally our lift arrived – an estate car full of stuff: boxes, crates, cartons and stacks of paper, that the man proceeded to cram into the tardis-like boot before we and our rucksacks were crammed into the back seat.

As we set off down the road and over the cattle grid the man asked how our walk was going and then said, "There's a bit of a problem."

"Oh yes?" said Chris in her 'what's that supposed to mean' tone of voice.

"Our son has unexpectedly returned home from hospital and we have had to put him in your room," the man explained. "He has had an operation on his foot, so he can't look after himself at the moment."

"Okay…" I replied slowly, in my 'uh I might have known!' tone of voice.

"So we have arranged with a friend of ours, who has a guesthouse in Denbigh to take you for tonight. It's the same price, she's very nice and will look after you, and in the morning my wife will pick you up and bring you back to Bwlch Penbarra."

As they had made alternative arrangements we could hardly complain and so settled back for the half hour drive into Denbigh. The man was very chatty and as we drove along the lanes of north Wales, paralleling the Clwydian hills he pointed out the different summits of the range. One part looked like a naked woman laying on her back, a very cold naked woman.

"That summit you can see is Moel Fammau and the one next to it is… oh, I can never remember the name. You'll be walking over those tomorrow," he said. "Moel Fammau has got a ruined tower on top of it and most of the others have cairns." So that explained the shape!

The guesthouse was on one of the main roads leading up into the centre of Denbigh. We hurried through our all too familiar rituals of tea, shower and laundry – how many times had we done that now since Chepstow? And then went out to explore the town and find something to eat.

Denbigh perches on a hilltop, the narrow twisting streets of old houses and shops tumbling down the slopes from the summit where castle ruins sit looking out over the surrounding valleys to the slopes of the Snowdon range in the west and the Clwydian range in the east and to the distant coast of the Irish Sea to the north. Denbigh was granted to Henry de Lacy by Edward I in 1282 following the defeat of those troublesome Welsh and it was de Lacy, the first Lord of Denbigh, who began to build the castle on its prominent hilltop position. Town walls were also built to protect Denbigh, with the castle located inside them; many of these walls still remain. Like most castles we had encountered on our walk, Denbigh Castle has witnessed a turbulent history: fought over by English and Welsh and later by Roundheads and Royalists. Today the castle ruins are owned and managed by Cadw, the Welsh equivalent of English Heritage and an admission fee is charged for entry to the castle ruins. Fortunately for us it was too late in the day for the ungated entrance to be staffed and we walked in for free to explore the ruins. We were not the only ones doing so; two elderly gentlemen wandered across the neatly mown green inside the circular ruins, and in the gatehouse, an unusual triangular building formed by the three polygonal towers, a small gang of local teenagers were loitering and chatting. The clouds had dispersed and the evening sun shone through the gaps and windows in the ruined walls, and cast long shadows across the lawns. In the distance, the sun warmed the heather covered hillsides and summits of the Clwydian Mountains, but the woman still looked cold.

It was in Denbigh that we saw the first seagull since Chepstow. It shrieked overhead, wings flapping and we ducked instinctively: I had been victim of a bombing raid by a nasty gull in Devon and did not wish to repeat that messy, smelly experience; Chris had been mugged for her fish and chips in Cornwall and was as equally unwilling as I to relive unpleasant events from one of our past walking holidays.

"Is that gull indicative of just how near we are now to the Irish Sea and the end of the walk?" asked Chris, craning her neck to see where the gull had gone.

"Could be," I replied, ducking as the gull flew overhead. "Keep your sphincter firmly clenched please!"

"Who? Me?"

"No, not unless you're about to take flight!" I tutted. "The gull could just be an inland scavenger and never have seen the sea in its life."

Having eaten a huge supper the day before, a huge breakfast and a huge packed lunch that day we were both ridiculously hungry and it was not long before we were thinking less of gulls and empty castle ruins and more of full stomachs. Friday evenings are not good times for finding somewhere to eat in a strange town, the bars were filling up with revellers and so we decided to try to find a takeaway. We settled on pizza choosing to eat it on a bench in the town centre as we had done at Chepstow, the only difference seemed to be that the evening felt colder – well we were considerably further north!

At a nearby off license Chris had purchased a can of lager to go with her pizza and we sat on the bench eating pizza and people watching.

"It's just occurred to me," said Chris. "But does Denbigh have an alcohol-free town centre?"

"Dunno," I mumbled, battling with a string of melted cheese that was threatening to drag half the topping off my pizza slice. "Why?"

"Because I am sitting here drinking lager! And oh, my goodness!" she exclaimed looking at the can. "It's extra strength."

"Good job I'm not drinking it then. You'd have to carry me back to the B&B."

But despite the lager it was me with my can of Lilt that spilt pizza first on my shirt and then down both of my trouser legs. Trying to carefully remove a slice of mushroom from my thigh only resulted in my smearing tomato sauce into the pale beige material.

"How did you manage that?" sighed Chris in despair.

"Missed my mouth."

"That's hard to believe."

"And then the mushroom bounced off the pizza box and ricocheted onto my trousers."

"And where did the tomato sauce come from?"

"Well, I think that must have been on my finger…"

"Poor Roger," said Chris, not for the first time.

We finished our meal and our drinks, carefully consigned the litter to a bin and made our way back down the hill towards the guesthouse. We returned to our attic room, up two flights of stairs; always on any of our walking holidays, if there are more than two floors in a guesthouse we will be in a room at the top of the house. It is almost as if people think walkers are going to be fit enough to make it up three flights of stairs if they have been walking all day. Whereas in reality, what we would really appreciate if not a ground floor room and a bath hoist, is a stair lift with inbuilt tea making facility.

It had become quite dark and on entering the room I switched on the light. But that also operated an integral fan, which kicked into noisy life and began blowing our maps across the room.

"You will have to switch the fan off with that chain," Chris pointed out, gesturing to a chain dangling from the combined light and fan. "I'm not tall enough to reach it."

I yanked the chain, which snapped off in my hand and fell under the bed. The fan continued to whir. I knelt down and began groping about under the bed until my probing fingers finally touched the chain. With some difficulty I balanced on the bed, wobbling about as I tried to fit the chain, eventually I managed to reattach it and carefully turned off the fan. Memories of a nightmare incident at a Scottish guesthouse involving a set of vertical blinds and its links of chains sent me into panic mode. On that occasion three of the vertical slats had broken off from their mountings and I was left wondering what to do as the blind seemed to go into self destruct mode; the irony was that for once, I had not even touched anything!

With the chain fixed, a cup of tea seemed like a good way to end the day. I collected the kettle from the tea trolley and headed for the bathroom but my toes got entangled in a loop of electric flex poking out from under the trolley. Off balance I staggered across the room dragging the trolley with me, to the accompanying rattle of cups, saucers and teapot. Chris sighed, tutted, shook her head and pointed out that it was her and not I who had consumed the extra strength lager. In the bathroom my run of mishaps continued as I yanked off the kettle lid, fumbled it and then dropped it into the toilet; yet another reason not to leave the lid up. The drink of tea, when I eventually made it, tasted a little odd – was it the bags, the water or the kettle lid?

Chapter Eighteen

From our bedroom window we could see the Clwydian Mountains, or rather the lower slopes of them; the tops were hidden by clouds. Were we in for a wet moorland walk that day? As we enjoyed a nice breakfast which included yoghurt from a local small producer, the sun shone on Denbigh in quite a promising manner.

We read the newspaper as we waited for our lift back to Bwlch Penbarra. The headlines were of the death of Mo Mowlam following a fall. A formidable figure in British politics she is likely to be remembered for the courageous way she overcame a brain tumour and for her key role in establishing the Good Friday Agreement in Northern Ireland. The two page special on this remarkable woman enforced the stupid piece on Tony Blair's holiday in the paper of the other day as the trivial bit of gutter journalism it was.

Our lift arrived at 9 a.m. before we could finish the article, and we were whisked back to the car park at Bwlch Penbarra. A couple just coming down from the mist-covered heights of Moel Fammau warned us that it was wet up there as they dripped past in damp waterproofs. Chris took a chance, opting not to put on her cagoule but wait and see just how wet it was, hoping I think that the clouds would lift. I, however, was already feeling quite cold after the warmth of the car and decided to put on my cagoule as much for warmth as dryness.

We set off up the steep hill, climbing steadily over the rough surface of millstone grit between heather clad slopes. The wind blew and my cagoule flapped, the hood slapping painfully into my face. At the old remains of the never-completed jubilee tower the wind chased the clouds away and we were able to look across the Vale of Clwyd towards the cloud covered peaks of the Snowdonia range. All we could hear was the sound of the wind. We lingered at the base of the tower, enjoying the peace and solitude and taking in the surrounding scenery. With Snowdonia at our backs we looked east, across the immediate slopes of conifer plantations, down to the Cheshire Plains and the Mersey Basin. A quarry scarred the near distance and further away we could see the Runcorn Widnes Bridge, the Stanlow Oil Refineries, the chemical works with their belching chimneys at Ellesmere Port and the deceptively small dot that was in reality the sprawling conurbation of Liverpool. To the east ugly man-made structures; to the west the beauty of rural north Wales.

Several people were out walking that part of Offa's Dyke Path that Saturday morning, but most of these walkers only went as far as Jubilee Tower before returning to their cars in the car park below. We were just two of the few who continued across the ridge beyond the tower. This was obviously a popular dog walking route and we had already met a few people exercising their pets. One man was trying to control his large, boisterous and totally disobedient dog but without benefit of a lead he was becoming increasingly unsuccessful; the more the dog ignored him the louder he shouted, to less and less effect. The dog was eyeing up the sheep with what seemed to us to be mounting hunger and we dreaded what might happen next. Why did the stupid man not obey the notices and just put his dog on a lead like all the other dog walkers had done'?

A woman jogged past us with her dog, this one sensibly on a lead. In a tangle of legs and lead the woman dragged, and was dragged by her dog, as she jogged down the slope away from us, and we watched with trepidation, expecting at any moment to see the pair pull one another to the ground. The woman must have been quite fit to jog up the slopes but one glance at her Lycra-clad figure certainly did not give that impression. Her lurid purple shorts and clinging vest clashed with the flowering heather and her ragged breathing broke the silence of the moorland. As she disappeared out of sight down the slope another woman appeared, this time walking with a male companion. This second woman did not seem to need to breathe, her strident and never ending voice cutting across the landscape like a foghorn through a thick sea mist.

A lone man was walking towards us along the rough path. Somewhere in his mid fifties, he looked every inch the veteran hill walker with his well-worn boots and sun-faded rucksack, unlike many of the fashion conscious walkers we had seen in the previous couple of weeks with their brand new gear and regulation bright red woolly socks and shiny leather boots. He stopped for a chat as we met up and unlike so many people who were keen to tell us where they were going but not interested in our walk, he was soon questioning us not only on our experiences on Offa's Dyke but on other long distance paths.

"Have you ever thought about walking abroad?" he asked. "There are some beautiful, well managed paths in Europe."

Just back from Switzerland, I remembered with longing the many yellow 'Wanderweg' signposts I had seen in the Bernese Oberland, perhaps Chris could be persuaded a wander through the Alps was a good idea! Forget Welsh cakes and dried apricots, think Swiss chocolate, rosti and fondues.

Slowly the sky to the west began to clear and the Snowdonia Range with Cadir Idris to the south became more discernible. The top of Snowdon was visible which, as anyone familiar to the area knows, is quite rare. By the time we were staggering down the steep gradient to the small lay-by before Moel Arthur, I had taken off my cagoule and was feeling quite warm. As at Bwlch Penbarra, a road bisects the range at this point and cars in the car park below us reflected the sunlight from their windows. We had almost drawn level with Denbigh, sitting in the valley to our west.

We stopped in the car park for a break, glad of a rest after the long hills of the morning. We took our time over lunch, basking in the sun and eating most of our remaining supplies of flapjack, biscuits and apricots as well as some of the packed lunch from the Old Rectory that we had been unable to finish the day before. A car drew up and parked nearby, grandparents and their young grandson getting out and proceeding to have their own lunch on a nearby wall. We watched them distractedly and I was beginning to think how nice it was to see grandparents taking their grandchild out for a picnic, perhaps teaching him a respect for the countryside, when my illusions were shattered as the grandfather hurled his empty banana skin into the heather. Banana skins and orange peel may be organic, but they take a long time to decompose. I remembered watching a red squirrel in the Lake District dragging a banana skin across the woodland floor and wondering if banana was ideal food for one of the rarest mammals in Britain.

The silence was absolute, no cars passed, no birds sang. The peace was shattered in the rudest of manners by the high pitched, deafening tones of the same strident woman we had seen earlier. She appeared round a bend in the hillside near the road and began marching towards us, talking incessantly to her companion.

"I only had two wees all day," she announced to her companion and the majority of north Wales. "Oh! John, I was soo hot. I was soo hot!"

Her monologue was beginning to sound decidedly dodgy and even John was laughing in a very embarrassed manner. We watched as they headed off across the road, climbing a curving path. Suddenly her voice rang out again.

"I'll tell you what, okay. I'm through now." As their retreating figures disappeared round the side of the hill her voice continued to drift back to us in piercing tones. Whatever she was through, speaking was not it.

Into view on the top of the hill we had descended a short while ago, there appeared a tiny figure. His descent of the slope was slow and careful, and as he gradually came nearer we could see he was limping quite badly. He negotiated the stiles with difficulty but carried on determinedly when he reached the road, crossing to continue along the footpath through the heather-covered slopes leading up to Moel Arthur.

It was a day of considerable ups and downs, not like the long steady ascent along Hatterall or the pleasant stroll across Hergest Ridge. With the Clwydian Mountains, we went up and down from one Moel to the next. That day was one of the most strenuous of the entire walk; Chris' GPS recorded a total daily ascent of over 2600 feet and descent of over 3300 feet during a walk of ten and a half miles; ascents, descents and miles that were made all the more difficult due to the rough, uneven surfaces of the paths on the moorland hills. But the efforts were rewarded by the changing profile of the Clwydian range as we advanced along its rippling back. The purple heather attracted bees and butterflies and the scent of the heather was intoxicating. With every gust of wind, pollen rose in clouds.

Our official route skirted around the eastern side of Moel Arthur, below its summit. On a whim we decided to take the branching path leading to the hilltop and its Iron Age hillfort, from where we could look down into the long valley to the west. Several other people had the same idea and they too strolled around the three defensive earthworks of this ancient hillfort. We stood for several minutes watching hang gliders swooping in the valley below us, whilst paragliders descended slowly on the thermals.

Rejoining the main path we continued northwestwards on a gradual descent to woodland, before climbing once again on the northern side of the wood. Mountain bike trails in the wood had attracted some rather fit young cyclists, and we dawdled across the tiny car park before the wood, admiring the scenery and the surrounding landscape and trying very hard not to look at the cyclists getting changed by their cars!

We contoured another hillside and suddenly encountered a shrew sitting on the path in front of us. As I carefully started to get out my camera the shrew scampered into the undergrowth, proving that shrews are obviously not as photogenic as bank voles. Bracken covered the hillside at this point, where before heather had dominated. The musty smell of the dry bracken hung in the still air. We stopped for a while, resting by a stile; the afternoon was becoming hot, a real contrast from the damp, cloudy and cold weather of that morning.

We were dropping down the western side of the Clwydian Range, leaving the summits and the hillforts further to the east. But the hills had not done with us entirely and we still had a few strenuous if shorter climbs before we would reach our goal that evening near Bodfari. With time to spare we stopped for a rest, sitting on a boulder at the side of the grassy path. The huge smooth boulder was a little too curving to make a comfortable seat and we clung on precariously, bracing ourselves with our heels as we sat looking across the tops of bright green bracken fronds to the Snowdonia mountain range on the western horizon. Snowdon's summit was once more hidden under a hat of cloud.

Field paths and quiet lanes carried us the last few miles towards Bodfari and our nearby guest house. Green woodpeckers called their by now familiar cry as we disturbed them in the trees. Just before the main road at Bodfari, where a tiny stream ran through fields, our presence disturbed four grey herons that perched precariously in the branches of trees lining the watercourse. They flapped away across the fields in a loose-limbed ungainly manner, struggling to gain height before coming to roost in more distant trees.

We crossed the road to face the final hill of the day, and the toughest: a very steep climb up a single-track road and then into fields once more. The fields had recently been mown, the grass left out to dry and it made for slippery walking on the steep gradient. We got lost for the first time that day in the last field of the day, somehow missing the gate and wandering about a bit in a tired, hot and confused manner, under the supercilious gaze of a family of walkers who seemed to know precisely where to go; by the time we found our way out I was more than tempted to tell them! We located the gate and left the field, climbing to reach another lane that led us to our guest house.

This was our last night, our last accommodation on Offa's Dyke Path. It is always nice to finish on a good note, to have an outstanding accommodation experience on your last evening, something to look back on with fond memories. If this were a narration with soft music playing, it would be at this point that the music would end abruptly with the screech of the stylus being wrenched across the vinyl. It might well be nice to finish on a good note but we were not about to.

This guest house, like nearly all our other choices, had sent us a leaflet and had its own website. The illustration on both the leaflet and the website had been sketchy to the point of incomprehensibility. No matter how often we studied the illustration we could not make out what the guest house looked like. Maybe warning bells should have sounded at that point, as surely if the building is attractive and well cared for then the owners would wish this to be reflected in their marketing literature? The details of what to expect were equally ambiguous: 'a warm welcome, antique furnishings, attentive hosts'. What did it mean? How should we attempt to translate it? The central heating might be on? The furniture was old, rickety and riddled with woodworm? Bribed warders in the Tower of London would be attentive to their wealthy prisoners before they went to the block.

We wandered along the lane in front of the house, trying to decide which of the several gates we should enter by, finally choosing to walk up the drive, passing an assortment of vehicles in the small car park. No one was about and with several doors to choose from we walked the length of the house looking for a door with a knocker or bell. The rambling house had seen better days. Much better. Before we could knock on any door an elderly man shuffled into view from around the rear of the property. His worn cardigan with its fraying sleeves and holey elbows, combined with his sagging trousers and scruffy slippers did nothing to fill us with confidence.

Chris introduced us and with an inarticulate grunt he shuffled back inside. An equally elderly woman emerged a minute later, summoned presumably by the man. Chris introduced us once again.

"Would you like a pot of tea?" asked the woman and to our enthusiastic agreement added, "Have a seat in the garden, I'll bring you out a tray."

"Good job we don't need the loo," I muttered as we settled ourselves at a rickety garden table that was covered in lichen and bird lime.

"Hmm, it is a bit unusual not to be taken to the room first," agreed Chris.

Ten minutes later the woman returned, carrying in best 'Mrs Overall' tradition a tray containing cups and saucers, a plate of warm mince pies, a milk jug and, strangely, a cafetiere of tea. She seemed friendly, if a little eccentric, as she proceeded to pour the tea and offer us the unseasonable mince pies. The tea was good and there was plenty of it, and so were the mince pies and the lady stayed to chat with us as we ate and drank.

"Did a mother and two daughters stay here last night?" asked Chris.

"Yes. Have you met them on the walk?" replied the lady.

"Several times," confirmed Chris. "And each time we have seen them the daughters looked extremely tired."

"Oh, they were last night!" exclaimed the lady. "It must have been after eight o'clock when they arrived. I felt so sorry for them. Never said a word, just came in and went straight to bed."

"They will have finished their walk today then," I commented.

"Yes, but I think they had had enough yesterday," replied the woman, becoming suddenly garrulous. "The father met them here and was walking to Prestatyn with them. That's their blue Ford in the car park. He's getting a taxi back to pick it up. At least today they did not have to carry all their rucksacks."

It is always nice to have a welcoming tray of tea and cake and that afternoon was no exception, but it could not hope to make up for the rest of our stay in that strange guest house. We were led through a maze of stairs and corridors to our room overlooking the front garden and the hills beyond. Left alone in our room we soon discovered that we were sharing the bathroom with at least two other rooms and that our bedroom had no tea making facilities and no sink. The furniture was old and worn and the beds were some of the most uncomfortable we had ever slept in, Chris' bed was the worst of the two, the shape of the springs visibly poking up through the mattress. Comments in the visitors' book were complimentary which made us wonder if our allocation of room was just unfavourable, or alternatively if the other guests were merely being polite or perhaps they had nothing better to compare this particular B&B with. Whatever the reasons, for us, that B&B was the worst of the walk and a rotten way to spend our last night. Not even the complimentary shower gel, shampoo and conditioner could make up for things. At least, with it being our last night we had no dreaded laundry to undertake and after showering and changing we went out for a meal.

We walked down the steepening lane to a pub in Bodfari, glad at least of a good meal. The pub was old and covered in creepers, inside we ducked beneath thick blackened beams to reach the lounge bar with its open fireplaces, oak settles, stone flagged floors and an eclectic mixture of dining tables crammed into every conceivable space. The meal was a long time coming, the service slow but friendly and the food, when it finally arrived an hour after we had ordered it, was worth waiting for. Both of us were incredibly hungry that evening and we started with homemade vegetable soup and freshly baked bread, before moving onto homemade chicken pie. We thought about dessert but decided that would be a little too greedy, and in any case it might be another hour before it was served.

Our walk back up the lane seemed to take much longer; surely the lane had got steeper? The last of the setting sun's rays had decorated the sky with streaks of orange and red, telephone lines and tree branches appearing in black silhouette against the colourful sky. We heard an owl and then had to duck as a bat swooped low over our heads. No longer hungry but now very tired the lane seemed much longer than it had on our descent; it was, in fact, over a mile back to the B&B.

A cup of tea would have finished the evening off nicely but I would have to make do with a swig of cold water from the bathroom tap. But first I had to get in the bathroom. The early night we had hoped for was delayed as we waited twenty minutes to get in the bathroom. Each time we heard the toilet flush, we hovered behind our bedroom door hoping to reach the vacated bathroom before any other guests did. But other guests must have had the same idea, and three times we lost the race to get in the loo. The situation was made worse as the toilet and shower room, although separate to each other, could only be reached by one door from the corridor; so anyone wanting only to use the loo had to wait for whoever was taking a shower to vacate the bathroom. It was a strange arrangement and very frustrating not only for us but for the other guests involved.

As the sound of the flushing toilet reached me for the fourth time, I darted out into the corridor but at the same time another guest had had the same idea and we found ourselves literally racing for the bathroom door. Hampered by a kettle, the man lost the race.

"Aw, god!" he exclaimed angrily.

"Look if you just want to fill your kettle, go ahead," I said, feeling guilty.

"No, it doesn't matter!" he snapped.

"Well, at least you've got a kettle," I snapped back before I could stop myself. Was this what a full bladder and a shared bathroom reduced people to, I wondered somewhat ashamedly.

Preparing to leave the bathroom, I knocked on the dividing wall, a signal to Chris, at the other side of the wall, to get ready. Her reactions were so fast we almost collided in the bathroom doorway, beating once again the man with the kettle and a woman wearing the skimpiest of nighties; the woman's appearance seemed to go some way to pacifying Kettle Man as he realised he had been beaten to the bathroom once more.

With clean teeth and empty bladders we attempted to settle down for a good night's sleep but that was made difficult thanks to the awful mattresses, the security light blazing through the window and the ongoing war of the bathroom. Doors banged, locks were shot, toilets flushed, showers taken, water ran and bare feet raced along the landing as fellow guests took their turns in the adjoining bathroom.

Chapter Nineteen

Six o'clock in the morning is not my favourite time of day. However, I do not like to lie in on holiday as I feel that is a waste of the day. But on walking holidays, when breakfast is at a set time, I usually get up forty minutes or so before that time. So getting up voluntarily two hours before breakfast that morning was a little out of the ordinary. Necessary though if I did not want to find myself in the situation of having a full bladder and nowhere to go. Having used the bathroom I then went back to bed for an hour.

At seven Chris and I both got up: with a cunning plan. Grabbing clothes, towels and toilet bags we went in the bathroom together. Whilst Chris used the separate toilet I showered and then we swapped. Ten minutes later with our modesty still intact we emerged from the bathroom to find kettle man waiting his turn. Trying to look like sharing a bathroom was no big deal we squeezed past him and scuttled back to our room.

"That'll give him something to think about," grinned Chris.

"Least he can have a cup of tea while he's thinking about it," I replied sulkily. Having to share a bathroom is one thing, but a bedroom with no tea making facilities!

We packed up our things and perched on the edges of the beds, waiting for breakfast time to come round and listening to the sounds of the other guests fighting for the bathroom. Locks were shot, latches rattled and feet pounded down the corridor.

"Good idea of mine, to get in there early."

"Of who's?" asked Chris.

"Well, you might have planted the seed in my head."

"Plenty of room for it!"

We were the first guests down to the dining room, if our plan worked out we hoped not to have to fight for the toilet after breakfast. The landlady appeared wearing what seemed to be a nurse's uniform, although I could not see it doing anything for any man's nurse fetish. She waved vaguely in the direction of a dusty sideboard and told us to help ourselves to either muesli or cornflakes, fruit and yoghurt, asked if we would like tea or coffee and then asked if we both wanted full English. Chris' request for just scrambled eggs on toast seemed to take the landlady completely by surprise and she left with an expression not dissimilar to Hatty Jacques in her fiercest matron role.

The dining room began to fill up with other guests, most of who seemed to be walkers. One party of two couples seemed keen to let everyone else know just how far they were walking and how wonderful they were, name-dropping and pontificating with increasing volume. Nightie Woman and her companion appeared and then Kettle Man arrived looking fraught and still damp from the shower. The fight for the bathroom was forgotten as the guests began a fight for the remaining crumbs of muesli and cornflakes and the last drops of milk.

I was only part way through my bowl of muesli when my cooked breakfast arrived.

"Oh, am I rushing you?" asked the landlady, plonking my plate of bacon, egg, tomato and sausage down on the edge of the table. Before I had a chance to say, 'yes actually you are' she had disappeared, leaving my fry up congealing as it cooled.

Chris' scrambled eggs appeared a few minutes later, served by a teenager who we presumed was the grandson. He bore a passing resemblance to the landlady. Then the family dog charged into the dining room, it too bore a passing resemblance to the landlady, proving the point that dogs do look like their owners. Small enough to get under tables as well as feet, the animal proceeded to sniff out scraps from any table willing to provide them or sloppy enough to have spilt them. It was only when the grandson tripped over the dog and almost threw a rack of toast at two of the guests that the landlady became aware of the dog's presence and ordered her grandson to take it outside. Farce ensued as great, lumbering, heavy-on-his-feet grandson proceeded to chase the dog around the tables and through the legs of guests and furniture alike. All this only enforced my surreal feeling that we were trapped in a Carry On film.

It was time to make a move and we left the pandemonium of the dining room for the emptiness of upstairs and the vacant bathroom. The dining room was still in chaos as we went downstairs to settle our bill. Leaving the guest house we were glad to be on our way, Prestatyn beckoned.

The day was already hot and sunny; it would be good to finish this predominantly dry walk with another day of nice weather. With only twelve miles to go, Offa still had some hills for us and we began with a gentle climb following the quiet country lane. Trees and hedges obscured much of the views but we watched goldfinches, wrens, blackbirds and blue tits flying between the trees and saw one of Offa's last squirrels crunching on hazelnuts in the branches above us. At a sharp right hand bend we left the lane, crossing a stile to climb the low hill of Cefn Du, site of yet another earthwork. From the summit we could see the Irish Sea shimmering silver in the hazy distance and through the binoculars we were able to pick out the five rows of wind turbines sited just off shore at North Hoyle Wind Farm. The blades spun lazily, reflecting the sunlight as they generated electricity.

There has been much controversy surrounding wind farms. Do they produce significant amounts of electricity? How many wind farms will be needed to replace conventional power stations? Wind farms look unsightly. All are valid points. But then again what cost nuclear power? What about the centuries needed for spent nuclear fuel to decay? What about pollution from coal and oil fired power stations? Is a wind farm any more unsightly than the marching legions of pylons that carry electricity around the national grid?

The wind farm at North Hoyle consists of thirty turbines and generates enough electricity annually to power over thirty-three and a half thousand homes. Put another way, an average wind turbine of 1 megawatt produces at least 2.5 million kilowatt hours of electricity per year: enough electricity from one wind turbine to provide the needs of almost six hundred homes. Wind power is seen very much as the future of electricity production in Britain, and the Government's own figures show that wind power will be cheaper than nuclear power by 2020. With Britain being the windiest country in Europe the arguments for relying more and more on wind generated electricity are powerful; in Denmark wind farms already produce 20 % of the country's electricity. The increased reliance on alternative forms of energy production is vital if we are to tackle the problems of global warming, and while many objections are raised about the aesthetics of wind farms it is worth remembering that global climate change, if left unchecked, will dramatically alter the appearance of the Earth on a worldwide scale. Obviously the location of wind farms needs to be undertaken with sympathy for the landscape, in a National Park or an Area of Outstanding Natural Beauty a wind farm would be out of place. But there are plenty of places where wind farms would not be detrimental to and can even be considered to enhance the landscape.

Quarries, open cast mines and conventional power stations are all far uglier than any wind farm.

Growing up, I remember that from many locations in my home town I could see cooling towers and chimneys; back in the sixties and seventies Burnley, sitting as it did on a coal field, was surrounded by several power stations, ugly polluting structures. In 1993 Coal Clough Wind Farm was built on the hills above Burnley. This wind farm, like all others I have seen, is not ugly and not polluting, sheep still graze on the land on which it is sited, something that is not possible with conventional forms of electricity production. The windmills can be seen in the distant from many locations, catching the light, catching the wind and generating clean electricity. Locals go for walks up there, for picnics, go to admire the wind farm, learn a little from the information boards and to look across the hills to the once industrial town nestling in the valley; the industrial town that was once hidden from those hills by the pollution of its smoking factory chimneys, belching power stations and busy collieries. The pits, the chimneys and most of the pollution have gone. Sadly so have many of the jobs associated with them. But the air is cleaner, the town is cleaner; now the majority of pollution comes from exhaust emissions as most people seem to have forgotten that legs evolved as a means of self propelled mobility and not merely to operate clutch, brake and accelerator. Perhaps that form of pollution, a major contributor to global warming, is what we should be concerned about now and not whether an environmentally friendly wind farm looks nice.

It would be several more miles before we got an up-close view of the offshore wind farm. We lost height to rejoin country lanes, crossing a minor road before getting back into fields once more. Sheep grazed the short grass, rooks scavenged and occasionally we heard the cries of gulls: slowly, slowly we were getting nearer to the coast. As we came in sight of a lone house the sound of gulls was obliterated by the sound of hammering and the noise of a radio. Madonna was belting out 'Papa Don't Preach' as an old man in baggy overalls belted away at a dilapidated tractor. Madonna seemed a strange choice of music for an elderly farmer but then I found myself wondering if perhaps her video to accompany 'Like a Virgin' might not be more to his liking. Still, he could hardly watch that video and belt away at his tractor at the same time without risking doing himself a mischief.

With the tune of 'Papa Don't Preach' going round in my head and the well remembered lyrics pouring tunelessly from my lips, (much to Chris' distress), we crossed a few more fields, scattered with grazing sheep and cattle and the odd small herd of ponies. Then, suddenly, we reached the noisy cutting of the A55, the main dual carriageway that snakes across the countryside of north Wales from Chester in the east, linking the seaside towns of Colwyn Bay, Llandudno, Conwy and Bangor, before merging with Telford's A5 to cross the Menai Straits into Anglesey and terminate at Holyhead. Traffic roared beneath us as we crossed the footbridge over the busy dual carriageway, and jet streams striated the blue sky as aeroplanes, tiny silver specks above us, undertook Trans Atlantic flights into and out of Manchester airport. On a clear day I have been lucky enough to fly across the North Wales coastline from Manchester, bound for Florida, and seen the beautiful patchwork of fields, mountains, moors and coast laid out below.

Once over the footbridge, the path dropped to meet a lane leading into the village of Rhuallt and immediately the roar of traffic was lost, the cutting acting like a baffle, cutting out the noise pollution. On that sunny Sunday morning few people were about, one man washed his car and a couple of ladies said friendly hellos as we walked down the quiet main street. Soon we had left the village, turning right at the crossroads and then taking a short, steep path up through shady coniferous woodland, ducking under the low hanging branches before emerging into full, hot sunlight in a field of gorse. We kept hopeful watch for lizards and slow worms, this seeming an ideal habitat for these reptiles but we saw none.

Chris' mobile began to ring and she unclipped it from her rucksack strap, fumbling to answer it before whoever was ringing disconnected.

"It's Merv," she said looking at the display. "He must be ringing to see where we are."

Chris' husband had spent the weekend staying at Conwy Youth Hostel and cycling along part of the north Wales cycle route. He was due to meet us in

Prestatyn that afternoon and drive us back home, thus saving us a tedious rail journey back to Lancashire.

"I don't know what time we'll get there!" exclaimed Chris in exasperation. "I'll phone you when we get nearer. We've still a few miles to go yet."

After the fields a quiet country lane ran for a mile or so along the north western arm of the conifer plantation and we walked along in the shade of the trees. But soon we left this lane too, climbing once more up to the rocky summit of Marian Ffrith, one of the last northerly peaks of the Clwydian range. Standing on the rock and grass covered peak we swivelled slowly through three hundred and sixty degrees, taking in the outstanding panorama. Somewhere far to the south, hidden behind many hills, many miles away was the Bristol Channel, the River Severn, Sudbury Cliffs and the start of Offa's Dyke National Trail. Chris' GPS read nearly 200 miles. According to the guide book this particular national trail was 177 miles long but how had that mileage been computed? The South West Coast Path Association recently commissioned a GPS survey of the South West Coast Path National Trail, only to discover that it was several miles longer than originally thought. Global Positioning Systems are remarkably accurate; we had no reason to doubt its precision and after all 200 miles sounds considerably more impressive than 177! From our vantage point almost 800 feet above sea level we had wonderful views of the North Wales coast, the wind farm and the red bricked, red roofed towns of Rhyll and Prestatyn. The end was now in sight.

We had ascended our last significant hill, Offa's last climb for us, and began a slow descent through cattle and sheep grazed fields to the old ruins of Marian Mill. We passed with interest the old mill race, the waterwheel and the crumbling building, walking along a bridleway that brought us out onto a quiet lane. At the next main road we crossed onto field paths once more that led us to the edge of the Clwydian range at a steep escarpment overlooking the flat coastal plains. We sat down here, at Prestatyn Cliffs, shrugged off our rucksacks for the penultimate time and indulged in our last Offa's Dyke lunch. Sprawling in the grass, serenaded by the calls of birds flitting between the nearby shrubs, we ate the last of the flapjack and the Welsh cakes, shared the last apple and chewed contemplatively on the dried apricots.

Neither of us had been looking forward to Prestatyn, expecting it to be much like Rhyll and the last time we had been there, on the way back from a weekend in Snowdonia with friends, that particular seaside resort had been most deserving of the title of 'Last Resort'. Normally the worst thing about ending a walk is the anticlimax – that dreary return to reality, life, work, washing. Unusually for both of us, the location was something we were dreading more than the laundry!

"Bet it's awful," sighed Chris.

"Yeah," I agreed. "Streets full of litter, buildings full of graffiti, promenade full of tacky stalls, sea full of scum."

"Oh well, we can hop in the car and Merv can whisk us away. We don't have to linger. In fact, I'll phone him now and give him an estimated time of arrival. How far do you reckon we have to go?"

"Not too far at all," I replied looking at the map. "It's half one now. I reckon by the time we've finished lunch and walked down this cliff, through the town and down to the beach it will be about three o'clock at the latest."

Chris phoned Merv and duly relayed our E.T.A. We finished all our food with the exception of a few remaining apricots and packed up the remains of lunch, heaving on our rucksacks and setting off for the last leg of our walk. The path followed the wiggling line of the edge of the escarpment, a mainly narrow dusty path running between bushes and bordered on the left hand side by a stout fence to prevent any nasty accidents. One path led off the main path, descending the slopes through ancient oak woods that clung tenaciously to the steep hillside. There was no signpost at this junction of paths and we hesitated, unsure of our bearings after the many twists and turns. Did we need to take this lower path? A family, sitting on a nearby bench watched our confusion before the dad asked if we were lost.

"Where are you looking for?"

"Prestatyn," I replied rather unhelpfully.

"We want to stay on Offa's Dyke Path," explained Chris with more clarity.

"Oh, right," nodded the dad.

"It's along there," the mum said, pointing to the left. "That path down there just drops straight to the golf course. You don't want that."

We certainly didn't. Thanking them for their help we carried on, passing almost immediately an acorn sign reassuring us we were going in the right direction. That always seem to happen: at a junction of paths where the dopey walker might get confused there is never a signpost but as soon as you get on a straight section of path with no possible escape to either right or left there will be a totally unnecessary signpost. Why? Is it just the quirky sense of humour of footpath officers?

We seemed to come out of the shrubbery and the steep path in a rush, landing in the leafy suburbs on the edge of Prestatyn. Our route through the town to the beach and the end of the walk was now straightforward; literally, all we had to do was follow this almost straight road right down to the shore. We found ourselves walking through nice suburbs of Prestatyn.

Merv suddenly appeared around a corner, walking towards us carrying something in each hand: bottled water! We rushed to meet him, not out of any sense of triumphant completion or for any joyful reunion. Both Chris and I were gagging for a cold drink. How did he know? Merv stood laughing as we gratefully took the offered water and gulped it down. We had endured some quite foul water during the previous two and a half weeks, that bottled water was pure nectar.

Feeling much refreshed we carried on down the main street. After miles of rugged paths, dusty tracks, scattered boulders, muddy dingles and root covered woodland rides it was a nice even, smooth, flat piece of pavement that tripped me up. I went over on my ankle, stumbling towards the edge of the kerb, arms wind-milling frantically and desperately holding on to my bottle.

"Are you alright?" asked Merv solicitously, putting a hand out to save me.

"Yeah, I'm okay," I replied. "Thought I was going to spill the rest of my water though!"

Most of the shops on the main street were closed, just a few open and making the most of the Sunday trading laws. Tubs of bedding plants filled the pavements, and suspended from the lamp posts there were hanging baskets full of begonias and flags with Offa's Dyke Path logo which flapped in the gentle sea breeze.

We crossed the railway line on an elevated footbridge, which was perhaps the worst part of

Prestatyn as railway stations often can be the worst part of any town with their accompanying litter and smell of diesel. But other than the diesel everything seemed to smell nice: the flowers, the people we passed, the tantalising smell of chips and vinegar emanating from a fish and chip shop, the sweet smell of the candy floss stall by the promenade, Merv smelt nice even though he freely admitted to an energetic morning spent cycling and sweating in the heat. Suddenly we too began to smell nice. How could we smell nice? We had been walking all morning in high temperatures and our clothes had only been hand washed for the last week. It didn't make sense but we definitely did smell nice, sort of a citrus aroma. And then it suddenly occurred to Chris.

"Julia?"

"Hmm?"

"You've not used the midge repellent have you?"

"No. The last time I touched the bottle was when I got my penknife out of my rucksack at lunch time."

"You didn't somehow open the top of the bottle, or invert it or something?" she asked.

"Omigod!" I gasped. "Is that what that smell is? Midge repellent?"

I hastily removed my rucksack and unzipped the side pocket, plunging my hand in to find the bottle of insect repellent. My hand encountered something wet and slightly greasy and my fingers closed around my penknife which felt unusually slippery. I pulled out the knife and a handkerchief and my notebook and pen and finally the opened bottle of insect repellent. Yes, the top had come open, yes the bottle had leaked and yes we certainly smelt a lot better than we had earlier. But citronella based insect repellent is rather pungent and as we sat down at a café on the promenade to enjoy a celebratory cup of tea we found that the Jungle Formula was keeping more than just insects away. People at neighbouring seats stood up and left, many leaving their ice cream Sundaes and disabled grandparents in their haste to escape the pungent aroma. Soon we had the promenade café to ourselves.

We went into the visitor centre and signed the Offa's Dyke walkers' book, adding our names to a long list of proud completers. The Leeds couple had added their entry and so had the Australian, finishing a day before we had, so he had survived his fossil hunt on the shifting scree slopes! The woman and her two daughters had not put their names in the book: did they not make it, had the visitor centre been closed when they arrived, or had they been too knackered to write anything when they eventually finished their route march?

We had one final thing left to do. Leaving Merv to guard the rucksacks, we unlaced our boots, kicked them off and peeled off our rancid socks. Then we raced down to the incoming tide and paddled our hot, weary feet in the grey waters of the Irish Sea. It was a fitting end to our long walk along the varied and beautiful Offa's Dyke National Trail. I had set out expecting to be disappointed, to miss the sea that had so characterised other long distance paths Chris and I had walked. Instead Offa's Dyke had exceeded all my expectations and had lived up to all the high praise and recommendations of other hikers. Even Prestatyn had not lived down to our expectations. But I had been right about one thing though – the sea was full of scum, of a low life, tattoo-covered, lager-swilling, Liverpudlian chav variety. Llangollen must be having a day off!

Acknowledgements

Thanks as always to Chris, for walking with me and putting up with my ramblings, smelly socks and dried apricot addiction. Thanks to Merv for his invaluable proof reading once again and for picking out all my glaring errors and even inventing a few! Thanks to Gary Harris for his help with the autorun sequence. Special thanks to good friends Mo McDermott and Julie Hammonds for parcel delivery and collection services, Julie's inherent ability to attract strange characters (well we are her friends, need I say more?) and for the additional supplies of dried apricots; with particular thanks for their much appreciated support for both Chris and I during a very difficult 2006. Thanks to the Offa's Dyke Association and their invaluable accommodation guide. Thanks to the YHA for deciding to close Capel y Ffin youth hostel the year after we needed it and not the year before - pity the poor OD walkers who come after us. Thanks to the many wonderful B&Bs along Offa's Dyke who provided us with copious amounts of tea and cake, special thanks must go to Kim of the Old Rectory Llandegla who really knows what weary walkers need and to Michelle Evans at Quarry House Newcastle who deserves to be running a restaurant.

Facts and Figures

Offa's Dyke was built between 757 and 796 A.D.

When built, it is thought the dyke would have measured some 27 metres in width and 8 metres in height from the bottom of the ditch to the top of the bank.

Offa's Dyke footpath follows the dyke for approximately 70 miles.

Depending on which book, website or footpath guide you happen to be reading Offa's Dyke National Trail is somewhere between 177 and 182 miles in length.

Chris' GPS recorded a mileage of nearer 200.

The Offa's Dyke Association was set up in 1969.

Offa's Dyke long distance footpath was opened in 1971.

Marks and Spencer's dried apricots contain less sulphur dioxide than the brand we purchased at Tesco.

Too much sulphur dioxide can cause impotence in rats. (So if you're thinking of opening a rat breeding business don't feed them dried apricots).

By the Same Author:

My Feet and Other Animals
© Julia R Merrifield 2003
https://tinyurl.com/y98fnuqx

When two friends planned a long distance walk on England's South West Coast Path they thought the toughest challenge would be the walking itself. But the biggest obstacles to be overcome were not the 630 miles of footpaths, or the soaring ascents and descents of the cliffs. They were the unforeseen factors that cannot be planned for but which transform a journey into an adventure. Factors such as a torn calf muscle, recalcitrant underwear, two days of torrential rain and gales, two weeks of the hottest July temperatures for years, high tech equipment designed to help but determined to hinder, the capriciousness of public transport and a host of B&Bs all competing for the title of Worst Accommodation in the West.

Walking Pembrokeshire with a Fruitcake
© Julia R Merrifield 2004
https://tinyurl.com/ycnuhgev

Two friends deliberated where to choose for their next walking holiday. How about somewhere different? How about somewhere exotic? How about somewhere foreign? How about Wales? But with countless people advising them where to walk that summer and with neither of them speaking a word of Welsh, had they made the right decision? On a hot August day they set off to walk the 180 miles of the Pembrokeshire Coast Path, starting from somewhere unpronounceable and finishing at a little place called Amroth, passing on the way lots more places they would struggle to enunciate.

Wales, a proud land with a proud past; a land steeped in history, a land of myths and magic, castles and cromlechs, dragons and double consonants, male voice choirs and Aled Jones. Follow their adventures as they search for ice cream vans and a Welsh dictionary.

Pedals, Panniers and Punctures
© Julia R Merrifield 2005
https://tinyurl.com/ybyfn8to

One woman, one bike, no backup and 1477 miles on a unique End to End adventure.

Since when did cycle touring become an extreme sport? Since it involved travelling by train. When one woman, more accustomed to long distance footpaths than long distance cycle rides, set out to cycle from Land's End to John o'Groats the first obstacle she faced was getting to the start. Between the start of her journey and the finish, 1477 miles later, she encountered not only ups and downs of terrain but mental and physical highs and lows as well.

Cycling the End to End is so much more than just sitting on something no bigger than, and as hard as, the sole plate of an iron and pedalling, as Julia was to discover. Every experience seemed to be about extremes: Cornish hills, Cheshire plains, busy Devon lanes, empty highland roads, downpours, droughts, smooth cycle tracks, hazardous cattle grids, psychedelic B&Bs and homely hostels. And when the terrain and the weather weren't against her the wildlife was: terrorising Labradors, formation herding sheep dogs, kamikaze squirrels, plagues of midges and road-senseless sheep.

With no backup, and just a bike and a puncture repair kit for company, that strangest of traveller, the lone female, set off to tackle the ultimate British cycle ride. If only she had got a pound for every time someone told her it was all downhill the other way she could have bought a lot more chocolate. As it was, sustained by copious quantities of tea and as much chocolate as she could carry she finally reached her wet and windswept goal.

By the same author but writing under her new name:

Cycling Across England
© Julia R May 2012
https://tinyurl.com/yc62pful

Two women, two bikes, no backup on a Sea to Sea adventure.

At the beginning of the twenty-first century two friends set off to cycle from coast to coast across England. For one, it was to be the first of many long distance cycle rides.

Cycling Across England is an account of the fun, the food, the mountains, the moorlands and the mathematics the two friends encountered along the way. From the Irish Sea, through the mountains of Cumbria and the Pennine uplands they travelled through a landscape of contrasts to finish their journey in the industrial northeast on the North Sea coast. Broken glass, slugs and arduous ascents were relieved by blackberries, an excess of pizza and delightful descents. Join them as they cycle across England on this iconic ride.

I've Cycled Through There
© Julia R May 2012
https://tinyurl.com/ybxf3gfj

That strangest of traveller, the lone female, is at it again. This time cycling through the heart of England from Bath to London to her home in Lancashire. For such a small country England was proving to be a land of contrasts and surprises; from the leafy lanes of Berkshire to the bleak moorlands of the north, spectacular scenery and post-industrial mill towns, dead divas and murderous mad men.

Throughout the six hundred mile cycle ride there was much that was quintessentially English: Georgian architecture and thatched cottages, William Shakespeare and Samuel Johnson, Bath buns and Yorkshire pudding, canals and Roman roads, Magna Carta and the Houses of Parliament, oh, and Maharajah's Wells and teams of huskies!

Share the experience, the food, the fun and the frustrations. Funny and factual by turns, this is a true account of a cycle journey home through the heart of England.

Walking with Hadrian
© Julia R May 2012
https://tinyurl.com/y9929ggz

A walk through time and fog along Hadrian's Wall.

Built almost two thousand years ago on the orders of the Emperor Hadrian and marking the northern-most boundary of the Roman Empire, Hadrian's Wall is one of Britain's most enduring ancient monuments and a UNESCO World Heritage Site. In 2003 a footpath following the line of the Wall was designated as a National Trail running 84 miles across England from the Solway Firth to the North Sea. Since then walkers have been coming to enjoy this long distance path in the wild landscape of northern England, and a few years later inadvertently choosing the foggiest week she could, Julia finally got round to walking the Wall.

Factual and funny by turns, 'Walking with Hadrian' is an accurate account of the history, culture, scenery and wildlife of Hadrian's Wall Path. Battling fog, maps, social networking and the encroaching perils of middle age, the author has added another book to her collection of traveller's tales.

Cycles and Sandcastles
© Julia R May 2013
https://tinyurl.com/yba8rbqz

Running two hundred miles from Newcastle to Edinburgh, the Coast and Castles Cycle Route promised to be a journey through millennia of turbulent history and fabulous scenery. It proved to be more than just ruined castles and wild coastline. More industrial heritage, more rain, more cross dressing stag nights, more stunning beaches, more wildlife, more grave robbers, more railways, more tea rooms and the Moorfoot Hills.

Close encounters with seagulls, precocious children, warrior-like toddlers and bathroom cleaning products were all in a day's cycling for the author as she pedalled north, passing remote beaches, wooded river valleys and more castles than you could shake a bicycle pump at.

Written with self-deprecating humour and a wry eye for detail, Cycles and Sandcastles is a narrative of the history, the scenery and the flavours of a bike ride through Northumberland and the Scottish Borders.

A Week in Provence
© Julia R May 2014
https://tinyurl.com/y7pruz4x

A much needed autumn break walking in the Verdon Gorge region of Provence turns into a fraught lesson in how not to speak French as the author gets to grips with the language of love, romance and strange combinations of Cs, Qs, apostrophes and genders. Written with her by now trademark self-deprecating humour, this, the author's tenth travelogue, recounts the beauty, the peace and the quieter way of life to be found walking in idyllic rural France.

Never a successful student of languages, but believing you ought to try, Julia displays an enthusiastic if dreadful grasp (or should that be stranglehold?) of the French language as the week unfolds. Whilst coping with a lack of underpants, some rather smelly food and the intricacies of French, A Week in Provence tells of the walks walked, the food eaten, the language butchered and the stretched patience of her long suffering partner as they embark on a walking holiday in south east France.

Bicycles, Boats and Bagpipes
© Julia R May 2014
https://tinyurl.com/y7hrnokp

Having cycled the length and breadth of the British mainland, it was time for a change. After seeing a little blue cycle route sign on the west coast of Scotland, Julia was struck with inspiration. The islands of the Outer Hebrides beckoned. There was just one problem, her boyfriend wanted to go too! Looking on the bright side he could be responsible for navigating and could take most of the luggage. Well, that was the plan. Little did she realise that with her boyfriend there also came his smelly footwear and holey cycling leggings.

Bicycles, Boats and Bagpipes is a detailed and often amusing account of a 500 mile cycle journey through the beautiful and remote islands of the Outer Hebrides and along the mountainous northwest coast of the Scottish mainland.

But it wasn't all about the cycling; there were the rare flower-rich machairs of the Western Isles, idyllic white sandy beaches, blue seas, wild moorland and ancient historic sites to explore. Wildlife to watch. Ferries to sail. Cake to eat and tea to drink. And throughout the trip the experience of isolated communities going about their daily lives, such a contrast from the hustle and bustle of home.

Bicycles, Beer and Black Forest Gateau
© Julia R May 2016
https://tinyurl.com/yctr5bbg

Not many people would consider cycling hundreds miles through Europe to be a relaxing holiday. Mike certainly didn't. But Julia did, she was peculiar that way. There was a challenge to be had in following the River Rhine from its source high in the Swiss Alps, through Germany, France and the Netherlands to the North Sea. But if Mike could not be convinced by mention of the varied scenery, the cultural diversity and the cake, what would change his mind? Finally it was mention of the hundreds of breweries in Germany that convinced him. Who knew, it might turn out to be very relaxing after all?

But as the couple were to discover, cycling on the continent can be very different to cycling in Britain. It was not just the language that would prove difficult to get to grips with, the rules of the road, the navigation, the continental heat and the alpine thunderstorms would test their patience as would tractor drivers and mosquitoes. But most challenging of all would be two weeks without a proper cup of tea. Would beer, gateaux and chocolate be enough to compensate?

Dawdling Through The Dales
© Julia R May 2018
https://tinyurl.com/y8kew292

The Dales Way long distance footpath runs for over eighty miles from Ilkley to Bowness-on-Windermere, encompassing the beautiful scenery of North Yorkshire and Cumbria and two National Parks. It is a varied walk of ever-changing scenery of lush river valleys, limestone pavements, moorland and mountains, and one undertaken by thousands of walkers every year.

When two friends decided to walk the Dales Way over a series of weekends they expected to complete it within a year, but life got in the way. For one of them, the Dales Way would remain an uncompleted long distance footpath.

With details of the scenery, the natural history and anecdotes about the walk, this book will give you a true flavour of walking this often overlooked yet delightful footpath. Light hearted but also darker at times, Dawdling through the Dales, like all of Julia's books, will make you laugh, but it might also make you cry. It is a true tale of walking, divorce, betrayal, depression and enduring friendship.

Cycling Through a Foreign Field
© Julia R May 2018
https://tinyurl.com/yc3rv2y7

In an overheated room in a sheltered housing complex in Burnley there is a small, carved wooden box. The box is a depository for memories, half remembered or forgotten entirely. Inside this box are two life times of old photographs, some sepia, some black and white, known and unknown ancestors; and laid carefully on top of them all sits a newspaper clipping, faded and torn at the edges, over one hundred years old now.

The clipping was taken from the Burnley Express which in 1916 was running a regular feature of Burnley families and the contributions they were making to the First World War. The clipping shows eight head and shoulder photographs of mother and father and six of their sons. One son is in a reserved occupation, one son is too young to fight. The other four sons are in uniform, serving soldiers in the Great War.

The occupant of this hot, stuffy little room and keeper of this box of memories is a lady in her late eighties, frail now and suffering from Alzheimer's Disease, her memory is fading like the contents of the box. She is my mother, Rose. The youngest son in the old newspaper clipping is her father.

In spring 2018 my partner and I set out to cycle the battlefields of Flanders and The Somme; to retrace our forefathers' footsteps and to find out a little of where they served, the conditions they endured and what had become of them during the First World War.

Find me on Facebook:

For excerpts from my books, photos and more information.

Julia R May Books on Kindle & Kobo

https://www.facebook.com/JuliaRMayBooksOnKindle?ref_type=bookmark

If you like what I do – let people know. If you don't – shh! ☺

Printed in Great Britain
by Amazon